MW01172782

Press Go

Lessons *Earned* by a Serial Entrepreneur

Bill Seibel

Copyright © 2021 Bill Seibel

ISBN 9798743855155

All rights reserved. No portion of this book may be reproduced, stored in a retrieval system, or transmitted by any form or any means—electronic, mechanical, photocopy, recording, scanning, or other—except for brief quotations in critical reviews or articles, without the prior written permission of the author.

Disclaimer:

The author strives to be as accurate and complete as possible in the creation of this book. However, its contents are only as accurate as his personal notes and memory of the events. The author does not warrant or represent at any time that the contents within are completely factual.

While all attempts have been made to verify information provided in this publication, the author and publisher assume no responsibility and are not liable for errors, omissions, or contrary interpretation of the subject matter within. The author and publisher hereby disclaim any liability, loss, or damage incurred as a result of the application and utilization, whether directly or indirectly, of any story, information, suggestion, advice, or procedure in this book. Any perceived slights of specific persons, peoples, or organizations are unintentional.

In practical advice books, like anything else in life, there are no guarantees of income made or results achieved. Readers are cautioned to rely on their own judgment about their individual circumstances and to act accordingly. Readers are responsible for their own actions, choices, and results. This book is not intended for use as a source of legal, business, accounting, or financial advice. All readers are advised to seek the services of competent professionals in the legal, business, accounting, and finance fields.

Published by Made to Change the World Publishing,
Nashville, Tennessee

Credits:
Editor – Stephanie Browning
Cover and interior design – Amanda Barrington

Printed in the United States and Canada

I'M DEDICATING THIS book to my wife, Carol, whose love and encouragement enabled me to achieve not only my boyhood ambition, but all of my dreams. Our life together reminds me of a story told about Winston and Clementine Churchill. As they walked through Knightsbridge, many passersby greeted the prime minister and engaged him in brief conversation. As they made their way through the crowd, Mrs. Churchill was hailed by a street sweeper, and the two of them spent more than a few minutes in a private discussion. Churchill was curious, and asked his wife, "What were you discussing with a street sweeper for such a long time?" "Ah...he was in love with me a long time ago," she said. Her husband smiled broadly and quipped, "You see, if you had married him, you would be the wife of a street sweeper today." Mrs. Churchill returned the smile and said, "But no Darling, if I had married him, he would be the prime minister today."

You'll meet Carol in many of my stories. After you do, I believe that you'll understand how important our partnership was, and is, to everything that we accomplish.

I'm also dedicating this book to my dear friends, whom I've forced to listen to my stories far too many times, always politely pretending that it was the first time that they heard them.

Table of Contents

A Note from Me to You

I'VE BEEN A serial entrepreneur for more than thirty years, and a storyteller my entire life. *Press Go: Lessons* Earned *by a Serial Entrepreneur* captures the lessons I've learned and earned along the way and punctuates them with stories that I hope make them easier to remember.

If you are **contemplating launching your first startup**, my book describes what that's like—not just how to get started, but what it feels like to be an entrepreneur: the highs and lows; the passion that drives you and the sacrifices that you're sure to make; the fear of failure that motivates you; and the excitement and pride that accompany a success.

For the **new entrepreneur or "intrapreneur,"** I've compiled the knowledge that I've acquired across the fifty-some startups that I've worked with. Reflecting on the questions that I faced at different stages of their growth, I've arranged what I've learned about launching, marketing, selling, scaling, and exiting to help you find your answers.

If, like most of my clients, you are a **serial entrepreneur**, you know that we all have much more to learn. We'll never master entrepreneurship, but we can always get better at it. I'm certain that you'll recognize many of the challenges I've faced, and perhaps I can provide a few new ways of thinking about them.

And if you are a **casual reader**, curious about the world of entrepreneurship and looking for a business book that's fun to read, I hope that *Press Go* takes you there, and that you enjoy reading my stories as much as I enjoy telling them.

Whatever your reason for picking up this book, I thank you for including me in your journey.

Acknowledgments

MANY PEOPLE HAVE contributed to this book. But it would never have been written without the advice and support of **Raj Echambadi** and **Mark Fuller**. They convinced me that I had much to teach, and that my stories conveyed my lessons in a way that made them fun to learn and easy to remember. They both strengthened my belief that I had what it takes to be an author and inspired me to do my best to reach that potential. Raj helped me make *Press Go* a better business book. Mark broadened my focus by helping me understand that my lessons weren't just about entrepreneurship—they're life lessons as well.

I also want to thank **Jim Sims** and **David Lubin**—the two mentors that influenced me the most. Both executives have launched enormously successful companies; I am fortunate that they took me under their wings and patiently shared their lessons *earned* with me. Each of them was as an advisor, a counselor, and a cheerleader—and played each of those roles precisely when I needed them the most.

Jim is best described as the CEO from central casting. Not only did he look the part, he was a role model for playing the part. Jim taught me how to see my world through the eyes of my customers, and to "always do the right thing."

David is better described as the college professor from central casting. Perhaps even a bit of a mad scientist! David taught me how to solve problems—both those that I had and those that I didn't know that I had. He provided tremendous value in many areas. But by pushing me to think three or four steps ahead, instead of just two, he made me a much better CEO.

To **Dan Ariely**, who taught me what's most important in life—the special memories that you create and share with those that accompany you on life's journey. Thank you for recalibrating the way that I think about keeping score.

To **Jim Cash**, whose research and teaching about the competitive impact that information technology can have on businesses inspired me to leave Air Products and become an entrepreneur. Thank you for opening my eyes to possibilities that I didn't know existed.

To **Larry Fish**, who grew Citizens Financial Group thirty-fold to become one of the ten largest banks in the United States; **Ron Shaich**, who, for three decades, never paused from his search for opportunities to continue to innovate and transform Panera Bread; **Bob Mack** who spearheaded Otsuka Pharmaceutical's effort to launch the first trackable digital medicine approved by the FDA; and **Jeroen Tas**, who challenged traditional thinking at Philips and leveraged the power of data and emerging technologies to transform their healthcare business. These four individuals embody the vision, courage, and resilience required to drive innovation in a large enterprise. Each of them is an entrepreneur— disguised as a Fortune 500 executive. Thank you for inspiring me to be a better entrepreneur, and for trusting me to help you achieve your vision.

People wonder how I remember the details of so many stories, and ask if I write them down. The answer is—I do. But my notebooks are also jam-packed with the words of wisdom and the stories I've heard from **Jim Barksdale**, **Richard Carpenter**, **Marc Goedhart**, **Andy Mellen**, **Bob Metcalfe**, **Bill McDermott**, **Nir Linchevski**, **Don MacDonald**, **Jim Robinson**, and **Thornton May**. Especially Thornton, who has a volume entirely to himself! Thank you all for providing me opportunities to learn from you.

Many thanks to my teammates that signed on with me to build a *special* company. Notable are **Ashkan Afkhami**, **Chris Harding**, **Michael Heffernan**, **Gajen Kandiah**, **Theo Schnitfink**, **Bret Siarkowski**, **Scott Snyder**, **Tony Tjan**, **Gus Vidaurreta**, **Mike Welsh**, and **Guy Yehiav**. I've learned much more in my time with you than you could ever learn from me.

Thank you to my friends and colleagues who invested their time to review my book and provided valuable feedback—**David Abdow, Jeanne Boudreau, Peter Cohan, Teo Dagi, Jody Davids, Robin Davis, Dave Dyer, Phil Perkins, Mike Pehl,** and **Cheryl Smith.**

Finally, I deeply appreciate the help of **Lucy Davis, Valentina Synen'ka,** and **Ellie Shefi** for ably bringing this book to fruition.

BILL SEIBEL - 221-6930

"THE PEEPLE"

MUSIC FOR ALL OCCASIONS

Introduction

Put it before them briefly so they will read it, clearly so they will appreciate it, picturesquely so they will remember it and, above all, accurately so they will be guided by its light.

– Joseph Pulitzer, editor

AS FAR BACK as I can remember, I've dreamed of writing a novel. I never aspired to becoming a famous author. In the coal mining town where I was raised, "famous" was reserved for items like Isaly's chipped ham sandwiches, not people. Most of the adults I knew were coal miners or steel workers, and I don't recall that any were famous. Becoming *just* an author would suffice.

A James Bond double feature triggered my first attempt to write a novel when I was twelve years old. My title was worthy of Ian Fleming: *Murder Ala Mode.* The first three chapters flew off my pencil. But when it came time to write the obligatory James Bond sex scene, I was lost. I put my manuscript in my bureau drawer and promised myself that I would return to it after I hit puberty. That never happened. Let me clarify. Puberty happened—but resuming my novel didn't.

In high school, I played keyboards in a rock band. That was the late '60s when groups like the Beatles, the Animals, the Monkees, the Eagles, and the Byrds dominated the music scene. We named our band "The Peeple." It sounded very cool at the time.

Having just turned fifteen, I was the oldest band member. Our bass player was twelve. Despite our youth, we were very good. Bars and clubs hired us. Crowds would come to hear us play. The Peeple consistently won local Battle of the Bands contests, although we did rig the audience. We generated buzz by renting a large bus and cruising the streets until we could fill it with teenage girls who promised to hysterically scream for us—if we could get them in for free. Our band even had a fan club, albeit it only had eight members.

Because of the buzz that we were generating, The Peeple were selected as one of the five top bands in Pittsburgh and were invited to perform at the Tea Rock. That was a highly promoted Battle of the Bands staged in front of several thousand people in a stadium at West View Park. But there was a catch. Every band had to play a set of three songs: an original piece, their own version of "The Tea Rock" (a song written by the sponsor, Lipton Tea), and a song of their own choosing. We didn't have an original song.

We were just kids and had no idea how to begin to write music. And we would be competing against experienced performers much older than we were. Two of them already had recording contracts. We were way out of our league.

Andy, our lead guitarist said, "Hey, Bill. I remember your telling me that you wrote a book a few years ago. We need you to write our original song."

"But I never finished the book," I explained. "I barely started it. And it probably wasn't very good."

"Listen. You're the oldest kid in the band and you've at least tried to write something. You're the best shot we have. Either you write a song, or we have to drop out of the Battle of the Bands." I reluctantly agreed. The music would be easy. Most of the songs in the '60s followed simple chord progressions. I just had to write a short story that flowed with the music. Perhaps my true path was to be a songwriter, not a novelist.

I began by studying the lyrics of recent hits and found that they ranged from silly to completely nonsensical. Do you remember "Alley Oop (oop, oop-oop)"? And "Purple People Eater"? Toss in "Snoopy vs. the Red Baron," "My Ding-a-Ling," and "They're Coming to Take Me Away,

Ha-Haaa!," and the answer became clear. Start with a silly but catchy title, select a simple chord progression, build in a good beat, and write lyrics that are catchy, repetitive, and ridiculous.

My first composition: "I Want to be a Tree."

I want to be a tree, come and be,

Be a tree with me.

We can grow forever and have leaves together

I want to be a tree.

I'll spare you the remaining verses.

Somehow, I convinced Fred, our lead singer, to go with it. We remixed "The Tea Rock" so it pulsated to a great beat, and we selected "Hey Joe" as our cover, remixing it so it came across as slow and soulful. It was time for the show!

We arrived at West View Park to find a large, raised stage surrounded by several thousand seats, and we quickly learned that the microphones would be connected to the amusement park's sound system to allow everyone in the park to hear the vocals. All the other musicians we met looked like professionals. They were in their late teens or early twenties, had been performing for many years, and were using top-of-the line equipment. It was intimidating. We had hit "the big time," and "the big time" was hitting back.

That's when Fred, our lead singer, looked at me and said, "I'm not singin' that dumb, fuckin' tree song. You sing it."

"Not me," I said. "You know God gave me the most off-key voice you've ever heard. The nuns didn't allow me to sing out loud in my grade school Christmas carol pageants. They ordered me to just mouth the words. No, not me."

Fred persisted. "There's no question that your voice sucks. But it's perfect for a novelty song. From the moment they hear you sing everyone will know it's a spoof. Besides, we're the third band to play, and we can sandwich it in as our second song. No one will even notice. Don't worry—you'll be great!"

As the amphitheater began to fill, the producers notified us of a change that made everything much worse. Instead of going third, they announced that we would open the show. And we were told to begin with our original song. I could not think of a way out.

The curtains came up, the stage lights came on, and we began our chord progression. The audience in the amphitheater, excited to hear the first of the top five rock bands in Pittsburgh, rose to their feet, and then...a wailing, off-key "I want to be a tree" filled the air across the entire park. I still relive that moment in an occasional nightmare. I'm certain that my fellow band members do as well. We tied for fourth place—or tied for last, depending on how you look at it. The next morning, everyone in the band resigned, and The Peeple never performed again. My path as a songwriter hit an abrupt dead end.

It was pretty clear that music would not take me away from the coal mines and steel plants, but I hadn't given up my hope that one day I would write a novel.

When I applied to college, I placed *practicality* ahead of *passion*, and enrolled in engineering instead of literature. I thought it would be easier for me to work as an engineer and be a part-time author rather than vice versa. I decided I wouldn't become a professional writer, but I'd continue to write. That never happened. Again, let me clarify. Getting a degree in engineering happened, but I didn't resume writing.

Time passed—twenty-seven years. In 1993, I relocated from Boston to Amsterdam to launch Cambridge Technology Partners–Europe. At that time, I'd been dating my now-wife, Carol, for three years after we first met at McCormack & Dodge. Unable to envision being apart, I proposed, and we departed for Europe two days after we were married. Carol planned an extended honeymoon beginning on the island of Sardinia that ultimately took us to our new apartment in Amsterdam.

Our second stop was Villa d'Este, a five-star sixteenth-century hotel in Lake Como, Italy. We decided to engage a private driver for three days to tour the countryside—from Lugano's lakeside and old town, to the fashion center in the industrial city of Milan. Guglielmo, our driver, was charming, very intelligent, and an excellent tour companion. After the first day, he felt like an old friend. Guglielmo attended the top schools in Europe. Instead of pursuing a career in business or science, he decided to live his life as a ski bum in the winter and a chauffeur in the summer. When I asked his age, he told me that he would turn forty-two on June 26 of that year. Carol turned to me and asked, "Isn't that your forty-second birthday as well?" I nodded. Our driver added, "What a small world. And even stranger, the name 'Guglielmo' is Italian for 'William!'"

We spent our remaining days together talking about the choices that we make in our lives. I could have been Guglielmo, and he could have been me. What made him decide to live a simple, carefree life? What made me decide to "press go" and relocate to Europe to spend five years working my tail off to build a company? We talked about choices—why you make them and where they lead you. I don't remember any of the tourist sites that we saw after that first day. But I remember my discussion with Guglielmo word for word.

Afterward, Carol asked me, "Didn't you always want to write a book? We just spent two days talking about choices. Why don't you write a book about our time with Guglielmo?"

Brilliant! Traveling by train for the next ten days would provide me with plenty of time. I snatched as much hotel stationary as I could cram into my briefcase and began to write a novel about chance encounters. What would life be like if I had chosen Guglielmo's path and he had chosen mine? What would we say to each other if we met again in ten years? Who made the right choice? And what does "right choice" really mean? Finding this incredibly easy to write, I completed 122 handwritten pages by the time we reached Cologne. Cologne is where I accidentally left my manuscript in the seat pocket of the train.

I never saw it again. I couldn't bring myself to try to recreate it. I wondered if someone found it in the train and turned it into a great novel. When I tell this story now, people occasionally say, "That sounds very familiar. I think that I read that book." More likely, the conductor tossed it in the trash. I wonder if he read it before he did.

Another twenty-seven years passed. In March 2020, Carol once again turned to me and said, "Didn't you always want to write a book? You enjoy working with entrepreneurs, teaching them what starting a company is all about, and what they should expect after they 'press go.' And they value and enjoy the time you spend with them and never forget the stories you tell to make your lessons come alive. Write a business book that's fun to read."

Not wanting to wait another twenty-seven years before Carol nudged me again, I decided to write a book that will help entrepreneurs anticipate and respond to the many challenges they will face in launching and scaling their companies. I've punctuated the important lessons with stories that will make them easier to remember. But I also wrote this book to share how it *feels* to be an entrepreneur—what to expect, what was fun, what sucked, what was exhilarating, what was scary, and how to keep score along the way. When I mentor entrepreneurs, the question they ask most frequently isn't about forming a board, raising money, or developing their customer value proposition. It's, "Is it supposed to feel this way? *Am I doing okay?*"

The odds of becoming a successful entrepreneur are based on both competency and seasoning. There are business lessons "earned" that come from "been there, done that." Or perhaps better said, "been there, don't do that again." Serial entrepreneurs are more successful than novices only when they apply their experience to their next venture. For me, success is about making a mistake, understanding and remembering what went wrong, and adjusting how I would approach a similar situation in the future. Mulligans and do-overs may violate the rules of golf, but, for me, they define the rules of entrepreneurship.

A number of behavioral traits, developed early in life, also improve the odds that an entrepreneur will be successful. They include work ethic, resourcefulness, the ability to improvise, the ability to build and grow relationships, the capability to juggle many balls while focusing on the few that are most important, and competitiveness driven by fear of failure.

I've worked with more than fifty startups—most of them technology-based. Regardless of where the lessons come from, I believe that most of my experience universally applies to any startup in any industry. And many of the lessons are *life lessons* as well. Serial entrepreneurship, like leadership, transcends the confines of a defining box.

Because professional services firms do have some important differences, I've included bonus material for readers considering launching a technology consulting company as Appendix—Lessons Applied to Professional Services.

• • •

Part I

Launching

It's kind of fun to do the impossible.

– Walt Disney

CHAPTER ONE

Lessons in "Tuepenerernr"-ship

The fishermen know that the sea is dangerous and the storm terrible, but they have never found these dangers sufficient reason for remaining ashore.

– Vincent Van Gogh

IT'S LATE AFTERNOON on April 13, 2000, one year after I founded ZEFER and quickly grew its revenue to $136 million—the fastest growth ever for a professional services firm. We are one of the darlings of the dot-com wave—profitable, growing revenue at 38 percent quarter-to-quarter, and doing impactful work for the Fortune 1000. My team and I have just completed ZEFER's initial public offering (IPO) roadshow consisting of ninety-eight presentations in eighteen different cities across five countries packed into fourteen business days. It's exhausting just to describe it. When we launched our IPO roadshow, analysts predicted ZEFER's enterprise value could reach $2.2 billion in less than eighteen months. I own an 8 percent stake in the company. If the analysts are right, my share of our IPO will be substantial.

My team has done everything possible to build and grow ZEFER and package it into an attractive IPO offering. But the choppiness of the stock market increasingly troubles us.

The Nasdaq has fallen eleven of the last thirteen days and we silently pray for an "up" day. After our final meeting on that fateful afternoon, I check with the Credit Suisse First Boston syndicate desk and am delighted to learn that the Nasdaq is up and our IPO deal is basically done! But over

Cover Story

Just how low will Nasdaq go?

Don't panic yet, but if index doesn't bounce soon, it'll be ugly

By Matt Krantz
and Adam Shell
USA TODAY

the prior three weeks, the market has often fluctuated dramatically as it nears the end of the trading window. And two hours remain before trading closes today.

Those two hours pass slowly. I watch nervously as the Nasdaq drops from a 120-point gain to an 80-point loss in the final hour of trading. My team drives to a hangar at a private airport in Houston to take our 4:00 p.m. pricing call with the syndicate desk, our banker, and our board.

4:00 p.m. comes and goes. So do 4:30, 5:00, and 5:15. Why aren't we hearing anything? At 5:30 p.m., the phone rings. ZEFER's IPO is having difficulty pricing in our range. If we lower the offering price, we can still get the IPO done. I quietly listen to the animated discussion that follows.

Our board, investors, and bankers all agree that we're competing in a crowded market that will only get worse. "ZEFER has to go public now to beat the rush and maintain our differentiation," they argue. One of our board members adds, "Since we invested this much time and energy and have come so close, we have to complete the deal." Everyone has a strong point of view, and so the arguments continue.

Finally, I interrupt and ask, "Whose decision is it?"

"You know how we all feel, but you're the CEO. It's your decision."

"How much time do I have to make it?"

"No more than ninety minutes," the syndicate head responds.

How do I weigh the alternatives? ZEFER is a shooting star on the eve of a huge public offering that has consumed a significant amount of management's time and effort. But we are faced with rapidly changing market conditions creating a very uncertain future.

What if we go public and the stock market crashes tomorrow? Perhaps the prophesized "inevitable burst of the dot-com bubble" has arrived. That seems like a low probability, but is it worth taking that chance? If the market continues to fall, will the value of our stock options plummet and distract our employees from building a great company? And what if the huge market swings are signaling a business recession? If our clients become skittish about their near-term future, will our revenue tank? And if that happens, do we want to try to recover while under the public scrutiny that comes with an IPO? Or will ZEFER need the liquidity from an IPO to stay afloat?

But if I pull our IPO now, will we permanently lose our chance to become public? If not, how long will we have to wait before an IPO door opens again, and do we really want to repeat the ninety-eight presentations in eighteen cities and five countries? And...will I lose my only chance to be the CEO of a public company and the payday that comes with it?

It's easy for me to see which option is better for my investors and for me, at least in the short term. But what's best for the company? And what's best for our employees?

I walk outside so I can be alone and think about how I got here. What made me decide, after more than twelve years, to leave a high-paying, secure, cushy job as an executive in a Fortune 100 company to become an entrepreneur? My motivation didn't hinge on making a lot of money. I could have done that without leaving. Instead, I left because I wanted to build a "special company."

My table stakes for a special company are that it generates strong financial returns which are sustainable through market disruptions. But it has to be much more. It must create significant value for customers and professional opportunities that enable employees to achieve their personal and professional ambitions. And if the company can redefine an industry by consistently achieving outcomes that the experts insist cannot be done— that's the biggest professional high any CEO can get!

Most importantly, a special company is aspirational. It's not yet who we are 100 percent of the time. But it is who we want to *be* 100 percent of the time. ZEFER could become that special company, and that belief makes my decision a no-brainer.

I reconvene the group and announce, "I've decided to pull our IPO." I silently count to ten before I continue. But no one says a word. "The only reason we're taking ZEFER public at this time . . ." I pause. "I repeat, the *only* reason is to take advantage of a highly valued market. If that's not possible, then let's benefit from operating as a private company until the right market conditions return."

Everyone supports my decision, and their support grows stronger the next day when it becomes clear that the Nasdaq had been on its way to its largest one-day correction ever. Our board and bankers resoundingly agree that my decision was both brilliant and courageous.

Sixteen months later, when ZEFER files for bankruptcy, my board fires me. Perhaps my decision wasn't so brilliant after all.

A Long and Winding Road

So, how did I find my way to that hanger in Houston?

I grew up in the 1950s in Bridgeville, Pennsylvania, twelve miles southwest of Pittsburgh, and lived there until I graduated from high school. Bridgeville was a coal mining town. Fifty percent of all of the coal mined in the US came from the 888 working mines that were within a twenty-mile radius. But thirty-eight major steel mills fueled most of the Pittsburgh economy, and comprised 60 percent of the male workforce. It's no wonder that almost everyone I knew as a child was either a steel worker or a coal miner.

My grandfather, Anton, dug coal for the National Mining Company until he died. Josephine, my grandmother, immigrated to the US from Lithuania in 1914 to become Anton's mail-order bride. It wasn't love that brought them together. It was the terror of a world war that was fast approaching her countryside farm. She gambled that becoming a

mail-order bride for a Bridgeville coal miner would be her fastest path to a safer and, hopefully, better life. On her first trip away from home, she voyaged across the Atlantic to New York for processing, and then on to Bridgeville where she met Anton for the first time.

Josephine and Anton only had one child. My mother, Albena, was born in their home and lived there her entire life. She married my father, Skip. After I was born, the five of us shared their two bedrooms. Our home came with mineral rights for the veins of coal that ran underneath it. I remember my grandfather mining it from a hill that bordered our property, hauling it to our coal cellar, and then shoveling it into our furnace every morning and evening to keep us warm.

My grandfather died of a heart attack in February 1956, a few months before I turned five years old. He was pruning branches in the big apple tree in our backyard and fell to the ground clutching his chest. The last time I saw my grandfather, he was demanding a shot of whiskey before he left for the hospital. His was my first funeral. I think that a child never forgets their first funeral. I know I'll never forget Anton's.

I had wondered if my grandparents ever fell in love. I never saw them kiss or hug or spend any time doing anything alone with each other. But I never saw them argue or raise their voices or be disrespectful to each other, either. On the morning before Anton's burial, my grandmother took me aside for a private chat. She was a very strong person but was unable to hold back her tears when she told me how much she loved him. Had she ever told him that?

Or were those expressions of affection not viewed as proper in their generation? In any case, Anton got his money's worth when he "bought" Josephine.

I was twelve years old when I first heard the word "entrepreneur." At the time, my mother was competing in a weekly *Pittsburgh Post-Gazette* puzzle contest where the editors scrambled the letters of an occupation. The puzzles grew harder every week. Undaunted, my mother continued to decipher them correctly. I remember the contest's final week. Sitting with my mother at the kitchen table, we opened the newspaper and saw "tuepenererenr" staring at us from the last page of the business section.

"Entrepreneur," she declared without hesitation, confirming my belief that she was the smartest person in all of Bridgeville!

"What does an entrepreneur do?" I asked, not quite pronouncing it correctly.

"They have an idea that they turn into a company and make millions of dollars doing it," Mom replied. It was clear to me that entrepreneurship would be a better path than working in the coal mines or steel mills. But it wasn't at all clear how I could get there.

I didn't hear the word "entrepreneur" again for another ten years, when I eagerly enrolled in Entrepreneurship 101 as a first-year MBA student at Carnegie Mellon University. A guest speaker taught our third class—a tall, gangly guy, with dark horn-rimmed glasses, wearing clothes that did not match. He introduced himself: "I graduated from Carnegie-Mellon twelve years ago with a PhD in Physics"—pausing just long enough for us to be impressed by his credentials. "And now I am founder and CEO of a company that sells playground equipment."

In concert, everyone in our class rolled their eyes and smirked. We all shared the same thoughts. "Who *is* this loser?" "What's *he* doing here?" And, "Now it's clear why his clothes don't match."

He continued. "I see the look on your faces. Before you judge me too harshly, let me tell you something. Only New York and Chicago have more Fortune 500 headquarters than Pittsburgh. And last year, only four Pittsburgh Fortune 500 CEOs made more money than I did."

He paused again as he scanned the room. "And I sell playground equipment."

I was hooked. My mother was right! I knew then that I wanted to be an entrepreneur, and I registered for every course that could prepare me.

As graduation neared, the founder/CEO of a local manufacturing startup offered me a job. I would be his protege and learn his business, bottom up, so I could succeed him when he retired in five years.

Over-the-top excited, I rushed home to tell my parents the good news. They had always been very supportive—until that moment. Mom shook her head while Dad said, "No. We didn't contribute to your education for you to work in a factory. Keep looking for a job until you find one where you'll wear a coat and tie to work."

That's how I landed at Air Products, a Fortune 100 company, in their career development program designed to groom high-potential new hires by rotating them through three departments during their first two years. Air Products' CIO convinced me to accept an initial assignment as a systems analyst in management information systems. I explained that I had no interest in information technology (IT) and did not even know what a systems analyst was. The CIO argued that, because I knew nothing about IT, this position presented the perfect opportunity for me to invest eight months to learn about it. His perverse logic intrigued me, and I agreed to start my career in the field where I was least prepared. After all, the rotation would only last for eight months.

My eight months in IT turned into more than twelve years. During that time, I was assigned to several roles where I was able to both learn and make a difference. That provided the pathway for me to move into executive roles. But I longed for a chance to make more impact on a business than an IT executive could have at a Fortune 100 industrial gas and chemical company.

I hoped I'd find my passion in the world of startups and left to join McCormack & Dodge (M&D) as general manager of one of their businesses. Everything was so different! And so much better! The energy, the passion for the corporate mission, the feeling that we could make decisions and get things done, and of course the beer kegs in the lobby that were tapped at 6:00 p.m. every Thursday and Friday—it was just as the twelve-year-old "tuepenerernr" had pictured life at a startup.

A few weeks into it, our sales vice president invited me to join her on a trip to an industrial glove company in the Midwest. Since this was my first sales call ever, naturally I was more than a bit nervous.

But I enjoyed it. I thought I did a good job telling M&D's story, and I seemed to connect with their CEO. But as my sales vice president warned, "You never know in sales until you get the order."

A week passed without any follow-up from our prospect. Then I received a FedEx envelope addressed to me. I opened it and found a $740,000 check to purchase M&D's software—made out to "Bill Seibel– McCormack & Dodge"!!! For the first time in my career, I experienced what it felt like to directly impact the business. I owned the profit and loss (P&L). This was *my* deal. My name was on the check! And I competed against our arch-rival MSA and won! That feeling hooked me for forever. I was on my way to becoming a serial entrepreneur.

M&D's rivalry with MSA was fierce. Both companies routinely interfered with each other's sales pitches and conferences by calling hotels and airlines to cancel their rival's reservations. Monash Research reported that MSA once disrupted a major M&D contract signing by calling the police to have our account manager arrested for delinquent child support.[1] Eighteen months later, after learning that the two companies were merging, I decided to leave to avoid an inevitable clash of cultures.

My next stop was MMS, where I stumbled into my first CEO role. Next, I joined Index Technology as executive vice president of operations. Index went public, reached revenue of $44 million, and merged with Sage Software to create a business with one hundred thousand users in ten thousand accounts across the world.

Soon after the merger, I joined Cambridge Technology Partners (CTP) as a member of the founding team. By the time I departed in 1998, the company had gone public (second best performing IPO of 1993) and grown to over $800 million in revenue, with four thousand employees in fifty offices and a $5 billion market cap.

ZEFER followed CTP. Then on to Demantra, my first business turn-around. After I pivoted our business to a predictive analytics solution that drove sales and operations planning, Demantra earned the *Best Business Turnaround* award. That recognition led to Oracle acquiring us.

Next, I launched Gumball, a consulting firm focused on helping startups scale their businesses rapidly. Ultimately, I served as a board member or advisor for more than thirty of my clients. Occasionally, those positions resulted in an operating role. As CEO of LogMatrix and OpenService, I led both to successful exits.

In 2011, I was lured into founding "one more startup." Mobiquity was named the fastest growing company in New England in 2015 and was acquired by Hexaware in 2019 for $182 million. That led me to launch Totality, an "internet of things" company that I rolled into Rocket Wagon.

And, God willing, there will be more to come.

Parting Thoughts

In business and in life, set personal standards that are aspirational. They may not define who you are 100 percent of the time—but they define who you want to be 100 percent of the time.

The next chapter explores what might hook you on entrepreneurship and where your path may lead.

· · ·

CHAPTER TWO

Getting Hooked—Why Start a Company?

It is a dimension as vast as space and as timeless as infinity. It is the middle ground between light and shadow, between science and superstition, and it lies between the pit of man's fears and the summit of his knowledge. This is the dimension of imagination. It is an area we call the Twilight Zone.

— Rod Serling's original opening narrative for *The Twilight Zone.*

Mobiquity's Founder And CEO Bill Seibel Is Unstoppable

Are You Cut Out to Be an Entrepreneur?

IT SEEMS TO me that Rod Serling's description of the "Twilight Zone" perfectly defines a startup. Launching a new venture presents both significant challenges and tremendous opportunities. On good days, running a startup can make you feel like you are a key member of a close-knit team that's on a mission from God to change the world. When your new product hits the market, or you win a new client or, better yet, one of your clients sends a handwritten note to thank you for doing a good job—that feels like you've just won an Olympic gold medal! And when momentum builds and you start to accomplish something that all the experts, industry analysts, and investors who turned you down insisted was "not possible," you feel unstoppable. That contagious energy triggers the biggest professional high that you can ever have.

But not all days are good. Most are hard. Sometimes you'll feel like Sisyphus, punished by the gods to push a rock to the top of a mountain only to see it roll back down again, over and over for eternity. But you can't allow bad days to get you down. I don't think Camus knew much about entrepreneurs, but he captured our spirit when he wrote, "Sisyphus' fate and his endless toil is not futile. The struggle itself toward the heights is enough to fill a man's heart. One must imagine Sisyphus happy." For an entrepreneur, it's not just about enjoying the reward of reaching the mountain top. It's mostly about savoring the experience of pushing that damn rock up the hill.

Why launch a startup? For the fame? For the money? For independence? If so, you're very likely to be disappointed.

The Small Business Administration reports that more than 627 thousand new businesses are launched in the US every year.[2] The pool of wannabes is even higher. A 2018 Qualtrics survey found that 32 percent of Americans had considered starting a new business in the past twelve months. But the survey also found that a vast majority of them never made it beyond the dreaming stage. The top reasons: overcoming inertia (44 percent); lack of capital (42 percent); and fear of going broke.[3]

Based on my experience with the founders that I've mentored, people who launch companies are comfortable taking risks and strongly believe in their ability to get things done. They are driven by the feeling of independence that comes with being their own boss, followed by the potential of wealth creation. For them, that potential outweighs the risk of failure and bankruptcy. In fact, I believe the fear of failure is precisely what drives entrepreneurs to be successful.

But the math supporting wealth creation doesn't work for me. The key word is *potential*. Investopedia reports that 90 percent of new businesses fail within the first three years.[4] In their 2020 survey, Startup Genome cautioned that four out of every ten startups were in the "red zone"— meaning that they had three months or fewer of capital runway.[5]

Of the 12 million companies launched in the US during the last twenty years, only 145 are unicorns.[6] Aileen Lee, partner and founder of Cowboy Ventures, coined the "unicorn" term in 2013 to describe startups that are worth more than $1 billion. The odds for becoming a unicorn, even for a venture-backed startup, are less than 1 percent.[7] Clearly, you don't have to be the founder of a company valued at a billion dollars to make money. Ten percent of startups stay in business or exit to an IPO or successful acquisition—sometimes even for an attractive return. But startups do not represent a rational financial risk-reward model. If you are thinking about starting a company for the money, buy a lottery ticket instead.

I also believe that "independence" is overrated. Startups create a number of dependencies. When I start a company, I recruit people to leave their jobs and join me. Their families depend on my making payroll. And in turn, I depend on these key employees to keep the business alive and stick with me. Especially in tough times. It's challenging to find the first customers. I'll do whatever they ask if it means keeping them. Occasionally, I've raised friends-and-family money that carries with it a commitment that I will not let them down. More likely, I'll raise money from professional investors. But that process carries a price: monthly board meetings, pre-board meetings and post-board meetings; frequent calls; and a daily pain in the backside. As soon as they decide someone can do better than I can, I'll be fired. And I'll lose my unvested equity. Independent? I feel like I am working for my employees, their families, my customers, my investors, and my board—more bosses and responsibility than I had as an executive of a Fortune 100 company. "Interdependent" is a much better word.

Don't "press go" to launch a startup unless it's your obsession. If you have created your exit plan before you begin, then it's not an obsession. If you are passionate about your work and love what you do, you'll spend every possible moment thinking about your company. You won't let anyone convince you that you won't be successful. Your confidence will become infectious and keep you and your team going when times get tough. And the lasting satisfaction that comes from achieving it will fuel you to do it again and again.

Here's a secret. Every time I decide to start fresh again, I envision building the special company that I described in my last chapter. I know that sounds idealistic, and I'm careful to accept that I may never achieve it. Setting my sights on a special company is a design point that I imagine from the beginning, communicate to my team, and reinforce every chance I get. It's the aspiration and ambition that hooks me time and time again.

How Will Your Life Change?

An unidentified student of Warren G. Tracy said, "Entrepreneurship is living a few years of your life like most people won't so you can spend the rest of your life like most people can't." Perhaps because of Carol's unwavering support at home and her many contributions to my startups, I don't see it that way. There were good days, and we celebrated those together. There were hard days, and we faced the challenges together. But I don't remember many truly bad days. Entrepreneurship, for me, is living most of my life doing exactly what I love to do. That's why I keep doing it.

But when you become an entrepreneur, your life *will* change. Before you take the plunge, ask yourself some critical questions.

- Can you become comfortable operating outside of your comfort zone? You'll face many decisions in areas where you have only limited knowledge and experience. Your employees, investors, customers, and partners will rely on you to make the right decision, and the success or even the survival of your startup will depend on it. Can you handle that pressure?

- Will the volatility of a startup frighten you? Or will it energize you? Startups are unstable. Things change—unexpectedly, rapidly, and often.

- Will you be able to balance your work and personal priorities and find time to take care of your family, friends, and your own health? The traditional notion of work-life balance isn't realistic when you launch a startup. Entrepreneurs rarely "come home from work." The boundaries between your personal life and work life will blur. Regardless of what time the phone rings, you won't be able to resist answering it. You'll check emails in the middle of the night to be sure you don't miss one that's urgent. You won't do this because you have to. You'll do it because you're in charge and you'll feel compelled to. Startups fall somewhere between a passion and an obsession.

What Makes an Entrepreneur "Serial?"

Sleeping Beauty's famous quote is sage advice for entrepreneurs: "If you dream a thing more than once, it's sure to come true." Perhaps that's why my casual LinkedIn search found 858,000 people who self-identify as serial entrepreneurs. Wow! But practically all of us will reach a point when we'll pause and wonder if we have one more startup in us. I reached that point midway through my six-month "paid garden leave" after selling Demantra to Oracle in 2006, I wasn't permitted to start another job because I had to be available in the event that Oracle needed me. But they never did.

Beginning in May that year, my family and I transitioned to our home on Cape Cod. Carol nervously wondered what it would be like to have me home all day, every day, from May through October. None of my previous breaks had ever exceeded two weeks, and Carol recalled that I would always become fidgety by day seven.

But the months passed quickly. The weather was perfect for a full agenda of activities: golf in the morning, Old Silver Beach with my family in the afternoon, cookouts with friends in the evening, frequently followed by good wine and great music at our firepit until the wee hours. And I checked off a list of household projects whenever I found the time. This summer was shaping up to be the best ever. I didn't want it to end. For the first time in my life, at fifty-four years old, I contemplated retirement.

Near the end of my time off, our close friends Michael and Peggy joined us for a long weekend. Friday was a late night for everyone. The firepit conversation turned to my brewing thoughts about retirement. Michael and Peggy were skeptical. "You'd go crazy if you retired," they both agreed.

Early Saturday morning, I was the last person to stumble downstairs. Carol was making breakfast while Peggy and Michael were having coffee. As I approached the kitchen, I heard Carol say, in a non-pejorative way, "Look at what Bill did to this kitchen drawer." Anticipating a compliment, I hurried into the kitchen so I wouldn't miss it.

I saw Carol opening and closing our "junk drawer," and doing it quite fluidly. Most people have a junk drawer somewhere in their kitchen. It's the one that has the big stuff—the spatulas and potato masher—mixed in with everything from rubber bands to tongs, pizza cutters, and ice cream scoops.

"This was the most mucked-up drawer in the kitchen," Carol continued. "Bill took the initiative to take out all the utensils, measure them, design an efficient, three-dimensional storage grid, build it in his shop in the basement, and install it! Now look. It's the most organized drawer in the entire house!"

I'm a blue-collar guy from Pittsburgh. For me, it couldn't get any better than this. My wife was bragging about something I had built with my own two hands. I pictured my father smiling down at me from heaven, proudly thinking, "That's my boy." I stood there quietly grinning.

That's when Peggy looked at me and said, "So this is what retired people talk about?" That was a dagger in my heart. My big grin turned into a blush of embarrassment.

We didn't talk about the kitchen drawer or retirement for the remainder of the weekend. But first thing Monday morning, I was on the phone searching for ideas for my next startup. My garden leave taught me that whatever I do in life, I'll never be bored. But the fear of being *boring* scared the hell out of me. I also realized that I'm a better CEO than I am a golfer—although that isn't a very high bar. And I still have that kitchen drawer hanging in my office to remind me of that.

What's It Like to Start a Company?

Several years later, prompted to "do just one more startup," I launched Mobiquity. After witnessing the massive change that occurred when the internet evolved from brochure-ware to e-commerce sites, I believed that large enterprise investment in mobile would follow the same path. So, I did what I always do. I reached out to everyone who I hoped might have a useful point of view to ask for their reactions to my idea. I started by calling Michael, joking that I had abandoned my kitchen drawer business to start another company, and asking him to join me as my cofounder. He agreed. By the end of the following week, we recruited another four team members.

A week later, I reached out to an executive of a large New York bank to test Mobiquity's value proposition and explore my hypothesis that mobile wasn't just about the simple $25,000 apps. Instead, it was a platform that could drive innovation within a business. Our call was brief. I told her that I was planning on launching a professional services firm focused on mobile for large enterprises. She immediately invited me to come to her office the next day so that she could learn more. I took that as a positive sign.

The next day, I began our meeting by asking, "Is mobile on the bank's radar screen? How do you envision the technology impacting your business? Are there specific projects planned?"

"We see mobile as a game changer," she began. "In fact, I'm looking for a partner to work with us on a very large, strategically important project." But before I could get too excited, she confided, "I've already spoken to an industry analyst who recommended thirty-five companies with the depth and breadth of experience to help."

As soon as I heard that, I began packing up. I was very encouraged that I was right about the opportunity. Mobile resonated with large enterprises and it appeared that they were prepared to invest in it. But I was disappointed that so many of the large, established consultancies were already pursuing it. I wondered if I was already too late. But the bank executive stopped me. "Wait," she said, "Don't leave. Tell me about *your* company."

I shared my view that mobile wasn't just about simple, gimmicky apps. It was a key component of a new technology stack (including social, internet of things, big data, and the cloud) that would enable companies to drive innovation that would transform their businesses. As I took her through our value proposition, her eyes lit up. "That's precisely what large enterprises need, and none of the other thirty-five companies seem to understand that. What the hell, I'm going to add you to the list. You're number thirty-six. What's the name of your company again?" I didn't want to tell her that we didn't have a name yet, so I said, "We're rebranding and changing our name. I'll call you tomorrow to tell you what we've decided." We were a semi-finalist for what was probably, at that time, the largest mobile project ever, and not only didn't we have a name—we didn't even have a company.

I called her the next morning to tell her that our new name is "Mobilocity." But before I could say anything, she interrupted. "Congratulations! We narrowed the list last evening, and you're one of ten companies that made the finals! You'll be pitching to our executive team in four weeks, and I've scheduled you to be the final presenter on the last day. Does that work for you?"

Does that work? Yessssssssss! I knew that we did not have a chance to win—but pitching to their executives would both force us to develop our pitch and serve as good practice. We spent the next three weeks defining our methodology and recruiting the remainder of our team, leaving us with just four days to create our presentation.

We met for dress rehearsal before our pitch. It was a good thing we did, because three of my new teammates didn't own a sport coat or a necktie. We stopped at a men's clothing store on the way to the bank.

When we arrived, security escorted us to a waiting area for check-in. That gave us a chance to peek at the sign-in sheet to see who we were competing with. As we suspected, we were up against the top firms in our industry. Twenty minutes later, the Mobilocity team was called into a large, plush conference room. Every seat was filled by a bank executive, and twenty additional people stood along the wall behind them. Even in this imposing setting, we weren't a bit nervous. We knew we didn't have a chance to win, and so had nothing to lose.

My team did a great job explaining our value proposition. The close was left to me.

"Thank you for your time and attention today. I know you have a very important decision ahead of you. I'm aware of the solid credentials of the other companies presenting today, and I'm sure they've told you about the impressive mobile solutions they've built for their clients." I paused to give them time to nod their heads.

I continued, "Mobilocity hasn't built anything for anybody." I paused again. "That's right, you heard me correctly. We haven't built anything for anybody. Not yet. We don't have any clients, and if you select us, you'll be our first." The audience chuckled, some louder than others.

"But what we *do* have are the lead architects and designers from four of the companies that pitched to you today. They are the people who designed and built the solutions that our competitors impressed you with. Our competitors may have case studies and references. But we have the people who created those case studies and references." Their chuckles had turned into intense stares.

"Our first team members chose Mobilocity because they believe in our potential and the track record of the individuals on our team. When our first client selects us, it will be for the same reason. And if it's you, we won't let you down. I promise."

What the hell—we had nothing to lose.

Three weeks later, our contact at the bank called to say, "Congratulations—you won! Our budget is $5.6 million, we're under a significant time crunch, and you need to start next week."

I had no idea that the project was that big—$5.6 million! It was like the dog chasing the school bus—what do you do if you catch it? This win would fund our company and put us on the map as a major player.

The major player. But could we successfully execute? In order to meet the bank's timeline, we had only two weeks to recruit, hire, and train an additional twenty consultants, and shape them into a high performing team. Was the contract worth that risk? A multi-million-dollar vote of confidence like this one confirmed my belief that the potential for mobile reached far beyond simple apps. And competing against all the established industry leaders and winning even though the ink hadn't dried on our business cards, confirmed my belief in our value proposition. I believed that Mobilocity had too much potential to take this level of risk. After celebrating with my team, I told them I would be calling the bank to decline. I explained that the project was way too big for us out of the gate, and, as a result, we faced a high risk of failing. "Building a successful company isn't just about winning a deal," I said. "It's about delivering value to our clients and building long-term relationships with them."

My team glared at me like I had lost my mind. They screamed, "You're crazy! Turn down a $5.6 million deal? So, what if we fail! We'll be $5.6 million richer!"

"Listen. We need to do the right thing," I argued. "We all believe that mobile is going to create a huge opportunity for professional services firms. If we launch our company with a project that's almost certain to fail, we'll lose our opportunity forever. Let's start with a project where we know that we can be successful."

"Bottom line!" they replied. "If you decline, all of us quit, and we'll do this without you."

But I remembered telling the bank's executive committee, "We will not let you down. I promise."

I declined the offer, and it turned out that my team hadn't been bluffing. All of them resigned on the spot. Well, everyone except Michael. The day before, Mobilocity could boast of the best team in the industry and the largest project. Then it became just Michael and me. But we hadn't lost everything. We were emboldened by a confirmation that we had identified untapped market potential and had developed a compelling customer value proposition. And we had constructed a methodology that we believed would deliver on it. We also had a reminder that you don't start a company for the money, even if it's $5.6 million. A company will only be successful if the founders are passionate about the work and committed to making its clients successful. Michael and I restarted the company, renamed it Mobiquity, raised money, and rebuilt the team.

In the six years that I led the company, we worked with several hundred clients, delivered many high-impact, award-winning solutions, and never *let one client down*. And "passion for the work" continues to be a big part of Mobiquity's culture today.

Parting Thoughts

- Entrepreneurship isn't a job. It's a passion. Don't start a company for the money. The math doesn't work. Do it only if it's your obsession. If you are passionate about your business and love what you do, you'll spend every possible moment thinking about it. Both life and business should be obsessions, and neither should have a time-stamped exit plan.

- If you decide to become an entrepreneur, your life will change. Can you become comfortable operating outside of your comfort zone? Can you handle the pressure? Will the volatility of a startup frighten you or energize you? Will you, and will your family, accept the change in work-life balance that's inevitable when entrepreneurs pursue their passion?

- Aspire to build a special company—one that you'll look back at years later, still very proud that you played a central role in creating it. That pride will make you want to launch a startup again and again.

- There will be days when the rock that you are pushing up the mountain rolls back down. You'll occasionally contemplate giving up. We all do. Steve Jobs said, "I'm convinced that about half of what separates the successful entrepreneurs from the non-successful ones is pure perseverance." Before you decide to quit, take a moment and reflect on why you started. Enjoy both the struggle and the result.

So, if you've decided to enter the "middle ground between light and shadow, between science and superstition, and between the pit of man's fears and the summit of his knowledge," how do you find the *right* business idea?

• • •

CHAPTER THREE

Eureka! How to Find (and Validate) Your Business Idea

The best way to have a good idea is to have lots of ideas.

— Linus Pauling, Nobel Prize-winning scientist

How Do Entrepreneurs Discover Their Idea?

SEVERAL YEARS AGO, I was sitting in the back of a red 1995 Honda, Uber-ing to moderate a panel at Harvard. As we approached Cambridge, Steve, my driver, turned and said, "I hope you don't mind me asking, but what are you doing at Harvard?

"I'm chairing a panel there. It's a joint session for Harvard and MIT students and alums. They've asked me to share lessons I've learned from the startups I've worked with," I replied.

"Have you ever 'launched' a company?" Steve inquired.

Coincidentally, I had drafted a precise answer to that question in advance as part of my introduction. "I certainly have. I've been an operating executive in fifteen startups—CEO of six of those, and founder and CEO of three of them. And I've been on twenty-four boards and an advisor to another twenty startups," I said proudly.

Steve didn't comment until traffic slowed his car, when he turned around, to look me in the eye and say, "So...if you're keepin' score the right way, the answer is three?"

"What do you mean?" I asked.

"Well, if you aren't both the founder *and* the CEO, it doesn't count."

I thought, "Who does this annoying Uber driver, dressed in a wrinkled t-shirt, cargo shorts and sandals, driving a beat-up twenty-year-old car, think he is by challenging my credentials and telling me how to keep score?"

"So how many companies did *you* start—Mister *Uber* driver?" I countered with a smirk.

"Five," Steve answered.

My ride was coming to an end. Intrigued by our conversation, I realized that Steve and I had more in common than first thought. Had I had more time, perhaps I could have benefitted from his experience. Then it hit me—perhaps the group at Harvard could also learn something from Steve. I asked him to take a break from driving and join my panel. He agreed, and the stories he told were almost as good as mine! That's when I realized that entrepreneurs are everywhere, or at least that's true in Boston.

Midway through the panel discussion, someone asked, "Where do good ideas come from?"

One of the panelists responded, "My best ideas come from my own experiences—problems that I see as an employee or as a customer. I keep an eye open for jobs that need to be done—but can be done better." I agreed with her. GoForth Institute cites that an entrepreneur's own experiences inspire 60 percent of new business ideas.[15]

But Steve disagreed. "It comes down to vision," he said. "Great entrepreneurs see opportunities where 'mere mortals' see only chaos."

I explained that I use a different lens. I'm not a visionary. I'm more of a historian. I look across megatrends, try to identify patterns between them, and connect the dots. I explore what worked and what didn't work in the past, and I apply those lessons learned. I think about how emerging technologies might change the game. I frame the opportunity by stating, "It's just like idea X, except for Y and Z."

The business ideas that I've helped develop include:

- professional services companies built on the disruption created by each of the last four major technology waves;

- software solutions covering a wide range of enterprise business applications, as well as security, predictive analytics, operations management, software development tools, retail loss prevention, process management, cloud management, and data warehousing; and

- hardware solutions that provide pipeline monitoring by drones, sustainable solar-powered water treatment systems, medical imaging, and digital audio equipment.

I've been blessed that sometimes my lens works pretty well.

What Makes an Idea a "Good Idea?"

It's widely accepted that the secret comes down to vision, execution, and luck. But I believe that execution and either vision *or* luck are more accurate.

On a red-eye flight to Boston in early 1983, Richard Carpenter jotted down a two-page thought piece outlining his theory that the CAD-CAM technology engineers had adopted could be successfully applied to software engineering. As Richard tells it, "I presented that concept at several conferences. Afterward, a number of attendees would approach the podium and ask for the 'product's' name and who to contact for a demo. That gave me a real sense of market interest—if only we could build what they wanted."

The tool set didn't exist, nor had Richard intended to create one. But based on the response, he realized he must have stumbled upon something. So, he launched Index Technology in 1984, and introduced

Excelerator, the first PC-based computer-aided software engineering tool. Excelerator was named *Software Product of the Year* by the American Federation of Information Processing Societies in 1987, and Index Technology went public in 1988.

The rapid rise of the E-Z Lyft golf ball retrieving device provides a more recent example. When the USGA Rules of Golf were revised in 2019 to allow golfers to putt without removing the flagstick, Niagara Precision, a small machinery shop in Ontario, wanted to make it easier to retrieve a golf ball with the flagstick in place. That idea marked their eureka moment.

At first, I didn't get it. My problem isn't getting my golf ball *out* of the hole. If and when my ball falls in, I'm pretty good at getting it out on my own. My problem is getting my golf ball *into* the hole. I've bought my share of devices that promise to help me with that.

Bad idea? Not after the pandemic hit. When golf courses reopened, as a way to limit the potential spread of coronavirus, players were no longer allowed to reach into the cup to grab their ball. E-Z Lyft happened to hit the market in April 2020, a brilliant solution to a problem the inventors never envisioned. Within two months, the device was installed in almost 10 percent of US golf courses.[16]

Sometimes *luck* trumps *vision*.

As We Say in Pittsburgh, "Does That Dog Hunt?"

Most new business ideas aren't good ideas, and some are really, really bad. Makes you wonder, "What were they thinking?"

What about Freewheelz, a dot-com e-commerce startup? The company promised a free, one-year lease to anyone willing to drive a car covered with advertisements and be bombarded by nonstop ads on a radio that could not be turned off. Skip Lehman, the founder and CEO, explained that he borrowed the business model from free TV programming financed by commercials. All an applicant had to do was go to Freewheelz.com and complete a 600-question survey that covered everything from eating habits to hair loss. To re-apply for a second year, applicants had to submit their tax returns, notarized video-store-rental receipts, and a stool sample.

Bad idea? Clearly. But it was a really, really good April Fools' Day prank devised by Ted Fishman, *Esquire's* contributing editor. For *Esquire's* April 2000 edition, Ted wanted to create a business idea so preposterous that everyone would immediately know it was a joke. David Granger, editor-in-chief, said, "We thought people would see immediately that the article is an April Fools' prank. But even before the story left the printer, people were asking how they could sign up for their free cars."

It got sillier. Before *Esquire* hit the newsstands, a Silicon Valley reporter on deadline heard about Freewheelz and desperately wanted to interview their fictitious CEO for a feature story. And a venture capitalist called Mr. Fishman to tell him that he had met three companies pitching similar ideas over the prior six months. *Esquire* received so many inquiries about where to apply for the free car that Fishman paid $75 to register the domain name Freewheelz.com and set up a website to explain the hoax. It averaged 5,000 hits per day. And Larry Butler, CEO of freecar.com, confessed to Fishman that he was so frightened by the prospect of this new competitor that he cried when he read the article. He eventually bought the domain name from *Esquire* for $25,000.

Who is dumb enough to buy a bad idea? I am. I scoffed at the Pet Rock (five million sold in six months, netting $15 million), and mood rings ($250 million in sales within four months). But in 1999, I felt compelled to purchase Swatch's Beat watch. In fact, I bought twelve of them, at $90 a pop, as a holiday present for each member of ZEFER's founding team.

I still have mine. It's a funky looking watch with an even funkier value proposition—to change the entire concept of time as we know it. Nicholas Negroponte, the MIT Media Lab founder, said in the 1998 announcement, "Internet Time is absolute time for everybody. Internet Time is not geopolitical. It is global. In the future, for many people, real time will be Internet Time." Swatch discarded the concept of the 24-hour day comprising 60-minute hours and replaced it with a measurement based on "Swatch .beats," a unit of time that divided the day into 1,000 units. An hour was redefined as 41.666 .beats, a minute became 0.6944 .beats, and a second amounted to 0.01157 .beats. Swatch eliminated time zones so it would be the same time everywhere in the world. They also moved the prime meridian from Greenwich to Biel, Switzerland, home of the Swatch factory. Are you beginning to understand why their scheme might have been a bad idea? It was not possible for me to use my new watch to tell time. And I couldn't get used to saying, "I'll be there in .6944 .beats."

Is it really that difficult to recognize when an entrepreneur has a bad idea? Lord knows that there are many successful companies whose value propositions seemed silly at first. An article titled, "18 of the Most Ridiculous Startup Ideas that Became Successful,"[17] asked, "If you were a venture capitalist and were pitched one of these ideas, what would your reaction have been?" The business ideas:

- It's like email or SMS, except that it does a lot less. (Twitter)

- It's another file sharing and syncing platform—even though the market already has a bunch of them that no one uses. It will only do one thing well, and you'll have to move all of your content to use it. (Dropbox)

- It's like the previous nineteen search engines that have either been abandoned or are commoditized money losers. Except we'll strip out all of the ad-supported news and portal features, so you won't be distracted from using the free search stuff. (Google)

It's not hard to develop an opinion, whether right or wrong, on the potential of a new business idea. The tough part is telling the entrepreneur, I mean the emperor, that he has no clothes. It's not easy to challenge a colleague who's passionate about his idea and is following his heart to tell him, "Your business concept sucks."

I've had more than a few bad ideas pitched to me, and one of the worst was a mobile app named "IJustDied." It was 2012.

"Can you say that again?" I asked the senior Fortune 1000 executive who scheduled the call with me.

"The name of my app is IJustDied," he said more emphatically. "Don't you get it? There are a lot of loose ends that need to be tied up after you die. And it's expensive if they're not taken care of quickly."

"Like what?" I asked. I still didn't get it. And frankly, I thought he might be pulling my leg.

"Like canceling your iTunes account. The deceased's family often forgets to do that. And if they *do* remember, they might not know the password. That costs several dollars every month. Add to that all of the other digital subscriptions with a monthly fee and things like Facebook or Instagram that you need to close down."

"That's it?" I asked.

"No," he replied. "That's the beauty of it. There are an unlimited number of use cases. For example, many people subscribe to their hometown newspaper just to look at the obituaries to see if anyone they knew died. With IJustDied, a message can be broadcast to all of your friends automatically. No need to subscribe to the local newspaper any longer!" He paused to gauge my reaction. After a moment, he said, "I bet if you think about the power of the app for a moment, you can think of other use cases. Go ahead and give it a try."

It was time for me to pull his leg. "I'm number thirty-two on the membership waiting list for my country club. When I drive by the clubhouse and see the flag at half mast, I know a member has died. And that means that I'm one step closer to getting in. Could IJustDied help me track that?"

"Great idea!" he boomed. "I hadn't thought of that use case. I told you that this would be easy. Try another one."

Clearly, he didn't get my joke. Perhaps if I tried harder... "What if I was on the run and wanted to steal someone's identity? Could I ask IJustDied to inform me whenever a blue-eyed male who was my age, height, and weight died—and get his name, address, and date of birth?"

The aspiring entrepreneur thought about it for a moment. "I'm sure the app could do that. How big do you think that market is?"

I dodged his question. "Okay. I now understand how IJustDied works, and I appreciate the breadth of use cases that it can support. But how do you monetize that?"

"Advertising," he responded without a moment's hesitation.

I was beginning to have quite a bit of fun with our discussion. "So, do you anticipate any difficulty in finding sponsors who want to target their advertising dollars at dead people?"

After a long pause, he said, "You have me there. I'll have to think more about that. But other than that, what's your take on my idea?"

I knew that nothing I said would deter him from his quest. "I think that it's a good idea," I fibbed. "But keep working on the business case. Perhaps if there's ever a worldwide pandemic, you might have something there." I ended our call and "died laughing!"

How I Find *the Next Big Thing*

I've already confessed that I'm not a visionary. I'm more of a historian. My track record in predicting the future is even worse than a Boston meteorologist's seven-day forecast. But you don't have to be a fortune teller to recognize when a new megatrend is taking shape. When things change, opportunities are born. And when they change a lot, investment themes emerge. I look for the major problems and opportunities that a megatrend creates, consider how technology could provide solutions, and form a hypothesis. Then I test my hypothesis with thought leaders and the people (consumers and business executives) who are likely to be impacted by the new trend. I'll go through dozens of iterations before I reject the idea or believe that I have it right.

Increasing life span is an emerging megatrend introduced to me by Dominic Endicott, founder of 4Gen Ventures. For the first time in recorded history, four generations will routinely be alive at the same time. In 1900, the average global human life span was thirty-one years. By the end of World War II, it rose to forty-eight. Today, with more than a billion people aged sixty or older, the average life expectancy is more than seventy. Lynda Gratton and Andrew Scott, in their book, *The 100-Year Life*, state that "A child born in the West today has more than a 50 percent chance of living to be over 105."[18] Can you imagine what our world will be like when more than half of our population is over one hundred years old? None of our social, political, and economic systems were built to accommodate an increase in life spans this dramatic. Employment, retirement, education, healthcare, transportation, housing, businesses, and business models will all have to be rethought and redesigned.

Trends that create pervasive challenges often lead to significant new opportunities. That's true with the advent of "4Gen." Dominic explains:

> People are not only living longer, they are healthier, more active and working longer than previous generations. In a 4Gen world, 85-year-olds willingly work thirty-hour weeks, homes adapt to an owner's age and ability, towns and cities are redesigned to be more people friends, and vehicles become our servants. A tsunami of trapped house equity is released, and entirely new product categories emerge—lifetime mortgages, hybrid long-term care, upgradable home modules, intra-generational wealth contracts, and multi-generational cruises. Colleges educate all ages and learning is continuous. Recreation replaces retirement; age-mingling supplants age-segregation. Death is dignified, and taxes are reasonable. Resources are used ever more efficiently, and emissions are willingly curbed.[19]

The intersection of these massive changes, along with advances in technology, will enable entrepreneurs to create the new business models that will drive the "next big thing."

To successfully address these opportunities, companies will need to adopt new mindsets. For example, most businesses target millennials.

Advertisers spend 500 percent more on them than all other age groups combined.[20] However, 116 million people in the US over age fifty spend $8 trillion annually and own 40 percent of disposable income and 83 percent of wealth. The over-fifty cohort will grow 45 percent by 2050, while the under-fifty population will expand by just 13 percent.[21]

If a newly hired S&P 500 chief marketing officer unveiled a marketing strategy to redirect attention and resources away from the largest, fastest growing, wealthiest demographic to the slowest growing demographic with the lowest disposable income, what do you think would happen? And would you be swayed from terminating them if they defended their strategy by saying, "But then we'll be in a very strong position when the purchasing power of that age group increases forty quarters from now"? And yet, for the last twenty years, driven by their quest for the millennial dollar, many enterprises have been skewing their priorities in precisely this direction. As a result, roughly 95 percent of marketing expenditures target 24 percent of the disposable income. Pareto would roll over in his grave.

I have faith that soon, many corporations will stop treating their older customers as an afterthought. Some forward-thinking enterprises are beginning to rethink their business models and reinvent their products and services to tap into this emerging market opportunity. "Age-tech," a digital means to enable longevity to be a blessing, not a curse, will emerge as a major new investment theme.

Only 35 percent of people over 75 report feeling "old."[20] Companies should not design products and services for "geezers." That's the kiss of death for any brand. Old people don't want to buy "old people products." The trick is to tap into this market using a multigenerational, "age-friendly" approach—create products and services that accommodate the needs and support the use cases of older consumers without being perceived as "your parents' brand."

A successful pivot could involve something as simple as a subtle change to an existing brand's messaging. For example, Petco recognized they were losing previously loyal older customers to online pet food delivery services. They realized that, for this population, lugging a sixty-pound bag of dog food from the store to a car was increasingly difficult. Petco made a simple, cross-generational change to their messaging: "You can order ahead, and when you arrive, we will carry your order to your car." Recent studies show that their traditional 4Gen customers are coming back.

Alternatively, a 4Gen strategy could require both a major change in a product or service portfolio and a new marketing approach. Recently, Disney Cruise Lines developed a new concept to entice baby boomers to organize cross-generational family reunions, advertising, "Discover fun and relaxation for everyone in the family on a Disney Cruise." They refitted their ships to offer "onboard accommodations designed with your family in mind," "dining for every taste," and "entertainment that targets every age." Ford Focus is another great example. Engineers wore "Third Age Suits" to simulate an older person's experience in the car and make the ride more comfortable. However, the car's launch targeted a younger market. As the features of the car became apparent to older customers, they also started to prefer the brand.

4Gen is a social, political, and economic movement yet to be shaped. Age-tech, projected to reach $2.7 trillion by 2025, will be the enabler. In 2018, two major acquisitions signaled that this new era is already arriving. Amazon purchased PillPack, an online pharmacy that sorts a customer's medications by dose and delivers them to their front door, for $753 million. Two months later, Best Buy acquired GreatCall, "the leader in mobile solutions for active aging," for $800 million.[22]

Digital spending by and for older citizens is already "the next big thing," and will continue to grow much bigger. The race is now on to create the next wave of billion-dollar age-tech companies.

Parting Thoughts

- Paraphrasing Isaac Asimov, the most exciting phrase to hear in science—the one that heralds new discoveries—is not "Eureka!" (I've found it!), but rather is "That's odd..." Most new business ideas come from life experiences that just don't seem "right" and "need" to be improved. My good friend Thornton May said it best: "Things sucking is the Mother of Invention." I use a different lens. My ideas come from paying attention to megatrends and anticipating the problems they might lead to. In either case, my advice is to focus on who is facing the problem, how you can solve it, and who would be willing to pay for your solution. Test your hypothesis, iterate, and retest.

- Don't get too excited when your colleagues tell you it's a great idea or dejected when you're told it sucks. You're sure to hear both.

- After you've decided to be an entrepreneur—and found a business idea that you're passionate about—how do you name your startup?

  - Select a name that won't pigeonhole you in the future. Would you think of calling "Western India Palm Refined Oil Limited" to lead you company's digital business transformation? Of course not. Fortunately, when they expanded from manufacturing and selling vegetable oil to Indian housewives, to becoming one of the world's largest IT companies, they were able to shorten their name to Wipro.

  - Make sure that the name is simple, easy to pronounce, and easy to spell. If not, it will be more difficult for your potential customers to find you.

  - Try to find a name that conveys an image. JetBlue is a great example.

- Connect your name to a story. Give your potential customers a cue that will help them remember you. ZEFER's name was tied to our belief that the growth of the internet was like a wind from the west that would change the climate of business. Mobiquity came from our conviction that mobile was becoming ubiquitous, making it a powerful force that enterprises could leverage to drive innovation. But it doesn't have to be that sophisticated. Cantina named their company after the tavern where, over drinks, they decided to launch their consulting startup. And the tavern's sign still hangs in the lobby.

- Finally, conduct a thorough internet search to ensure that your name is available and not too similar to that of any of your competitors.

Now that you've signed up to pursue your passion, and have locked onto a business idea that may be "the next big thing," are you ready to step into the CEO role, build your team, and lead them to a successful outcome? The next chapter discusses how life changes on the day that you become a first-time CEO. I wish that someone prepared me for that reality twenty-five years ago.

• • •

CHAPTER FOUR

What's It Like to Become a CEO?

I knew exactly what to do. But in a much more real sense, I had no idea what to do.

— Michael Scott, fictional CEO of the TV series, The Office

CEO-ship

ACCORDING TO A 2013 *Harvard Business Review* survey, there are more than fifteen thousand books on leadership in print.[8] Cairnway reports that Amazon currently offers 57,136 books with "leadership" in their title.[9] And articles on the topic continue to number in the thousands every year. 'Nuff said. There's nothing more I can add to this body of knowledge. I've read my share and still proudly display the classics on my office bookshelf. Just as a medical degree on my doctor's wall gives me confidence in his care, my book collection provides the credentials to "prove" I must be a good leader, right? Actually, none of them prepared me for how my life would completely change when I assumed the role of a first-time CEO.

How Does it Feel to Become a CEO for the First Time?

It feels like you are unprepared and unqualified for the job—an impostor waiting to be caught. If 70 percent of people report experiencing "impostor syndrome" at least once in their lives,[13] I would expect that an even greater percentage of first-time CEOs feel that way. In fact, a survey by Vantage Hill Partners reports that impostor syndrome scores as the biggest fear that all CEOs face.[14]

CEOs typically respond to the angst of impostor syndrome in one of two ways. Some procrastinate because they are paralyzed by self-doubt. Others (typically more successful) respond by over-preparing. If you ever worry that you're unprepared and unqualified to be a CEO, you are far from being alone. As the actress Tina Fey quipped in a 2010 interview, "I've just realized that almost everyone is a fraud, so I try not to feel too bad about it." If you feel like an impostor, keep in mind that almost everyone else feels the same way. The important thing is to be aware of how you respond to it.

My First CEO Gig

My first CEO gig is a secret. At least until now. I've kept the details to myself for more than thirty years. They don't appear on my resumé or LinkedIn profile, even though their absence creates a three-month gap in my work experience. I can live with that. After I tell you the story, I think you'll understand why.

I joined MMS, a software company, as COO on Monday, October 16, 1989, two days before their quarterly board meeting. Both of the company's investors invited me to share my first impressions over dinner after they flew into Boston from San Francisco that Tuesday night.

Discussing first impressions after only two days on the job with investors whom I had never met required tact—and two drinks in the bar before they arrived. Our conversation was casual until the lead investor's phone rang. As he scurried away from our table, I heard him say, "Oh no. Oh my God. Do you know if everyone is okay?" The other investor rushed out after him.

I sat there by myself for thirty minutes, wondering what happened and where dinner would go from here. They returned together and nervously told me that a 6.9 magnitude earthquake had hit San Francisco. Phone service was disrupted, so they were not able to reach all of their family members. They decided to return to their hotel to keep trying. Before leaving, they said, "We planned on spending time with you this evening and then again tomorrow afternoon. But we know you'll understand that everything's changed, and we're flying back to San Francisco tomorrow right after the board meeting. We're sorry we won't have more time together." I nodded to signal my understanding.

They continued as they put on their coats, "Before we leave, we need to tell you that we're going to fire your CEO tomorrow at the board meeting. He has no idea, so it's important that you don't say anything to anyone before we announce his termination and his successor."

I gulped and asked, "Who is his successor?"

"You are," they said as they dashed out of the restaurant. "Oh, by the way, congratulations!"

I didn't see that coming. I had learned a lot about succession planning as I worked my way up to an executive level at Air Products. And I was pretty sure that this wasn't the way it was supposed to work for a new CEO.

I spent the rest of the week meeting everyone in the company, beginning with my direct reports. Max, my chief information officer, was on the road through Thursday, so I scheduled a get-to-know-each-other meeting for 11:00 a.m. the next day. In the meantime, my other direct reports related stories about him that were, let's say, "unusual." Before MMS hired him, Max was an explosives and hand-to-hand combat specialist in Delta Force, the elite, special-operations force designed to "kill or capture high value units or dismantle terrorist cells." I asked, "Why was he kicked-out?" The answer was, "Mental stability and anger issues."

When Max joined MMS, he learned that a local gang was harassing a company team working on a project in Mexico. He volunteered to travel there to join our crew. The gang members were never seen again. Although Max didn't know much about IT, the CIO position was unfilled, and, as a reward, he was promoted to fill it. I thought back to when I joined IT at Air Products without any relevant experience. The good news—Max and I shared something in common. The bad news—I was in charge of a CIO who knew nothing about IT and who was a one-man killing machine too unstable to trust to dismantle terrorist cells. I expected this to be a management challenge.

When I walked into Max's office, I noticed he wasn't wearing a jacket and tie like everyone else. He was dressed in camouflage fatigues. His head was shaved, and he had a raven-black beard. Max was sitting at a desk cluttered with parts of I'm not sure what. On the corner was a picture of him with his girlfriend, but not your typical cute, cuddly picture. Both of them, garbed in martial arts robes with black belts, were airborne in the midst of Mae Tobi Geri kicks.

Max invited me to sit down. As I looked around, every chair was smashed. I decided to stand.

"Why are we here?" Max barked in a gruff voice.

"I'm here to learn more about what you do at the company and discuss what I need from you, and how I can help you be successful."

Max pounded his fist on the desk and shouted, "No! You should use our first meeting to get to know me better."

Caught off guard and already a bit intimidated, I stuttered, "Okay. So, tell me about yourself."

Max launched into his story, telling me about his tours of duty and the sequence of misadventures that got him kicked out. He talked about his interest in education and how he landed a job as a teacher in an elementary school.

I asked, "What did you teach?" I could tell by Max's scowl that he didn't like my question.

He shouted, "I taught kids! Good teachers don't teach subjects, they teach kids. I get very angry when people ask me that question."

I hurried to change the subject. "If you loved teaching, why did you leave?" I asked.

"I was fired," Max said as his expression changed and his face grew red. "I hated all the fucking paperwork—the lesson plans, grading papers. All that paperwork made me snap." I decided it wasn't a good time to tell him about the new, weekly status report I planned on introducing.

I figured it might be safer if we adjourned to the cafeteria. At least I would feel more secure with people around. We brought our lunch trays to our table and sat down. Max said, "I notice that you forgot to get a knife." As I began to stand up, he pulled a switchblade out of his boot and tossed it onto the wooden cafeteria table. "Here—you can use mine." Yep, this was going to be a management challenge.

Later that afternoon, my investors called to ask how I was doing and to inform me that they had unilaterally reached a deal for IBM to distribute our product. "IBM will sell a lot of our software," they said. "So, we no longer need a salesforce. You should begin to terminate them." I knew DEC, our biggest buyer, would drop us as their preferred vendor the minute they heard about the IBM deal. The tradeoff didn't seem logical, and it was risky to double down on that bet by terminating our sales team. But what did I know? I was just a first-time CEO.

At the end of the day, Paul, my CFO, asked if I would like to join him for a drink after work. "Barry (our sales vice president) and I are going to Froggy's, a local watering hole." I said, "Great idea! Let's leave now."

After our second drink, I overheard Barry ask Paul, "Anything new with our international accounts receivables issue?"

I jumped in, "What international accounts receivables issue?" I hadn't heard about any problems.

"Should we tell him?" Barry asked.

I asserted my newly bestowed authority. "I'm the CEO now. You *have* to tell me."

Paul reluctantly began filling me in. "Three of our distributors in Germany, Israel, and the Middle East were shot and killed at precisely noon last Saturday. The authorities are just beginning to investigate, but they suspect our guys were laundering weapons—buying them in Israel, moving them through Germany, and reselling them in the Middle East. They must have upset the wrong person, and all three were assassinated at the same time, apparently to send a message. And now, I'm not sure how we're going to collect our receivables. You're the CEO—do you have any ideas?"

I briefly considered sending Max in to sort this out. But I didn't. On my way home, not quite sure which part of my first week was real, which was a well-thought-out joke, and which had been a bad dream, I reflected on my recruiting process. Until now, I had believed that my due diligence was thorough. But I'd never thought to ask, "Is the company engaged in illegal international weapons laundering?" Or, "Just wondering, are any of my direct reports mentally unstable trained killers?" Or, "Any plans to walk away from our only strategic partner while disbanding our salesforce?" Should I add those questions to my list when I interview for my next job?

I began to look for that job the next day. Clearly, I had joined the wrong company and needed to get the hell out of there as quickly as I could.

I stayed at MMS for only three months, but that was more than enough time for me to learn that life changes quickly when a person becomes CEO. You have to pick your words carefully. All of a sudden, employees monitor every remark that comes out of your mouth and attribute wisdom to whatever you say. They watch everything you do, and your actions set the standard for their behavior. Most first-time CEOs feel like an imposter, waiting to be found out. I know that I felt that way. And it's lonely on that stage. All the colleagues you confided in are now direct reports. Do they pose confidentiality risks if you ask for their advice now? Are they still comfortable sharing confidential information with you? Is their advice now colored by their own personal and professional agendas? And your board doesn't fill that gap. It's not as if you can approach them and ask, "What should I do?"

The only advice I can provide is to get over it. That's just the way it is.

How to Be a Great CEO for Your Startup

Based on my experience mentoring many startup CEOs across a wide range of industries, I believe there are seven proficiencies that drive their performance.

1. Make Tough Decisions

As CEO, you are where the buck starts stops—and starts. As your company grows, making tough decisions is what you do all day long. Over time, you will learn to distinguish between decisions where you "could kick yourself" for getting it wrong, and those where you "could shoot yourself." Focus on the latter. Learn to delegate the former. While everything matters, some decisions really do change a company's trajectory—sometimes in unrecoverable ways. Those decisions need to be your focus.

Understanding the difference between decisions based on an analysis of risk and those driven by uncertainty helped prepare me for my first CEO gig. Shortly after I turned thirty, I was promoted to director of manufacturing materials management at Air Products. Moving from an IT staff position to managing 240 people represented a huge change in responsibility. All but twenty of them were union workers in our two manufacturing plants. Their average age was three years older than my parents.

A few weeks into the job, Charley, my purchasing buyer, interrupted a meeting when he barged into my office. His voice was always gruff, and he barked, "We need to talk now. You have a *big* problem." Charley went on to explain that we were scheduled to ship three LNG heat exchangers before the fiscal year ended, but our traditional supplier was unable to deliver the key component we needed to manufacture the units in time to meet our deadline. Heat exchangers were a highly profitable product for Air Products. Every unit we shipped added ten cents to our earnings per share. If a shipment was delayed, we would miss the earnings expectations that we set for the quarter, and our stock could plummet.

"You need to make a decision," Charley growled. "We can stay with our preferred supplier. We know they fabricate quality components, and until now, they've always delivered them when they promise. But if you wait for their shipment, you'll cause Air Products to miss our second quarter's earnings," emphasizing *you'll*. He continued, "Or you can decide to place the order with a Japanese supplier we've never used before, so we don't have any experience with their quality or their delivery track record. They say they'll get us what we need on time. But if the component is defective, Air Products will miss its earnings estimates for the entire year." Charley paused, looked me in the eyes and sneered, "What's your decision?"

This felt like a Kobayashi Maru, the fictional Star Trek exercise designed by the Starfleet Academy to test the character of cadets by observing how they perform in a no-win scenario. Nothing in my short career had equipped me to make this decision. So, I recalled my handy MBA training and said, "Thanks Charley. I now understand the problem. Give me your detailed staff analysis of each scenario."

Charley scowled at me. "That *was* my detailed staff analysis. Now what's your fuckin' decision?"

CEOs often don't have the information they need to make the right decision. A 2014 survey from Korn Ferry, cited in the *Harvard Business Review*, identified key behaviors that dramatically raise the odds that a CEO will be a high performer. Topping the list was decisiveness with speed and conviction. "Legends about CEOs who always seem to know exactly how to steer their companies to wild success seem to abound in business. But we discovered that high-performing CEOs do not necessarily stand out for making great decisions all the time; rather, they stand out for being more decisive. They make decisions earlier, faster, and with greater conviction. They do so consistently—even amid ambiguity, with incomplete information, and in unfamiliar domains. In our data, people who were described as 'decisive' were twelve times more likely to be high-performing CEOs."[10]

It's important for CEOs to understand the difference between *risk* and *uncertainty*. Risk can be measured and predicted, while uncertainty cannot.

Playing blackjack is an example of risk. Before taking another card, a skilled player can calculate the odds for each possible outcome and use them to guide how they play the game. Applying that process to business, a CEO can:

- identify a risk in advance by analyzing history;
- assess the probability of it occurring;
- perform a cost-benefit analysis of alternatives; and then
- make a decision.

Uncertainty is different. It can't be measured in quantitative terms using past models. Probabilities can't be applied to the potential outcomes, because the probabilities are unknown. Therefore, when facing uncertainty, it is difficult to predict a future outcome.

Charley was right about the heat exchangers. A detailed staff analysis wasn't possible. I just had to trust my gut and make a "fuckin' decision." I decided to hedge my bets by asking him to negotiate favorable cancellation terms with our preferred supplier and place an order with both vendors.

2. Be a Member of the Away Team

When you become a CEO, it's easy to forget about the field and trap yourself in your corner office, busy with lots of meetings and decisions, many of them important. But if you become completely disconnected from the front lines, you lose an important perspective while distancing yourself from the action and much of your team. That detachment makes leadership much harder. Instead, continue to be a member of the Away Team.

3. Be a Gap Filler

Conventional wisdom dictates that CEOs should tell their teams, "Don't bring me your problems; bring me solutions." How many times have you heard someone say that?

I don't subscribe to that approach. Sure, I want my team to do their best to solve the problems that confront them, and I don't want them to automatically use me as a crutch. But I also don't want them to be afraid to ask for my help—and I make that clear. When they turn to me, I don't offer to fix everything, but I do add my experience to theirs to help them solve the problem. I try to be a "gap filler."

Often, I'll ask for my team's help. If I'm struggling to figure out what to do, I'll walk through the building and recruit a group of "volunteers" to join me for an ad hoc brainstorming session. At Mobiquity, where our employees called themselves "Mobsters," my ad-hoc group of volunteer advisors became known as "Bill's Consigliere." Each member brought perspectives and insights that I didn't have. They often helped me figure out what was best to do, and all of us learned from that experience. Not once did they say to me, "Don't bring me your problems..."

The Kauffman Ewing Institute's research suggests that older founder/CEOs are more successful because they "bring significant assets in the form of personal experiences, business skills, and experiences with challenges that may seem insurmountable to a first-time founder." Kauffman goes on to report that, "The average entrepreneur of a successful startup is forty-five years old when they launch it. People over age fifty-five are twice as likely as people under thirty-five to launch a high-growth startup, and the average age of a founder of a successful startup with over $1 million in revenues is thirty-nine." The report concludes by stating, "Previous industry experience and startup experience had less impact on firm survival prospects than did owner's age."[11]

I tell my team that we're in this together. If you're stuck, bring your problem to me. I'm pretty good at helping you solve it.

4. "Make Shit Happen"

CEOs who are serial thinkers can methodically build a successful company over a long period of time. They manage their companies incrementally, step by step by step, and aren't looking to radically disrupt the status quo. They qualify as successful small-business owners, but not as successful entrepreneurs.

I once served on the board of a company founded by a CEO who built a very profitable professional services business. He reached $10 million in revenue, but it took him more than twenty years to get there. The CEO was a serial thinker, not a serial entrepreneur. Coming from an engineering background, he carefully plotted his progress, solving problems one step at a time. He summed up his own leadership style as "do no harm." Mine is "make shit happen."

When we first met, he confided that he needed to fill two gaps in his leadership team. "First," he said, "I want to replace my head of design. After that, I'll hire a vice president of sales."

"Why 'after that?'" I asked. "The two positions don't overlap. Tell your recruiter to search for both at the same time. You don't have to wait to find your sales vice president until after you replace your head of design."

"I like to focus on one important thing at a time," he responded.

After nine months on the board, I surfaced an outstanding candidate for vice president of sales, an exceptionally strong executive who could eventually replace the CEO. Although the design head was still in place, this sales executive prospect was too good to pass up. And it still wasn't clear to me why the timing of one hire was dependent on the timing of the other. I was part of negotiating the candidate's salary, had a very successful meeting, and called the CEO to ask him to make the formal offer and close the deal. A week later, the candidate contacted me to complain that he hadn't received a call. I followed up with the CEO who said, "Last week was very busy. And this week I have to focus on preparing for our company's holiday party. Then I'll need a few days of downtime after that. Tell him that I'll call sometime next week." Of course, we lost that candidate. Ultimately, it took almost three years to replace the design head. Sometimes "do no harm" does a lot of harm.

Not taking step B until you have successfully completed step A may eventually get you where you want to go. A deliberate, one-step-at-a-time approach may feel less risky, but it will take much longer. Remember, in a startup the tortoise seldom beats the hare. I'm not debating the importance of focusing or setting priorities. But I've found that the CEOs of fast-growing startups that I've advised are comfortable juggling a lot of balls in the air at the same time. They must—to move the needle. Accepting that some balls will drop, they believe the most important ones won't. Roy Ash, founder and president of Litton Industries, said, "An entrepreneur tends to bite off a little more than he can chew hoping he'll quickly learn how to chew it." Entrepreneurs subscribe to the airline overbooking theory of time management. Airlines typically overbook flights because they assume some passengers will not show up. In my experience, successful CEOs overbook their to-do lists because they assume that priorities will change and some tasks will be dropped. A key byproduct is that a sense of urgency becomes contagious across their organization.

I'm not suggesting that you attempt to do everything that comes to mind all at once. Successful CEOs must be selective and be comfortable saying "no." They need to focus on doing a very small number of things really well, and that discipline requires saying "no" to a thousand other temptations. But that "very small number" needs to exceed one priority at a time.

5. Teach

Harvey Mackay, author of the *New York Times* number one bestsellers, *Swim With the Sharks Without Being Eaten Alive* and *Beware the Naked Man Who Offers You His Shirt*, said, "A mediocre person tells. A good person explains. A superior person demonstrates. A great person inspires others to see for themselves." Great CEOs are teachers who demonstrate every chance they get. Their teams perform at a much higher level as a result. Storytellers make great teachers because good stories are easy to remember. It's really cool to hear someone retell a story I told years before and be able to relate it to a situation they are facing today.

Great CEOs also teach by placing their employees in theoretical situations and asking them how they would handle it. Soon after I joined McCormack & Dodge (M&D), the software company recognized that it faced a difficult year financially. The executive committee, chaired by founder/CEO Frank Dodge, planned to meet one afternoon to decide what, if any, preemptive actions M&D should take. I was a member of the management committee. Our weekly meeting was scheduled for the morning of that same day. One of our members shared a draft of the actions that the executive committee was contemplating. They included a hiring freeze, a reduction in the merit pool budget, a 25 percent bonus pool reduction, and a 10 percent reduction in the overall expense budget.

The management committee meeting resembled a corporate mutiny.

- "If we reduce our bonus pool or our merit pool, we'll signal that we don't care about our employees, and all the good ones will leave."

- "We're overworked now. There's no way we can ask our teams to do more. A hiring freeze will crush us."

- "I'm not going to be the one who delivers that idiotic message to my team. Let the executive committee do it."

- "If Frank were here, I'd tell him to his face."

That's when Frank Dodge unexpectedly walked into the room, leaned against a wall, and calmly asked, "Mind if I join you?" No one said anything. Frank broke the silence. "What's the management committee discussing this morning?" Frank knew exactly what we were talking about. "I'd like to give you some context." For the next ten minutes he explained the challenges that M&D faced and their potential impact on the company. He finished by asking, "What should we do?"—emphasizing *we*.

Without hesitation, one of the vice presidents who had been quite vocal in opposition a few minutes earlier said, "I think we should consider implementing a hiring freeze," and another said, "Consider? No, that's something we *have* to do." A third called out, "We should eliminate the bonus pool for the year." Followed by another member who added, "Yes, and defer all merit increases for the next six months."

I was stunned. The management committee was recommending measures more draconian than the executive committee had been considering. And they weren't kissing up. I could see that all of them totally reversed their positions when Frank presented the problem from the company's perspective, and they felt responsible for helping to solve it. It had become *their* problem.

After a few minutes, Frank said, "Spend some more time discussing what you think we should do, then email me your recommendations. I'll take them to the executive committee this afternoon." He walked out as casually as he had walked in, comfortable in the knowledge that he could count on his vice presidents to make tough decisions when they had to, and confident we would stand by him when he most needed our support.

I was the newest member of the group, so I had to ask, "What just happened here?"

Someone said, "It's easier to understand why a tough decision has to be made when you're the one making it."

6. Continue to Learn

Know when you need help. Find the balance between self-confidence and willingness to take feedback. I don't simply ask myself, "How could I have handled that better?" I ask others for their opinions as well.

7. Provide Clear, Frank Feedback

While preparing to conduct an exceptionally difficult performance review with one of my direct reports, I wondered, "What would Bill Parcells do?" The "Big Tuna" provided some insight in a *Harvard Business Review* article in 2000.

Bill Parcells, former head coach of the New York Giants, Dallas Cowboys, and my New England Patriots, won two Super Bowl championships. He developed nine head coaches, and three of them—Tom Coughlin, Sean Payton, and Bill Belichick—later won Super Bowls on their own. Here's what he said about developing his coaches and players.

> You have to be brutally honest with people. You have to tell them the truth about their performance, you have to tell it to them face-to-face and you have to tell it to them over and over again.
>
> Confrontation does not mean putting someone down. You need to put it in a positive context. When I told a player that he could do better, I'd tell him, "It's in your best interest that you succeed, and it's in my best interest that you succeed. We really want the same thing." Once you set that context, you can be brutally honest without fear of offending someone. It's much more valuable to them to have a leader who's absolutely clear and open than to have one who soft-soaps or talks in circles.[12]

I scheduled that tough performance review and decided to give Parcel's approach a try. Vic, a member of my Cambridge Technology Partners–Europe leadership team, was based in our London office. I scheduled his performance review for 5:00 p.m. at the White Cross Pub in Richmond, Surrey. I selected the White Cross because it's on the banks of the River Thames, a tidal river. Every evening, the river overflows its banks and floods the walkway into the White Cross, making it impossible to leave for ninety minutes. Even if Vic became angry and wanted to leave, I knew he would be stuck with me until 7:00 p.m.

I began the review as I thought Coach Parcells would, saying, "Vic, it's in your best interest that you succeed, and it's in my best interest that you succeed. We really want the same thing. Your work is outstanding, but there are three observations that have been consistently brought to my attention that are holding you back. Can I have your permission to be brutally honest with you?"

After Vic nervously nodded, I continued. "You dress badly."

"I dress better than you," Vic responded defensively. "Who told you that?"

I replied, "Several of our clients who are executives complain that your suits don't fit, your neckties don't match, and they're not tied properly. Vic, I'm from Pittsburgh. That shit doesn't matter to me. But four clients have told me that you 'don't look like an executive,' and I don't want that to hold you back." This was even more difficult than I had expected.

"Okay," Vic said as he chugged his pint and ordered another. "You said there are three bits of feedback."

I took a deep breath and said, "Your teeth are bad."

"My teeth are bad? What do you bloody mean 'my teeth are bad?' Everybody in the UK has bad teeth."

"Vic, your teeth are brown. They're not supposed to be that color. Clients and members of your team joke about that behind your back," I said.

"This can't get any worse," Vic muttered. But it was about to.

"Vic, you smell badly. Many of our employees have asked me not to assign you to their team because of that."

"I smell badly?" Vic said loudly enough for neighboring tables to hear him.

"Is it a cigarette smell? I know I smoke too much."

"That might be part of it. But it's more of a body odor smell," I said.

"Could you describe it more clearly?" Vic asked.

Our chat had become almost unbearably uncomfortable. I felt the urge to run away, but remembered that we were all trapped by the high tide.

"Vic, you smell like you don't shower enough. Let's leave it at that. Just shower more frequently."

Vic and I sat quietly for a few minutes while he took it all in. Then he took a breath and said, "No one has ever told me any of that. Not any of my managers. Not even my wife of twenty years. That's probably what's held back my career. Thank you for telling me. I know that it was as difficult for you to share as it was for me to hear."

We had time for another pint before the Thames receded and spent the evening talking about the exceptional quality and high impact of Vic's work. On the way out, he smiled and said, "I still think I dress better than you do."

"You probably do," I responded. "But I smell better!"

Afterward, I wondered what Vic would do with that feedback. Was it too much? But he took it to heart and sincerely appreciated my candor. On the rare occasions when I see him, he still greets me with, "How do I smell today?" and breaks into a laugh.

Parting Thoughts

The morning after you first become a CEO can be a daunting experience. It's okay to feel that way—most first-time CEOs do. You'll soon hit your stride if you follow this advice.

- Over-prepare while you continue to learn.

- Become comfortable making decisions. Teddy Roosevelt said, "In any moment of decision, the best thing you can do is the right thing, the next best thing is the wrong thing, and the worst thing you can do is nothing."

- Don't lock yourself in a corner office and forget about the field. Be a member of the Away Team.

- Solve problems *and* teach. You can do both at the same time. Engage with your team to solve their problems and help them learn in the process. In business and in life, never stop teaching and never stop learning.

- Be a CEO who's absolutely clear and open, not one who soft-soaps and avoids confronting the real issues. Telling someone the truth is not the same as putting someone down.

- Don't be a serial thinker. Press go. "Make shit happen!"

After you decide to be the founder/CEO of a startup, the next step is to build the team that will join you on your journey.

• • •

CHAPTER FIVE

How to Build Your Team

The secret to successful hiring is this: Look for people who want to change the world.

— Marc Benioff, CEO, Salesforce

Without a Clear Objective, You Can't Design the Team to Achieve It

IN 1985, I was director of IT at Air Products. Our corporate headquarters was located in Trexlertown, Pennsylvania—a small town surrounded by cornfields. I lived in an eighteenth-century remodeled farmhouse, fifteen miles away in New Tripoli. Most of its five hundred residents were Pennsylvania Dutch farmers.

Exploring New Tripoli was like being transported to a fascinating new world. Soon after I moved there, I saw a poster in the window of the general store announcing that month's "Liar's Contest." My curiosity compelled me to attend. Every pew in the local church was filled. The pastor stood at the front and announced each contestant. Every one of them told a preposterous story, accompanied by applause that was proportionate to the tallness of the tale. The pastor determined the winners. I found it odd that the local church awarded its parishioners for breaking the Ninth Commandment. But then again, I found many things in New Tripoli to be odd.

The Leather Corner Post Hotel in nearby Orefield hosted more lively entertainment. The crowd there was deceptively subdued when I entered the barroom. But as soon as someone deposited twenty-five cents in the jukebox to play the "William Tell Overture," they erupted. Apparently, this song was the boomba national anthem. Everyone darted to grab their own customized boombas from a hook on the wall. A boomba is a Pennsylvania Dutch "musical" instrument built by attaching a tambourine and bells to a wooden pole with a spring-loaded base (much like a pogo stick), with cymbals that crash as the boomba is bounced. I found it to be the perfect musical instrument to play after a few beers.

I could cite many more examples of what makes the Pennsylvania Dutch culture fascinating. But it's also a *careful* culture that is hesitant to let outsiders in. For example, New Tripoli municipal regulations required Town Council members to operate a snowplow during winter storms, effectively preventing "outsiders" with nine-to-five jobs from running for office. Only a farmer in off-season could commit to that.

My son, Jason, was nine years old at the time. I volunteered as an assistant head coach for his Little League baseball team, hoping that would lead to my making friends with the locals. The coaches were scheduled to meet at the New Tripoli Hotel to draft our teams. I admit that I'm more competitive than most people are, so I invested quite a lot of time scouting the kids, discussing them with my son, and assembling my draft board. On paper, I had a kick-ass team, and I was ready!

I arrived at the New Tripoli Hotel early. Originally built in 1771, it was a "country bar" unlike any of the establishments I frequented in Pittsburgh. All of the coaches and assistants were already there and more than a few beers ahead of me. Several of them had brought their dogs. I found Don, my head coach. I introduced myself, and sat next to him on a tattered, beer-stained couch with my draft board sprawled on my lap. The head coaches drew numbers out of a bucket to determine their drafting positions. We were fourth out of five.

Team 1 selected the boy at the top of my list, giving me an early confidence boost in my scouting ability. Team 2 picked the next player on my list, and Team 3 followed by selecting my third. It was our turn, and I turned to Don to give him my input.

"Good choice," said Don. Instead, he called out a name that I didn't recall. I checked my draft board and saw this boy was listed near the bottom. Team 5 followed by picking the player I had recommended to Don. The beginning of the second round went the same way—every coach selecting the player that I would have picked. Again, I turned to Don to give him my input. And again, he said, "Another good choice," then called out a name from the bottom of my list. The third and fourth rounds played out identically.

Frustrated, I took Don aside. "I spent hours scouting the kids and assembling a draft board," I said. "Every other coach's selections are spot-on with what I recommended. What am I doing wrong?"

Don smiled before he responded. "Bill, this is your first time coaching, right?" I nodded. Don continued, "What you are doing wrong is that you're drafting the best players." I became even more confused. Don's smile broadened. "What *I'm* doing is drafting the players with the hottest-looking mothers. You see, at this age, all the kids develop and get a lot better during the season. You never know what you'll end up with. But if you start the season with ugly mothers, sure as hell you'll end the season with ugly mothers."

Said another way, you need to decide on your objective before you can build a team that can accomplish it.

How Do You Pick Your Team? The "No Asshole Rule"

My next opportunity to draft a team was the fall of 1998. ZEFER was a new and evolving startup idea that I shared with David Lubin, former co-chair and managing director of Renaissance Solutions, a large and very successful consulting company. If ZEFER became a reality, he planned to join the company as vice chair.

There was no shortage of people who wanted to join our team, and both David and I knew how important it was to make the right hiring decisions. David reserved a large conference room for a day, and we invited fifteen potential team members to develop ZEFER's business model and explore how we would work together. Not only were they a group of very talented individuals, they brought building blocks that David and I knew would have an important impact on our growth. All the puzzle pieces that we needed to build a special company would be in that room. I was excited about the world-class team that we were about to assemble.

As the day unfolded, it became increasingly difficult to get the group to stop focusing on what was in it for them. All of our attempts to reach synergy became dead ends. The members of our dream team were more worried about their roles and titles than architecting a company that we could build together. They just didn't "play nicely." Instead of developing the framework for creating a special company, our discussion deteriorated to reporting structure, compensation, and who would be entitled to a private office.

I adjourned the session early. As David and I walked to the parking lot, I asked, "So what did you think about our dream team?"

David didn't hesitate. "They are the biggest group of assholes that I have ever met."

That's when we coined the "No Asshole Rule." We were confident that the population of talented people was large enough that we could always find and hire people who weren't assholes. After terminating discussions with our dream team, we institutionalized the "No Asshole Rule" at ZEFER. If any interviewer felt that a prospective employee failed that test, regardless of how talented, we would move on.

How Do You "Get the Right People on Your Bus?"

Twelve years later, Michael and I were developing Mobiquity's business model and assembling our team. We followed the traditional startup team model: Hire people who have worked with you before. Include in the mix someone who can sell, a technologist who can communicate and is also a bit of a hacker, someone good at business operations, and a marketeer who knows how to craft an engaging customer value proposition. However, our original team members weren't working out as well as I hoped. Michael helped me recognize why.

He began, "Bill, when you become excited about a new business idea, you'll test it with business colleagues you respect. If they share your enthusiasm and express interest in joining, you'll say, 'Get on my bus!' As your business concept matures, the skills and experience that you need on your team will become clearer. When that gap becomes too wide, you'll look at your team and wonder, 'How did all of these people get on my bus? And how the hell do I get them off?'"

Michael nailed it. The original Mobiquity was composed of friends and colleagues who were interested and available. They could help me get "Mobilocity" off the ground but weren't the right team to make it the rapid-growth, impactful leader in the industry. It was a stroke of luck that they all resigned over our disagreement about the New York bank opportunity. Michael and I capitalized on that exodus and began our search for world-class contributors who shared our passion and had the specific skills that we now knew we needed. I took it a step further and decided that, for my first ten hires, I'd only recruit people I'd never met before. I would contact my network and ask, for example, "Who is the top mobile strategist in the world? Where do I find the top mobile user-experience and mobile development executives? The best marketing and sales executives for an early startup?" As soon as I heard the same name three times, I'd call that person, introduce myself, explain Mobiquity's value proposition, and invite them to get on my bus. To my surprise, only one of the ten "strangers" I contacted turned me down.

Isn't It All About the Talent?

Now I really did have a dream team, and I posted this announcement on Mobiquity's website:

> I'd like to announce the birth of our new baby Mobiquity at 5
> p.m. today; it weighs approximately 1,900 pounds (+/- a few
> ounces). Although a bit harried, all twelve parents are doing fine.

I quickly learned that my dream team came with a new set of challenges I hadn't anticipated. Every member was an alpha dog, accustomed to being the smartest person in the room. Our discussions were high-charged, intellectual debates. Our pace was breakneck. Everyone was aligned to accomplish the same goals, but each individual saw their role and their discipline as the most important in achieving them. I wondered how that would play out in our first engagement.

Soon after Mobiquity launched, I found out. We landed a small consulting gig with a major retailer in Ohio. If successful, it would lead to a significant project or perhaps many projects. It was a foundational opportunity, one that could prime us to build our new company. Our team worked hard to prepare, and all of us believed we did a good job of delivering what we promised. However, I felt that something was a bit off.

Our sponsor, the CIO, emailed me a few days after we completed our project to tell me they would not continue our relationship. He explained, "Everyone you've assembled is amazingly talented. Your deliverables were outstanding. However, we just didn't like working with your team. We found them a bit arrogant and condescending. I'm sure that Mobiquity will do well. But not with us."

I wasn't sure what I should do. How would I share the CIO's message with my team? Should I rewrite the email and "sugar coat" it so I wouldn't demotivate them? I remembered a phenomenon called the Dunning-Kruger effect. It describes a cognitive bias where teams that are aware they don't know much are very productive, whereas teams that think they know it all are dangerous. I knew what I had to do.

I have no idea how I made the connection, but a scene from the 1960 movie, *The Alamo*, came to mind. John Wayne, playing Davy Crockett, wrestled with how to convince his volunteers, vastly outnumbered by General Santa Anna's army, to stand and hold the Alamo. He decided to assemble them and read a letter written by Santa Anna. "Your volunteers do not have a chance against my well-trained army. They are cowards that will turn and run when they hear my first cannon shot. Either surrender now, or I'll have them all hung by their necks before dark tomorrow."

Davy's volunteers reacted predictably. Inflamed by Santa Anna's letter, they banded together and declared that they would never retreat. That's when Davy confided, "Santa Anna didn't write that. I did. But if he wrote a letter, that's what it would have said." The volunteers' resolve didn't change, and they held the Alamo for thirteen days.

If that trick worked for Davy, perhaps it would work for me. I rewrote our prospect's email to amplify the CIO's message, called a debriefing meeting, and read it to them.

> Dear Bill –
>
> I am writing to inform you that we have decided to not move forward with Mobiquity. The work that you delivered was first class. However, we found your team to be the most conceited, arrogant, and opinionated consultants that we have ever met. I'd advise you to adjust their full-of-oneself attitude and teach them how to work as a team. Tell them to stop throwing around their pedigrees. No one at McKinsey or IBM brags about their titles or advanced degrees. Neither should you. Instead, let your intellectual horsepower carry you.

I waited for anyone to respond, but the room was silent for an uncomfortably long time. Finally, someone broke the silence. "I am so embarrassed. I had no idea that we came across that way. We need to change. What should we do?"

That was my cue to talk about dream teams that failed, despite their great pedigrees.

- The 1980 USSR Olympic ice hockey team, having won fourteen gold medals, two silver, and a bronze in the previous seventeen Olympic Games, lost to a team of US college kids.

- The 2004 Yankees, who added superstars Alex Rodriguez, Gary Sheffield, Kevin Brown, Jon Lieber, and Javier Vazquez to a roster already boasting Derek Jeter, Mariano Rivera, Jorge Posada, Hideki Matsui, and Mike Mussina, lost to my Boston Red Sox in the playoffs.

- The 2004 US Olympic men's basketball team consisting of Allen Iverson, Tim Duncan, Stephon Marbury, Carmelo Anthony, Dwyane Wade, Amar'e Stoudemire, and LeBron James barely beat Lithuania for the Bronze medal.

- The 2006 US All-Star team was eliminated from the World Baseball Classic after losing to Mexico, South Korea, and Canada.

The lesson was the same in each of those stories. Commitment to the mission trumps talent.

Without prioritizing personal chemistry, shared values, trust, and mutual respect, any team, especially a dream team, is likely to fail. As Coach Herb Brooks said when he was criticized for passing on the USA's most celebrated college hockey players in 1980 in lieu of building a team based on personal chemistry, "I'm not lookin' for the best players. I'm lookin' for the right players."

(Note: I never told my Mobiquity team that I rewrote the email from our first client. So please let that be our little secret.)

How Do You Get Everyone on the "Same Page?"

We endured ups and downs while building a culture based on trust and shared values. It's not possible to successfully execute until everyone on the team aligns behind a common mission and set of values and recognizes how their individual roles contribute to the bigger picture. My leadership team often complained that a member wasn't "on the same page as the rest of us." That seemed like an overgeneralization to me, so I decided to write down what it actually meant to be on "the same page" and ask everyone to confirm their commitment with a signature. New members also had to sign before they joined. And if any executive's behavior was inconsistent with our agreement, it was okay for anyone on my leadership team to call them on it. This is what I came up with:

The Same Page – November 11, 2013

- We have a very narrow, unpredictably short window to build our company. That requires significant effort, a strong commitment and a very high sense of urgency, at least for the next several years. Personal sacrifices will be required.
- "In the end, it's the attention to detail that makes all the difference. It's the center fielder's extra two steps to the left, the salesman's memory or names, the lover's phone call, the soldier's clean weapon. It's the thing that separates the winners from the losers, the men from the boys and very often, the living from the dead. Professional success depends on it, regardless of the field." Over prepare and sweat the details.
- There is no such thing as a Tier 2 customer. We treat every customer as if they are our most important customer.
- We have a passion for our work. However, we measure ourselves by our client's success, not whether or not we developed an award-winning work product. It's all about making our customer successful.
- We listen to our clients. We present them with alternatives – and potential risks and rewards that accompany each. We then tailor our methodology to deliver what they want – even if we don't believe that it's what they need.
- When multiple disciplines are involved, there will naturally be tensions about trade-offs. When that occurs, the executive in charge of delivery makes the final call.
- We follow through on all our commitments.
- We are constructive and supportive when working with our colleagues. As a team, we can accomplish much more that we can as a collection of individuals.
- Act as if Mobiquity is your own company – because it is. But we must also be aligned with our investor's objectives.
- We are honest and transparent in all of your communications.
- Maintain confidentiality.
- When in doubt, "do the right thing."

I found that clearly defining "the same page" immensely helped to get my team to accept and live by the shared values that were important to Mobiquity. Our version is not transferable. Every team in every company has to create their own pact.

What Does a Chief Spiritual Officer Do?

Organic Valley, the nation's largest farmer-owned organic cooperative and one of the world's largest organic consumer brands, reinforced my belief in the importance of shared values. I visited them at their La Crosse, Wisconsin, headquarters soon after they selected Demantra's software to drive their demand planning process. Peter, the CFO, gave me a tour while he talked about their business and shared how they began in Kickapoo Valley as a farmer-owned cooperative "not driven by profits but driven by principles." As we walked down a long hallway, I saw a barefoot man in a white robe hugging everyone who walked by. He looked like Gandalf from *The Lord of the Rings*.

"Who's that?" I asked Peter.

"That's Jerome. He's our chief spiritual officer," Peter replied, followed by a wink.

"What's a chief spiritual officer do?"

Peter smiled and said, "Just watch him. He's doing it."

We continued toward the man, and as we approached him, he lurched forward to embrace me, whispering something about "the power of we." Peter explained, "Our values all tie back to our roots as farmers. 'The power of we' means being a good neighbor and lending a helping hand to whoever needs one. He's reminding us that we are a family-owned business, even though we're owned by 2,000 farmer families."

"How did you find him?" I asked.

"He found us," Peter replied.

"Just one more question, Peter. What's the career path that leads to becoming a chief spiritual officer? What did he do before he came here?"

He paused for a moment, then said, "I think he came from Wall Street."

Damn. I was hoping Peter would reply, "He was an entrepreneur from Pittsburgh who launched a number of technology startups."

How Important Is Culture?

I've seen many CEOs reject applicants because they're not a cultural fit. Culture is important—but be careful how you define it. I think of culture as the beliefs and behaviors that determine how a company's employees and management interact with one another and handle business transactions. It has nothing to do with the music they listen to, their age, how they dress, or how many tattoos they have. Diversity is invaluable to any team, but it's even more critical for a startup team. That's why I think "shared values" is a better way to think of it.

I'll talk more about that in Chapter 18.

Parting Thoughts

- Don't hire assholes. The pool of talented people is large enough that you can avoid hiring someone who does not add to the energy and cohesiveness of your team. CB Insights reports that the number three reason that startups fail is "not building the right team."[23] And the "No Asshole Rule" isn't limited to startups—it's a life lesson as well.

- Don't invite anyone to get on your bus until you have a clear sight on where your bus is going and the skills and roles that you'll need to drive it there.

- Commitment to the mission, personal chemistry, shared values, trust, and mutual respect are key success factors in designing a team.

- Think "shared values" instead of "culture." If you agree that shared values are important, take the time to write them down. Get everyone on the same page. Discuss the document with your team and prospective employees and formalize buy-in with signatures. Give your employees the okay to call out a team member if their behavior is not consistent with that set of beliefs.

Now that you have launched your startup, decided on the opportunity that you want to pursue, and recruited a team to help you execute your plan, it's time to articulate your value proposition to your prospective customers.

• • •

Part 2

Marketing and Sales

You have to tell a story before you can sell a story.

– Beth Comstock, former vice chair,
General Electric

CHAPTER SIX

How to Craft Your Customer Value Proposition

People don't buy what you do. They buy why you do it.

– Simon Sinek, author

How to Make It *Irresistible*

YOUR STARTUP'S CUSTOMER value proposition (CVP) explains why your prospects should buy from you. It doesn't state what you do; it clearly and concisely frames why you do it. When you pivot to a new business model, your CVP will change. It requires a lot of thought and discipline to get that "right" not just at the very beginning, but at each and every pivot point. Without a compelling, clearly articulated value proposition, your prospects will have a difficult time understanding the connection between the problem they're trying to solve and the value that your product or service delivers.

Crafting your CVP sounds straightforward. But startups typically do not do a very good job at getting their value proposition right—simply because they don't invest much time crafting it. As a result, their CVPs are:

- inward-out, stating what the product or service does without creating a connection to the outcome that their prospect is seeking;

- not connected to a prospect's budget;

- aspirational—but not backed up by actual results;

- polluted with noise and sound bites—making the message undecipherable; or

- not differentiated, so they sound like everyone else's CVP.

I've asked more than fifty CIOs and CMOs how they select a technology partner. Their answers consistently confirm that a startup will lose business if their CVP misses the mark. Cheryl, a Fortune 100 serial CIO, described it best:

> I ask one of my key lieutenants to narrow the field of potential partners by reviewing their websites. I tell them to assess positioning, case studies, blogs, and points of view. I want them to provide me with a list of the five to seven companies with a value proposition that targets the specific problem we are trying to solve, and with the credentials to back up their promises.

> That's when I take over. I'll review the websites of each finalist to select the three that I'll invite to pitch. I don't have a lot of time to invest, so their positioning has to be clear. I look for what differentiates them and map that to the capabilities that I'm looking for. I also look at how they describe themselves to see if they feel like a good fit.

Think about your CVP as if it were your company's resumé because it is. Explain that your product or service is like _____, but better because _____. That explanation positions what you offer in a category that a prospect knows how to buy, while also differentiating it within that category.

YERP

Theo, a close friend, and I were having dinner in Antwerp, chatting about the company he had recently launched. "I named it YERP," he said proudly.

"What the hell is a YERP?" I asked.

"I got the idea when I saw a cartoon of George W. Bush in *De Telegraaf* soon after he became president. It depicted him deplaning Air Force One as he arrived in Europe for the first time, saying, 'Well this must be YERP.' It's Texas slang for Europe. I want my startup to be viewed as a European company that provides consulting services to American businesses. Do you get it?"

I didn't, so I asked, "Does Y-E-R-P stand for anything?"

"That's the beauty of it," Theo responded. "It can stand for many things: Your European Resource Provider; Your European Revenue Partner...the possibilities are endless."

My friend spent the next two hours taking me through one of the most detailed, well-thought-out businesses that I had ever encountered. He explained that YERP was organized organically. He handed me YERP's forty-five-page DNA design guide while he explained it to me. It was what "traditional" businesses might call their employee handbook. In order to be hired as a YERP-ean, recruits had to be voted into a Cell—a group of people who agreed to tie their individual compensation to the performance of their team. Employees could be voted out by Cell members at any time. Cells retain a percentage of the revenue that they generate and choose how to allocate it to its members. They create their own Cell Charter to define their rules and business model. Once a Cell grows to fifteen people, it would undergo mitosis and split into two Cells. YERP wasn't set up with a hierarchical structure. Instead, it was designed as a "transparent self-organizing organism." The Cells received support and direction from the Brain (the senior leaders who set direction), the Conscience (which sounded a lot like a traditional human resources group), the Senses (employees who monitor and interpret internal and external changes, then send change requests to the Brain), and the Nervous System (individuals who embody YERP's culture and have been voted in by the Cells—reminding me a bit of a labor union). The last page in the DNA guide captured, in one sentence, the essence of YERP's model: "No matter what we decide today, tomorrow things might be different." After my friend finished, he sat back in his chair, crossed his arms, and smiled, waiting to hear my reaction.

"Amazing," I said. "I'm not sure I agree with all of it, but it's certainly very interesting. And the detailed thinking that you invested in YERP, and the analogy to a human organism that you've built your model on is comprehensive and really impressive. But we haven't talked about what your company does for your clients."

Theo looked confused. "I'm not sure what you mean."

"What services do you provide? How does that help your clients? Why do they hire you? You know, that kind of stuff."

"I don't know yet. I'm waiting for the Brain to figure that out."

Laughing out loud, I replied, "Staying with the organic human body metaphor, who is the asshole that decided to leave that out of the anatomy?"

What Made Cambridge Technology Partners' CVP *Irresistible?*

In the early 1990s, IT projects consistently suffered from significant cost and schedule overruns. In 1994, the Standish Group published its *CHAOS Report*, which stated that only 16.2 percent were completed on time and on budget with all of the required functionality. Project overruns in the US averaged $59 billion each year, and 31.1 percent of IT projects were abandoned, never to be completed. "The cost of these overruns and failures is just the tip of the proverbial iceberg. The lost opportunity costs are not measurable but could easily be in the trillions of dollars."[24] At that time, every business executive knew that their most important IT projects were likely to fail. And they were resigned to the fact that there was absolutely nothing they could do about it. That was, until Jim Sims launched Cambridge Technology Partners (CTP). CTP was a consulting company focused on designing and developing client-server solutions for businesses. In 1992, soon after I joined them, I had my first experience crafting a value proposition.

CTP's sister company, Cambridge Technology Group, generated all of our sales—until our relationship abruptly dissolved. Suddenly we were left with sixty employees and no sales engine. Jim Sims quickly pivoted to Plan B. He called three of us into his office, explained that we would build our own go-to-market capability, and said we'd start by crafting our customer value proposition on the spot.

I remember asking, "How are we going to do that? None of us have ever been a consultant before."

Jim responded, "That may be true, but everyone here has been a victim of consultants. Let's write down what we don't like about consultants— and then we'll do the opposite."

Jim continued, "I'll begin," and handed me a marker. "I don't like consultants who say they're the experts, but when they're wrong, the customer has to pay the price. Bill—write down 'Fixed Price.'" Our marketing executive jumped in, "And I don't like consultants who take too long before they generate anything of value. Write down 'Rapid Application Development.'"

I was beginning to get the idea and added, "I don't like it when they get their hooks in you, and you can't get rid of them." Jim chimed in, "Good one. Let's call that 'Empowerment.'"

He continued, "I don't like it when consultants say they're your 'partners' but change their tune as soon as a project encounters a major problem. Large projects almost always run into problems. When that happens, I want us to always do the right thing."

"But how do we define 'the right thing'? That seems really ambiguous," I asked.

"Everyone knows in their gut what 'the right thing' is," Jim replied. "We learned what it means in kindergarten. If we do the right thing, our clients will respect that, and they'll probably do the right thing as well."

"But what if they don't?" I asked.

Jim responded, "Then we'll *still* do the right thing and then choose not to work with them again."

We continued down that path for well over an hour, having fun with the process and assembling quite a list. Jim took the marker and highlighted the differentiators that he felt were the most important, then said, "Okay! That's the list. We're done here. Now, Bill, it's your job to figure out how we can deliver on it!"

CTP's CVP led with Rapid Application Development and Fixed Price/Fixed Timeframe—and was backed up by Empowerment and Always Do the Right Thing. It was successful because it:

- addressed a major problem that threatened all enterprises, since the majority of IT projects at that time faced significant cost and schedule overruns, and a high percentage were complete failures;

- emotionally connected to our prospects' abiding frustration with consultants;

- was sufficiently differentiated so that none of our competitors could replicate it;

- was clear and concise, with no noise; and

- highlighted who we were and what we believed in.

Where Did Our CVP Lead?

- Instead of revenue significantly declining that year, it grew by 87 percent to $36 million—and that was before I learned how to sell!

- The following year, CTP expanded to eleven offices, grew revenue to $56 million, and went public with the second-best performing IPO in 1993.

- By the time I departed CTP in 1998, the company was earning over $800 million in revenue, with four thousand employees in fifty offices and a $5 billion market cap.

Should You Modify Your CVP for New Markets?

When entering a new market, re-evaluate your CVP to make certain that it still works, and be willing to modify it. Sometimes even a simple alteration can improve the appeal to a new audience. When CTP launched in Europe, revenue growth was slow until we realized that Europeans were, at least at that time, more risk-averse than Americans. I realized that they valued fixed-price, fixed-time contracts more than rapid development. I simply reversed the sequence of our CVP to lead with Fixed Price/Fixed Timeframe, followed by Rapid Application Development. Perhaps it was a coincidence, but after we made that tweak, European revenues skyrocketed to $100 million in four years.

It's not always that easy. It took me years to reposition Demantra as a predictive analytics company targeting the sales and operations planning market. But in every case, it comes down to continuing to test and iterate your message until you're convinced that your new market finds it engaging. Make every word count.

What Made ZEFER's CVP *Irresistible?*

When I moved on to launch internet consulting firm ZEFER, I began by acquiring a small firm founded by recent Harvard Business School (HBS) graduates. Their CVP was "Be honest. Do you have a clear vision for your Internet strategy?" The words perched on top of a cool pair of eyeglasses.

It was easy to see why ZEFER's growth was initially slow. Startups were taking market share from Fortune 1000 firms and creating astronomical market valuations. Large enterprises didn't know how to respond to the dot-com boom. CEOs might have felt compelled to develop an internet strategy to keep board members and shareholders off of their backs, but they were hardly game to trust a group of inexperienced young people— even if they were brilliant and had Harvard pedigrees—to formulate a major step-out strategy for their enterprises. More importantly, merely delivering an internet strategy falls far short of meeting the real need: enabling a Fortune 1000 enterprise to exploit the opportunities that the ubiquity of the internet offered. I revised ZEFER's CVP by blending the dot-com DNA of the HBS grads with an experienced delivery team skilled in large enterprise architectures. The result: "ZEFER brings dot-com thinking to the F1000."

Crafting a CVP that blended internet strategy with world-class delivery:

- achieved the outcomes that the Fortune 1000 companies were wrestling to reach;

- connected emotionally to the CEOs by creating a path for them to enter the dot-com world;

- was differentiated; and

- was clear and concise.

ZEFER was the first strategy-led internet professional services firm; yet, within six months, sixty-four competitors entered the space. Though they copied our services model, they couldn't compete with the attention that our customer value proposition captured among Fortune 1000 executives.

Organic growth accelerated quickly, and ZEFER grew revenues to $136 million in less than eighteen months—growth that remains a record for professional services firms.

What Made Mobiquity's CVP *Irresistible?*

In 2010–2011, most large enterprises developed a mobile strategy. In many instances, CEOs acted because they felt pressured by their boards, customers, and employees to "do something." Creating a mobile strategy checked the I'm-doing-something box, while avoiding the investments, risks, massive changes, and long-term focus characteristic of true business transformation. Some enterprises skipped the strategy phase altogether. Instead, they "innovated" by conducting experiments and proofs-of-concept. These "Random Acts of Mobile" rarely generated any real business benefits.

I believed that the potential for mobile technology extended far beyond simple, silly apps. Mobiquity's vision was to "make mobile matter." We saw mobile as a key component of a new technology stack—mobile, social, cloud, internet of things, and big data, and analytics—that would become a platform for driving innovation across the Fortune 1000. Our CVP, "We build enterprise-class mobile solutions that help you run your business—and in many cases, transform the way that you do your business" resonated.

We didn't have any problem securing meetings with senior executives. They asked good questions during our presentation, appeared to understand our point of view, and seemed enthusiastic about engaging us. But in the end, few actually hired us.

Eventually I realized that our prospects didn't have a budget for "enterprise-class mobile solutions that help you run your business—and in many cases, transform the way that you do your business." But all of them did have budgets for mobile apps. So, we modified our CVP by adding "and we build apps" to the end.

Once again, adding one simple phrase made all of the difference. Within a few years, Mobiquity was recognized as the fastest growing company in all of New England—and sold for $183 million.

Parting Thoughts

- Think of your startup's CVP as the first page of your resumé. Invest the time to make certain that every word clearly conveys who you are, and focus on what would matter to your customer. Make it easy for them to understand what you do, why you are different from your competitors, why those differences matter, and how you are uniquely positioned to help them. Test it with advisors.

- Write your website content to support your CVP. Forrester reports that "82 percent of technology buying decision makers said that it is 'important or very important' for sales reps to have relevant examples or case studies to share."[25] Data shows that the fewer calories prospects need to burn to figure out what a company does, the more the company will sell.[26] Carefully eliminate any noise in your messaging—stuff that isn't clear or that the prospect doesn't care about. Again, test it with advisors.

- You have to *tell* a story before you *sell* a story. Storytelling is the most effective way to influence people. We're hardwired to react to a story. According to Donald Miller in his book, *Building a StoryBrand: Clarify Your Message So Customers Will Listen*, always make the prospect the hero in the story and always make your company the guide.[26]

- You might have to modify your CVP when you enter new markets. Needs, priorities, and values differ across vertical markets and geographies.

- Make sure your CVP is tied to a budget category. Your prospects will be able to make a better case for buying your product or service if they're armed with a business case. Remember Willie Sutton's reply when asked why he robbed banks: "Because that's where the money is."

- Research the websites of your competitors to learn how they are attempting to reach the market and to understand their differentiators.

- Back up your value proposition with evidence. Make certain that it focuses on what you do well, not on what you would *like* to do well.

- Constantly monitor and continue to adjust your positioning as you learn more. Even small changes in words and tone can make a significant difference in getting noticed and winning a deal.

- Make certain that everyone in your company knows your CVP and can articulate it; consistently convey it across your website, marketing collateral, and sales decks; and ensure that all of your blogs, whitepapers, and case studies emphasize and support it.

- And remember that "always do the right thing" isn't just a soundbite. It's a principle that's as important in life as it is in business.

As you scale your startup, you'll transition from founder-led sales to a professional sales team, which I cover in the next chapter.

• • •

CHAPTER SEVEN

Who's In Sales?

I have always said that everyone is in sales. Maybe you don't hold the title of salesperson, but if the business you are in requires you to deal with people, you, my friend, are in sales.

– Zig Ziglar, author and salesman

The Chant

IT WAS BOTH my first week at Cambridge Technology Partners (CTP) and my first all-hands meeting. Kris, our sales and marketing executive vice president, bounced to the front of the room and shouted, "Raise both hands if you're in sales." All six of our account executives obeyed. "Wrong! We are *all* in sales! Everyone—put both hands in the air." Apparently, we had no choice. Kris began to lead a chant, "We are *all* in sales. We are *all* in sales..."

I was immensely annoyed. I had been on dozens of sales calls and had my share of wins under my belt, including the $740,000 check with my name on it. But I wasn't "in sales." I was a technology and operations guy. Most of my colleagues felt the same way. We didn't know much about sales. In fact, we weren't sure if there was much to know. At that time, classes in sales were uncommon in business schools. Had they been offered, you wouldn't have caught me registering for one of them even though I would have assumed I could earn an easy "A."

Everything my colleagues and I knew about sales came from our experience on the job. Sales executives schmoozed with prospects to book meetings for us, most of which were a waste of time. As soon as we closed a deal, they disappeared, leaving all of the heavy lifting to us. And based on the clothes they wore, their Rolex watches and the cars that they drove, the sales team apparently was paid more than we were. *Everyone is in sales?* I beg your pardon.

Embracing Sales Is a Shared Attitude

My attitude about sales changed the day that I terminated CTP's European joint venture. My two team members and I found ourselves solely accountable for launching our business in Amsterdam—with the nearest sales executive 3,500 miles away. With no clients, no prospects, no partners, no office or infrastructure, and no one who could speak the local language, I pondered, "How can I make this work?" As we drove along the A10 highway that circles Amsterdam, the answer came to me. I turned down the radio and enthusiastically shouted, "Raise your hand if you are in sales!"

After three long months of cold calling, we won our first deal. That was our big break! Our client was a small company, but it was a division of Unilever, one of Europe's largest corporations.

Howard, our vice president of technology, Carol, and I were scheduled to arrive at Emmerich, a ninety-minute drive across the German border, at 8:00 a.m. on a Monday. That was also the day that Rik, our first European hire, would join our team. He had graduated from Eindhoven the previous Friday. Even though he didn't have consulting experience, we planned to bring him with us as a show of force.

On Saturday, two days before kickoff, our new client's division president called me. In a trembling voice, he informed me that Fritz, our sponsor, had passed away in his sleep the night before. Unfortunately, our project would have to be postponed indefinitely. I was stunned. This was our only deal in the pipeline. We couldn't lose it. That's when I discovered that sales is the art of overcoming objections.

I argued that our engagement could go forward without Fritz. In fact, Fritz would want it that way. This project was his legacy. What would Fritz say, looking down at us from heaven, if we abandoned it?

I began to believe that I might have a chance. But the division president continued to object, "I don't know. Most of Fritz's team are members of the church choir, and they will be rehearsing for Fritz's service on Monday and Tuesday. And his funeral is Wednesday. Next week will be too choppy."

"Not for us," I confidently replied. "We can work around that. We'll schedule our work sessions to align with your availability and use any downtime to work internally."

I paused, "Let's do this for Fritz."

We arrived on Monday to meet our new sponsor, Fritz's replacement. Because Fritz could speak nine languages fluently, I assumed that everyone in Germany could. But his replacement spoke only two—German and Dutch. The rest of his team just spoke German. My team only knew English, except for the first-day-on-the-job Eindhoven grad who spoke English and Dutch. That generated an entirely new slate of objections.

Since we had traveled a long way to get to Emmerich, I convinced our client to give us a try. We asked a question in English. The new kid translated it to Dutch. Our new sponsor translated the Dutch to German. The Germans discussed the question for what seemed to be an eternity. Then their answer was translated from German to Dutch, then Dutch to English. I was pretty certain that the ten-word translated replies weren't capturing all of the context.

But we got through the design sessions and delivered a solution that significantly improved the quality control of their production process. In fact, our client won an award that year. Unilever named their project as one of the top technology initiatives across the more than four hundred brands that comprised their empire. Ultimately, Unilever became our largest client not only in Europe, but worldwide as well. I finally understood what Kris had intended with his chant. Sales is a shared attitude. Startup teams who understand this truth are better positioned to uncover new opportunities and overturn objections.

What Defines the Art of Sales?

After my return to the US, CTP engaged a consultant to conduct interviews to determine the characteristics of a top sales executive. Like every good consultant, ours told us precisely what we already knew.

1. Listening skills

In their sales calls, CTP's most successful account managers spent 80 percent of their time asking open-ended questions and listening. They were most concerned about understanding the prospect's problem, the business impact of solving it, the organizational context (i.e., the budget, urgency, sponsors, and decision-making process), and their professional ambitions and potential objections. A sales call's success was inversely proportional to the percentage of time that an account executive spoke.

2. The ability to overcome objections

Before David Lubin joined me at ZEFER, he was co-chair and managing director of Renaissance Solutions. A group of executives was visiting Renaissance to finalize a decision about engaging them for a large consulting project, but the deal hit a roadblock. The account manager ran to David's office to ask for his help. "Mr. Lubin," he began, "I'm very close to closing a $1.5 million deal. But the client is digging in about our price. They're arguing that Renaissance is, by far, the highest priced consultancy that's bidding on their project. Can you join the meeting to discuss reducing our price?"

David followed his account manager to the meeting room and walked to the head of the table. He began, "I understand you believe that we are one of the highest priced consulting firms in the world. I can assure you that no matter how hard and how long you search..." David paused for effect, "you will never find anyone as expensive as we are."

The account manager's face turned pale. David went on, "And that's because there is not another consulting firm that will have the impact on your business that we will." He went on to explain what Renaissance would do differently, and the client signed the contract before they departed the building.

It doesn't always work to draw a line in the sand. While at ZEFER, a colleague and I were negotiating a partnership with the CEO of one of the top technology firms in Italy. If we successfully closed the deal, we would gain access to most of the top businesses in the Italian market for the first time. But we hit a sticking point. We felt it was important to operate under our own brand, while our potential partner demanded co-branding.

After two days of haggling, the negotiations reached a stalemate. Their CEO called me aside. "Mr. Seibel, I am sending for a car to take you and your colleague on a tour of the countryside, followed by lunch, as my guests, at Rome's very best restaurant. Then we can reconvene at the end of the day to conclude our negotiation. All I ask in return is that you permit me to call you 'Bill,' and that you call me 'Angelo.'"

I was puzzled. "But Angelo, we have had two days of intense negotiations, and I thought you were becoming annoyed with me. Why are you being so gracious now? Are you open to dropping your joint branding demand?"

"No," he said. "I just wanted to get to a first-name basis so that when you return from lunch, I don't have to say, 'Go fuck yourself, *Mr.* Seibel.' That sounds too formal. I'd rather say, 'Go fuck yourself, Bill.'"

That was the end of our Italian joint venture.

3. Staying engaged for the entire sales process

Poor performing account managers disappeared prematurely to chase their next opportunity. Top sales executives stayed engaged with the deal until it closed—and called the plays along the way. Even when, in the middle of the night, the consultants were putting the final touches on the technical solution, the top sales performers were there with them—if only to bring them coffee. They owned the pursuit to the very end.

4. Persistence in spite of rejection

We found that, on average, prospects tended to respond after seven sales calls, whereas most sales executives gave up after six attempts. Top performers were better at dealing with rejection and not giving up. I asked one of Mobiquity's early clients, "Why did you select us?" She replied, "Tim tried to reach me more than twenty times. Early morning. Middle of the day. Late at night. I admired his persistence and decided to give Mobiquity a chance because that was the only way I could stop him from calling."

5. Asking for the deal

That step might seem obvious, but many sales executives stop short. They pitch their product or service, then expect the prospect to take charge and ask to buy it. Not everyone is comfortable, at the moment of truth, asking for the business.

I admit that I was uncomfortable taking that step. Karen, ZEFER's marketing vice president, successfully booked a meeting with Chad, the CEO of the largest bank in Boston. Karen instructed me, "This is a CEO-meets-CEO meeting. It's about beginning to build a relationship. It's not about selling anything. It's too early to 'talk business.' That would offend Chad and make the meeting very uncomfortable." Karen was always right, so I happily agreed to her terms.

Karen and I were escorted to Chad's office and informed that he would join us as soon as he finished a call. A few minutes later, he strode into the room, said hello to Karen, shook my hand and said, "I see that you recently raised a significant amount of money, more than $100 million. What bank do you use? I'd like you to deposit your money here."

Stunned, I looked at Karen and said, "She told me it's too soon to talk business."

Chad laughed, "It's never too soon!"

"But...but Karen said that pushing now would offend you...make you feel uncomfortable."

Chad laughed even harder. "Bill, we're both businesspeople. I'm comfortable asking for your business. If I can do it, you can do it. Now, is there anything that you'd like to ask me?"

Do Sales and Promiscuity Have Anything in Common?

After departing CTP, I raised $100 million to launch ZEFER, the small internet consulting firm founded nine months earlier by recent Harvard Business School graduates.

The $100 million was to be wired in sixty days. A startup CEO who had served as a fighter pilot in the Air Force once advised me, "A good pilot never runs out of fuel before he lands." As ZEFER's new CEO, my job was to ensure that the company had sufficient cash flow to last until that wire arrived. Reflecting on everything that I had learned about sales processes and management at CTP, I scheduled ZEFER's first sales pipeline and forecasting meeting. All six of the original ZEFER founders who attended appeared a bit uncomfortable, precisely how I wanted them to feel.

"Tell me about the first deal in the pipeline," I began.

"That's Helen's deal. Her father is the CEO of a major Boston-based retailer. And he told us we could build his company's new e-commerce site."

Good start! That deal would most likely happen. It could even be large. But selling business to your father didn't seem to be a very scalable business model.

"Tell me about the next deal in the pipeline," I continued.

"That's Dave's deal. Dave's Harvard Business School class meets at a bar in Cambridge on the first Thursday of every month. The last time they met, Dave bumped into a classmate who was starting a dot-com company. He promised Steve that ZEFER could build his website—if he receives funding."

Uggghhh... It seemed quite unlikely that that deal would see the light of day. And finding leads on the first Thursday of the month at a bar in Cambridge did not seem like a very scalable model. I began to worry.

"Tell me about the third deal," I said with hope in my voice. "Where did it come from?"

"That's Franklin's sister's deal. Franklin's sister is dating that guy."

Now I was worried. Could I keep ZEFER alive long enough for the $100 million to arrive? Hope was rapidly shifting to panic. I asked, "How many more deals are in the pipeline?"

After a long pause, someone said, "Only one more."

I crossed my fingers and, hoping for the best, asked, "Where did that deal originate?"

Another long pause—and then the reply, "Franklin's sister is dating him, too."

I adjourned the meeting and left the building to walk around the block. ZEFER's pipeline was not what the founders had projected when I agreed to acquire them. It seemed unlikely that we could sustain our startup until our investor's funds arrived. I pondered, "Should I walk away?"

But I didn't. I reflected on the grit that the ZEFER team demonstrated in holding their startup together for their first nine months. ZEFER had not yet built a scalable go-to-market model—but I could help them with that. More importantly, they had an immensely strong shared attitude that *everyone is in sales*. Each member of ZEFER's team was looking for, and working to close, opportunities with their parents at home, with former classmates in bars, and even with the men who dated Franklin's sister. I remember joking a few months later, "If Franklin's sister wasn't such a flirt, ZEFER would not have survived."

Although no one ever led a chant, the power of *everyone is in sales* pervaded ZEFER and played a huge role in our success.

Do Sales and Puppy Dogs Have Anything in Common?

I was wrestling with how to break into a new major account. Our prospect offered tremendous potential, and I knew that ZEFER could help them. But nothing I tried seemed to work. I asked my sales executive, "What if we offered something for free? Would that help them recognize the benefit of working with us? Or would that make us look desperate, and cheapen our value proposition?"

David Lubin happened to be chatting with someone in the hallway and must overheard me. He walked into my office, carrying a look that I had seen many times before—something between a smirk and a smile. I knew that I was about to be mentored. He paused and said, "Let me tell you about the *puppy dog close*."

"Soon after I cofounded my first company, the local Xerox salesperson dropped by to convince us to lease a copying machine. As a courtesy, we gave him enough time to pitch its benefits. We explained our financial situation and politely declined. Three months later, we closed our first funding round. The next day the salesman was there to congratulate us and ask if we were now in a better position to consider leasing a copying machine. We told him we hadn't had time to do our vendor assessments but hoped to get to it soon. Anyway, we had a copy shop in Harvard Square, the site of our cool new office, so we weren't in a huge hurry."

"He replied, 'I understand that you must be too busy to spend your time thinking about nonessentials. But I'm hoping you could do me a favor. I've just received a larger than expected shipment of the Xerox 9700, our latest model, and I don't have enough space to store all of them. I have one in my car. Could I leave it here? I'll retrieve it in about a month, and you can use it for free until then, no strings attached.' WHY NOT?! It was an offer that we couldn't refuse, so we accepted."

"A month went by, then another, and another. We went through several boxes of paper. And once again, the Xerox salesperson stopped by unexpectedly. 'I'm here to retrieve my copying machine. I nearly forgot about it, and I need to return it to inventory today.'"

"We panicked. There was no way we could survive without that machine. We used it many times every day. It was built into our infrastructure, and we couldn't remember doing business without it. There was no way we were giving it back. Screw the vendor assessment. We signed his leasing agreement on the spot."

David paused while his smirk-grin returned. "That's the *puppy dog close!*"

"Brilliant," I said. "I get your point. But why do they call it that?"

David continued, "Suppose you're in a pet store, and your child begins pleading for the puppy in the window. You know that puppies are a lot of work, and so you don't think it's a great idea. But the clerk gives you a deal that's hard to refuse—take the puppy home for a few days. If it doesn't work out, bring it back with a no-questions-asked money-back guarantee." David paused for effect, "Bill, how many people do you think will return that puppy?"

"Not many," I guessed.

"Not many at all," David replied. "In two days, your child will have fallen in love with it, named it, and adopted it as part of your family. Once your product is in the hands of a customer, and they experience the benefits of owning it—especially if there's an emotional component attached—it's sold."

David continued, "I later used the *puppy dog close* when my startup was trying to introduce our interactive learning technology to the market. Our hardware platform was expensive, and it was bundled with an extensive library of interactive learning courseware focused on IT training. There weren't many competing systems on the market—but there were a few. Our prospects always wanted to engage in a lengthy analysis to decide which hardware platform to buy. That slowed our sales process to a near halt. Then it occurred to us—*puppy dog*. Let's just give the IT training departments our entire system and let them begin using it. We'll give them the courseware that's in high demand for their live classes. In three months, we'll come back and say, 'we're here to pick up the gear, useless you want to rent it.' No bake off, no hardware procurement—just rent the puppy. Sales went nuts!"

David walked to my white board, picked up a marker, and continued, "Let's think through how you can entice that high-potential prospect with a puppy dog proposition. My bet is that it will significantly increase your odds of success."

How Not to Find a Great Sales Leader

At Demantra, I interviewed RJ for a sales role. Midway through our chat, I was convinced that he was perhaps the best sales leader I had ever met. He was poised, articulate, handsome, well-dressed, and had done his homework both on Demantra and on me. Knowing I was a huge Penn State fan, RJ told me his story of Joe Paterno trying to recruit him as a linebacker at "Linebacker U." I was hooked from the very beginning. He followed that by clearly articulating Demantra's value proposition. RJ concluded our discussion by taking me through a long list of senior executives that he had personal relationships with—all of whom he believed would quickly become customers.

Being from Pittsburgh, it's very easy for me to trust people. I value handshakes more than signed contracts. I don't lock the doors to my home. My car keys can always be found under the front seat. And I sincerely believe that everyone will do the right thing. But RJ seemed too good to be true, so I personally checked his references. He sent me a long list of celebrity CEOs, annotated with their private mobile numbers so that I could call them directly. All five of the references I contacted were stellar. And every one of them expressed a strong interest in doing business with Demantra as soon as RJ joined our team. I hurriedly composed a job offer as vice president of sales for the western region of the US, and RJ accepted.

RJ didn't generate any sales during his first three months. Although I was surprised, I attributed that to the long sales cycle typical of enterprise software. But after RJ chalked up zero new business in months four and five, I became increasingly concerned. He pushed back on my requests to fly to the West Coast to accompany him on sales pursuits, convincing me to call into them instead. I conferenced into six meetings in month six. Every one of them was hosted by a Fortune 1000 CEO, and RJ consistently demonstrated his mastery in each of the key characteristics I outlined in the previous section. I regained my confidence!

But month seven came and went without RJ closing any business. I informed him that I would fly to San Francisco as soon as possible—and that was not open for discussion. RJ reluctantly agreed and promised to send me his schedule so I could organize my travel logistics. But he went dark. I called him again and again and again—and only reached his voicemail. RJ also ignored my emails.

The silence continued for two weeks. Irene, my human resources executive, became increasingly worried and called RJ's local police department to report him as a missing person. The police promised to send a car to his home that day.

A few hours later, the police called to report that RJ was fine and was playing basketball with friends in his backyard. That's when I finally realized RJ was scamming me. Duh! It turned out that he was "working" for five software companies at the same time. His reference calls with the celebrity CEOs were staged—orchestrated by RJ's friends using burner phones. The sales meetings that I asked to join were also hoaxes. RJ knew that his scam would eventually be discovered. But until then, he was drawing five substantial salaries. And after he was fired, he knew he could quickly find another sucker.

After we terminated RJ, Irene re-contacted the police to file charges for fraud. The officer laughed and said, "We don't arrest people every time a company like yours makes a stupid hiring decision." I saw his point.

I still believe that RJ was the most talented sales executive that I ever met. He certainly sold me. Unfortunately, he chose to apply his skills and talent in other ways. More than a year after I terminated him, I received a call from the CEO of another software company. "You don't know me," he said. "But I saw that you announced in a press release several years ago that you hired RJ. I hired him nine months ago because I thought that he was perhaps the best sales leader that I had ever met. But he hasn't closed any business. How did he perform for you?"

I sometimes wonder if RJ is still out there, and how many other software CEOs have fallen for his ruse.

How to Find a Great Sales Leader

It's challenging to find the right sales leader. The head of sales has to push hard, but also fit in. It's a high-risk position because if revenues fall short of projections, the CEO will save their own skin by blaming and terminating the sales vice president. It's no surprise that the average startup CEO fires four sales vice presidents before settling on one that's a keeper.

I've found that the following interview questions provide insights that will increase the odds of hiring a great sales leader.

1. "Take me back to the time that you first joined sales. When did you first know sales was for you?" I never hire a sales leader who didn't begin their career as a bag-carrying salesperson. I follow that with, "What made you a successful salesperson?" And next, "What have you learned since then?"

2. "Tell me about the most difficult sales deal that you've ever closed. What did you do to eventually win it?" I'm looking for how skilled the sales executive is in the *art of sales*. I follow that question with, "Tell me about the second most difficult..." Then, "Tell me about the third most difficult..." Good candidates often have prepared an answer for the most difficult. A few may even be ready for the second most difficult. But when I ask about the third, I learn a great deal about the candidate.

3. "How big is your Rolodex?" I really don't care how big their Rolodex is. I believe that's overrated. If you bought a Volvo from a car dealer, and your salesperson contacted you a year later to say, "I'm now working for Audi. Would you like to buy one," would

you? Buying something from a salesperson in the past has very little to do with a client's desire to buy something different from them in the future. At best, they'll take the call.

But I do care about the salesperson's ability to build new relationships—much more than I value those they've built in the past. And the size of their Rolodex is a good indicator of that.

4.   "Explain your current company's go-to-market model. Where do new leads come from?" I'm asking to determine if the candidate's approach is consistent with the go-to-market model that is the best fit for my company. Does the candidate depend heavily on marketing? Or do they rely on inside sales to tee-up new opportunities? Are they a *farmer* or a *hunter*?

5.   "Tell me about the sales teams you've built." I want to learn what the candidate believes are the characteristics that define a great sales team; the process that they follow to recruit them; and how they shape their hires into an effective team. I follow that by asking, "How do you manage a sales representative who isn't performing?" Then, "How and when do you know that someone you've hired won't be successful?" Finally, I smile and ask, "How and when will I know whether or not you will be successful?" That leads to a discussion of what the candidate believes they will accomplish—and how quickly. I learn how thoroughly they understand the go-to-market challenges that I am facing.

6.   "Describe your favorite boss and what made them your favorite." I'm exploring what motivates the sales executive, and what they need from me to help them be successful. I follow that by asking, "What is the best advice that you've received from that manager?" That helps me learn how the candidate processes feedback.

7.   "Reflecting on your professional career, what are you most proud of?" I find that's the best question to end my interview. It's a softball. But it also helps me better understand what motivates the sales executive. I've had candidates who answered:

- "I tripled sales;"

- "My team tripled sales;"

- "I didn't give up on an underperforming salesperson who I believed had potential—and they eventually blossomed;"

- "I developed a new go-to-market model that increased both leads and close rates;" and

- "The solution that I introduced to a client was a game-changer for their business."

There is no correct answer. But understanding what drives a candidate's professional ambitions helps you decide if they are a good fit for your company.

In summary, these seven questions help me evaluate a sales executive's skills and experience, their ability to build a strong team and drive the go-to-market model that I've invested in, and the support that they need to be successful. For me, it beats "sell me this pen."

What Is the *Science* of Sales Management?

I learned the science of sales management from Curt, CTP's US sales vice president, and one of the best sales leaders that I've ever worked with. Curt held pipeline and forecasting meetings every Friday at 8:00 a.m. Eastern Standard Time—5:00 a.m. for our West Coast sales team. Attendance was mandatory. He followed a rigorous process designed to keep all of the forecasted deals on track. Curt challenged everything. "Where did that opportunity come from?" "Why do you believe we'll win it?" "How big is it, and how do we scale it to something bigger?" "What's the decision process?" "Who owns the budget?" "Who are we competing against?" "Why is that different from what you said last week?" And on and on...

Curt followed Shane Gibson's rule: "Always be closing... That doesn't mean you're always closing the deal, but it does mean to always be closing the next step in the process." He described his management style as "tough." His sales team affectionately described it as the "pimp" style of management. In their words, "One day he would beat the hell out of me and do it publicly. The next day, he would smother me with love." Although I couldn't imagine that his style could be effective with any other discipline, it certainly seemed to work for CTP's US sales team. And Curt was masterful at it.

Will Sales Evolve?

Willy was executive vice president of sales and marketing at one of my tech consulting companies. He began his career as a bag-carrying account executive and built a career successfully running sales for half a dozen technology companies. Willy had sales in his DNA. His father was a career account executive, and Willy's first job was working for, and learning from, him. His father named him after the lead character in the 1949 play, *Death of a Salesman*. I regard him as the best sales vice president I've ever worked with.

But Willy wasn't getting the traction that he and I expected at our new company. We were riding the "Brains" consulting wave, where the smartest people in the world gather to solve new problems that no one had solved before. As a result, our company's partners and thought leaders both found and closed the deals with many of our clients. Our geography-based sales force and high field-marketing expenses weren't paying off, driving a much higher cost of sales than we could afford. I believed that we needed to rethink our go-to-market strategy. Willy disagreed. "Actually, we should double down on what we've been doing, not stop. This model has worked since my father taught it to me thirty years ago."

His words got me thinking that sales is both an art and a science, and success relies on a delicate dance between the two. Over time, does the art change? Does the science? Do both evolve? Or, as Willy believed, do both the art and the science remain unchanged?

I'm not sure who invented the art of sales. If I had to guess, I'd pick the serpent in Genesis that convinced Eve to eat the apple. But I do know who invented the science of sales: John H. Patterson.[27] In 1884, when he founded the National Cash Register Company, Patterson introduced a selling approach encompassing the sales training manual, canned sales pitches, assigned territories, sales quotas, sales pipeline meetings, direct mail, industrial advertising, public relations, and testimonials. Although many of his fundamentals remain intact, the science of sales—the go-to-market model, sales management processes, tools and technology enablers—has come a long way and will continue to evolve.

Inside sales models have emerged for less complex solutions that don't require customization, buy-in from a number of key executives, or large capital investments. Josiane Feigon, author of *Smart Selling on the Phone and Online*, confirms that inside sales is significantly less expensive than the traditional sales model. "The average cost of an outside B2B sales call is $215–$400 per call. An inside call, on the other hand, averages only $25–$75."[28]

Only 35 percent of an account representative's time is actually spent selling.[29] New sales and marketing tools aim to solve that sales productivity problem. And there are a lot to choose from. In 2020, ChiefMarTec referenced more than eight thousand marketing technology solutions,[30] while Sales Hacker identified the "Best 150+ Sales Tools."[31] Eric Quanstrom, CMO of CIENCE, went as far as predicting, "In the next three to five years, the sales function will be completely based upon artificial intelligence."[32] Yes, Willy, the science of sales is evolving.

Parting Thoughts

- When attempting to get agreement on your point of view, listening is much more effective than talking. That doesn't just apply to sales—it's a life lesson. F. Scott Fitzgerald's quote is more important today than it ever was before: "The test of a first-rate intelligence is the ability to hold two opposed ideas in mind at the same time and still retain the ability to function."

- The science of sales can make a good account manager much more productive. But it doesn't "take the sales out of Sales." The art of sales—the skill sets (questioning, listening, ability to overcome objections, creativity), personality traits (empathy, competitiveness, persistence, trust, transparency, confidence), mindset (partnership, relationship), behavior (research, preparation, quarterbacking, closing the deal) are fundamentals that I believe will always be key to success. Sales will always be personal.

Now that you can articulate your value proposition, you've convinced your team that *everyone is in sales*, and you understand both the art and the science of a successful sales strategy, how do you find your first client? The next chapter destroys the business school myth of triaging your prospects.

• • •

There's No Such Thing as a Tier 3 Client...at Least Not in the Early Days of a Startup

Pretend that every single person that you meet has a sign around his or her neck that says "Make me feel important." Not only will you succeed in sales, you will succeed in life.

— Mary Kay Ash, founder, Mary Kay Cosmetics

Forget What You Learned in Business School

I KNOW WHAT you're thinking. *Of course*, there are Tier 3 clients. All of us learned about them in business school. They're the ones that are small, without a huge budget, perhaps not as forward thinking as our other clients. Tier 3 customers can easily cost us as much money as we can make from them. On the other hand, Tier 1 customers are those that match our "best-fit" customer profile. They are the targets of our sales and marketing engines, and we do whatever we can to never lose one of them. If a Tier 3 customer leaves, we see that as no real loss.

Seems logical. So why do I have a problem with that? It's because a startup is an organization in search of a repeatable and sustainable business model. If your business model is still evolving, so is your best-fit customer profile. For startups, especially in the early days, it's more important to be opportunistic than to focus on the quality of your prospect. In my experience, opportunities are really hard to come by in a new business—and you can't afford to squander them. Pursue all of them with an equal sense of urgency.

Landing Cambridge Technology Partners' First UK Client

One year after launching Cambridge Technology Partners (CTP)– Europe, I decided to expand from Amsterdam to the UK. I remember one of my colleagues arguing against it. "The UK isn't really part of Europe," Thornton said. "It's an historical theme park off the coast of Europe." But I had an opportunity to hire Steve, a London-based sales executive, who had a prospect that he believed was *qualified*. Besides, everyone spoke English. What else did we need? I flew to London to open our UK office and pitch to Steve's qualified prospect.

When I arrived at Heathrow, Steve picked me up. Sixty minutes into our drive I asked, "Didn't you say our prospect was based in London?"

"No," Steve said. "Just outside of London." Five hours later, we arrived in Liverpool.

The drive gave Steve plenty of time to brief me on Beacon, the "qualified" prospect that he had uncovered. He explained that Beacon was a trading company. When pressed for more details, Steve told me that they were in the business of buying and selling dead animal hides. They had a group of seven buyers who took calls from people who, for example, wanted to sell six zebra skins. They wrote the details on sticky notes of specifically designated colors: blue for hides, yellow for fur, and pink for "other." I was afraid to ask, "What's included in 'other'?" Next, they posted that "deal" on a board they shared with their team of seven sellers. The sellers then contacted their potential zebra skin customers and attempted to make a deal. Beacon received a commission on successful transactions.

I'll grant you that Beacon was technically a trading company. But it was a trading company with one of the least politically correct, most abhorrent business models ever created. What was Steve thinking when he asked me to fly to London, drive five hours to Liverpool, and pitch to a tiny company that couldn't possibly have an adequate budget? Hadn't Steve learned not to waste time on Tier 3 customers?

I didn't think things could get worse—but that's because I had never been to Liverpool before.

Liverpool had not yet recovered from the decline that began in the mid-1970s when changes in shipping routes, restructuring of their heavy industries, and containerization led to an obsolescence of the city's docks and an unemployment rate approaching 20 percent. An average of twelve thousand people each year were leaving the city, and 15 percent of its land was vacant or derelict. That led to a significant surge in heroin use and other crimes. The worst section of Liverpool was the dock area. That's where Beacon was located.

It was a damp, cloudy day in January, and it was already getting dark when we arrived at 2:30 p.m. We entered the Beacon lobby and immediately noticed that all the decor—the rugs, the furniture cushions, the lampshades—were made out of dead animal hides. The light switches, crafted out of what looked like deer hooves, were the creepiest. It could have been my imagination, but the lobby carried the pungent scent of damp animal fur.

Beacon's managing director—I'll call him Jonathan Vaughn—invited us into a conference room to meet the buy and sell team leaders. They explained that their manual process was time-consuming and made it difficult to support the many time zones where their suppliers and customers operated. That was my opening to explain the advantages of a three-tier client-server architecture. Ten minutes into it, I noticed the blank faces in the room, and realized that the company was run by sticky notes and didn't own a single computer. No one had any idea what I was talking about.

Hoping to engage the audience, I paused to ask if there were any questions. Thank God there was one. The lead buyer asked, "Is it true, Mr. Seibel, that if we use one of these computers, we can get some sort of a disease?" It didn't occur to me until later that evening that he was asking about computer viruses.

We adjourned to produce a $90,000 proposal to automate their buy-sell process, and I handed it to them as we hurried to our car to catch the last Amsterdam flight out of Heathrow. No way did I want to spend the night in Liverpool. Beacon signed the contract the next day, and CTP–Europe had won our first UK client. My attitude abruptly changed. Perhaps Beacon was not a "best-fit" client. But they were our only UK client. I organized an office party to celebrate. After our last round of drinks, my implementation team asked me, "What does Beacon do?" I smiled and said, "They are a trading company just outside of London." Best to let them find out more when they got there.

Roll the clock ahead six months. We had won four more UK clients, all in less exotic businesses than Beacon's. But having Beacon as our first UK client made it much easier to win our second, third, fourth, and fifth deals. In the late spring, when I was on my way back to Heathrow to return to Amsterdam, I had time to sort through the mail in my briefcase. Near the top I found a letter addressed to me.

Dear Mr. Seibel,

I am writing to thank you for the work that you and CTP–Europe performed for Beacon. We were losing revenue to our competitors and on the brink of failing. But thanks to the 24x7 trading system that you built and implemented in record time, our growth has skyrocketed, and we have regained confidence in our future. Thank you for being a huge part of our success.

—Jonathan Vaughn, Esq., CEO – Beacon

I thought, "I'm not sure we made the world a better place, but I'm delighted that they valued our work." Even though Beacon wasn't an attractive company to me, they kept sixty workers employed during a difficult economic time in Liverpool. I was proud that we helped them survive. Thank you notes like that one are rare, so I folded the letter and put it back into my briefcase.

On my flight, I thought about that letter, opened it again, and reread it. At that time, the biggest consulting opportunity in Europe was driven by large banks looking to build 24x7 trading systems. None of the consulting firms had made a dent in that market. It occurred to me that Beacon sounded like the name of a financial institution, and Jonathan Vaughn, Esq., could easily pass as the name of a bank CEO. And his thank you letter referred only to a successful 24x7 trading solution that CTP–Europe built, without any mention of dead animal hides. Hmm...

I called Mr. Vaughn the next morning, thanked him for his kind letter, and asked if I could publish it verbatim in that week's *Financial Times*. He thought the *Financial Times* was an unusual choice, but gladly agreed.

Within six weeks, CTP–Europe won two European banking clients and built a robust pipeline of financial services opportunities that drove much of our growth for the next two years—without ever misrepresenting or exaggerating the work we did for Beacon.

Parting Thoughts

I find that many startups attribute their success to an early opportunity that turns into something quite unexpected. It's easy to justify walking away from a prospect that falls short of your "ideal customer" profile. I certainly felt like running when I entered Beacon's furry, musky lobby on that damp, cloudy day in January.

The business school theory of Tier 1 customers overlooks the importance of the network effect for early-stage startups. The successful launch of a business relies on more than the value of any one customer. It also depends on the opportunities that the first customer can lead to. As long as your business model is evolving, pursue all opportunities with an equal sense of urgency.

My next chapter explains why it's important, as your startup grows, to evolve from an opportunistic mindset to a focused sales approach.

• • •

CHAPTER NINE

When Does Focus Become Critical? And How Do You Do It?

"Opportunistic" selling can be addictive since it brings in cash. But, like with any addiction, to become healthy again, you need to kick the habit.

– Brian Turchin, founder and CEO, Cape Horn Strategies

When Should You Change Your Go-to-Market from Opportunistic to Focused?

CHAPTER 8 ARGUES in favor of treating any potential customer as an important prospect in the early days of a startup. But that opportunistic sales mindset needs to evolve as your business model matures.

As your sales team grows, they'll need to focus their efforts in order to be productive. The sales executives should prioritize which accounts to target and think through how to position your value proposition to engage each one of them. Furthermore, you should standardize the processes used to qualify sales opportunities so your company can allocate scarce resources to win the "best-fit" clients and increase the accuracy of your revenue forecasts.

Founders can continue to be opportunistic. But the sales team must become both structured and focused. When I was traveling the world to validate ZEFER's model, I met Jim Barksdale, Netscape's CEO. I was visiting the company's headquarters the day they held their "going away" celebration. They had just been acquired by AOL for $10 billion. Technically it was a great exit, but the ending was bittersweet for employees because Netscape's culture and their identity wouldn't survive. Jim reiterated his words of advice that had become famous: "The main thing is to keep the main thing the main thing." He explained, "Every business has a profit engine that lies at its core. And that engine is invariably simple if you strip away everything extraneous."

Contemplating ZEFER

In 1998, I departed Cambridge Technology Partners (CTP) to contemplate the launch of ZEFER. Because this would be my first "real" startup (at least according to the way Steve, the Uber driver, kept score), I had to create a business model, craft and validate a value proposition, build a team, raise funding, identify my initial prospects...and so on. Best for me to hunker down at my home in Cape Cod until I could figure it all out.

Our Cape home is on Old Silver Beach in North Falmouth. We're located there because that's the beach where Carol vacationed when she was growing up. Residents from Boston seem to spend their summers in one of four locations—the Cape, the North Shore, New Hampshire, or Maine—depending on where their parents spent their summer holidays. If you vacationed on Cape Cod as a kid, you wouldn't be caught dead going anywhere else. I got that. Old Silver Beach was where Carol created many of her childhood memories. So, it's where she dreamed of building new ones with our family.

Cape Cod was also the perfect place for me to reflect on what I wanted to do with my new startup and construct a plan for getting there. To get to the Cape, you have to drive over one of two bridges that cross the Cape Cod canal. And when you do, legend has it that you leave all of your troubles and worries on the other side.

Before long, I developed a routine, beginning with an early morning walk on Old Silver Beach. August rolled into September, and the summer crowds rapidly disappeared. Old Silver was deserted in the mornings, except for a young man who appeared to share my same routine.

After a few days of passing one another, we began to smile and wave. That degree of intimacy normally takes a while to achieve in New England. A few days later, we stopped to introduce ourselves. I asked my new acquaintance, Tom, "Are you taking an extended vacation? It's usually pretty deserted here off-season."

Tom said, "No. I just retired."

"Retired?" I responded. "You look much too young to retire—unless you were the founder/CEO of a blazing hot dot-com rocket ship..."

He smiled and said, "No. I ran sales for a CAD/CAM company."

I thought that he must be kidding. "CAD/CAM is an old technology. It's been around for decades. How could you possibly afford to retire?"

Tom looked a bit embarrassed. "I developed a scalable customer qualification process and value proposition that was easy for my sales team to understand and execute."

I explained that I was starting a new company, and that "a scalable customer qualification process and value proposition that was easy for my prospective sales team to understand and execute" might come in handy. "What did you do, and how did you do it?"

Tom's face reddened. "It's so simple that I'm embarrassed to tell you. I'm afraid you'll laugh at me." Before I could respond, he turned and walked away.

In the following days, our morning routines continued. But now, when we passed, I'd call out, "Are you ready to tell me? I promise I won't laugh." As it turned out, that was a difficult promise to keep.

The Three Smokestacks

After a few days, Tom relented. "Okay. I'll tell you." He talked while we walked. Tom explained that he gave his sales team five simple rules.

1. Make sure that you are driving on a highway by 8:00 a.m. every morning. You can decide which highway and which direction to drive.

2. Keep driving until you see a building with at least three smokestacks with smoke coming out of all of them. If you see only two smokestacks, keep driving down the highway. If you see three, but smoke is only coming out of two, keep driving down the highway. But when you see three smokestacks that are all smoking, get off at the next exit, turn around, go back to that building and pull into the parking lot.

3. If it's easy to find a parking space, turn around and continue driving down the highway. If the parking lot is crowded, find a place to park, even if you have to park illegally.

4. Walk around the perimeter of the building and peek in the windows. Look for a large room filled with slanted tables with someone sitting at each table. If you can't find that room, don't assume it's on a higher floor. Go back to your car and continue driving down the highway. If you find the room but there aren't people sitting at every table, get back on the highway.

5. If you haven't left yet, walk to the front door, ask to see the head of engineering, and hand them our brochure that explains how our CAD/CAM system can dramatically improve drafting productivity.

I thought his scalable customer qualification process was probably the dumbest thing I'd ever heard.

Tom saw the look on my face and continued. "Let me explain. Before I took charge of sales, we followed the 'solution selling' model that most companies use. Our sales executives cold-called prospects, hoping to arrange a meeting. That meeting had a dual purpose: to introduce our company and our capabilities, and to land a second meeting. At the second meeting, our sales executives would go into more detail on the range of problems that we could solve, citing case studies as confirmation.

The objective at that point was to land a third meeting to discuss the prospect's specific opportunities—which could fall within a very wide range—including drafting and engineering productivity, 3D modeling, finite element analysis, dynamic modeling, simulation/testing ..."

"Next, the sales executive would collaborate with our chief technology officer to review the prospect's requirements and develop a customized approach for addressing them. If the fourth meeting was successful, it could lead to meeting number five (refining the solution and approach), meeting six (pitching the customized solution to a larger group), and finally meeting seven (pitching to the decision maker). That process takes a lot of time. The account manager has to manage the opportunity down the sales funnel, customizing the offering to eliminate obstacles along the way. Time is never a friend during a sales process. In fact, only two to three percent of the opportunities ever successfully make it all the way through."

I was beginning to understand. Rather than trying to solve every engineering problem that CAD/CAM can address, customizing the solution for the buyer, and managing his way through the accompanying long and complex sales cycle, Tom created a value proposition that directly addressed a problem that most large engineering companies face.

Tom wrapped up. "It may take a while for a sales executive to find his three smokestacks. But when they do, the odds are significantly higher that they'll win the deal—in much less time, and with much less investment."

I identified with the long sales cycles, significant investments, and low rates of success that characterize the traditional sales funnel. Was Tom sharing, verbatim, his proprietary solution to that problem? Or were "three smokestacks" just a metaphor? Or perhaps Tom was just pulling my leg? Regardless, the more that I thought about it, the more value I found in his approach.

I never saw Tom again after that day. I continued with my morning walks on Old Silver Beach, but he was never there. To this day, I have no idea what happened to him. I didn't have a chance to ask the dozens of follow-up questions that were whirling through my mind. How do I find *my* three smokestacks? Where do I start? How could I build on Tom's story to create a process to help me create a "focus" for my startup sales teams?

My Process for Helping You Find *Your* Three Smokestacks

Begin by identifying a problem that you believe your company can solve better than anyone else.

Identify the market niche facing that problem. Define it narrowly so you can dominate it. When Jack Welch was CEO of General Electric, he exited every market where GE didn't rank first or second. Jack's approach wasn't driven by ego. Rather, he knew that when a GE division was number one or number two in a market, customers recognized their name and flocked to them, making sales much easier. But it's much harder to get that first meeting when a company ranks third or lower. Select your initial market niche with two questions in mind: First, is it sufficiently narrow to allow your business to become one of the top two competitors within twelve months? And second, is it expandable to larger niches (for example, new geographies or verticals for the same product) that will support your growth ambitions?

Identify the target customers in that market niche. Learn everything about them that you can. What do they read? Which conferences do they attend? Who else do they do business with?

Capture, analyze, and share these customer insights with your sales team. Identify the three smokestacks that will help your sales team know where and how to find them.

And of course, equip your sales team with an engaging but simple customer value proposition that targets a prospective customer's problem and links your solution to their budget.

Parting Thoughts

The traditional sales funnel is a long, expensive, unpredictable process that delivers only a small percentage of the opportunities that surface. "Three smokestacks" is, of course, a metaphor. It's hard to find actual smokestacks these days, even in Pittsburgh. The key takeaway is to identify a problem common to many of your prospects and match it with a solution that you can credibly deliver—and then target the prospects with that specific need. If your startup can create the right focus, your prospects are more qualified, and you will enter the sales funnel 75 percent of the way through. What are your three smokestacks?

Chance encounters often lead to new ideas, new contacts, and occasionally new business. Read on to learn how you can maximize those opportunities.

• • •

CHAPTER TEN

How Do You Build Your Network?

Networking is not about just connecting people. It's about connecting people with people, people with ideas, and people with opportunities.

— Michele Jennae, artist, healer, author

Are You an Accomplished Networker?

NETWORKING COMES NATURALLY to some. Others find it daunting. I was a member of the "others" group. I found it uncomfortable to stand alone in a crowded room where everyone else seemed to know one another. And if I found someone to chat with who, after a few minutes, excused themselves to join another conversation, I felt abandoned, and my self-esteem was a bit shaken. "Why didn't they chat with me all evening? Perhaps we could have become friends."

But I knew that networking was something I had to do for professional reasons. Failure to build and leverage your network is cited as another reason why startups fail.[23] In today's world, networking is a necessity. "A mountain of research shows that professional networks lead to more job and business opportunities, broader and deeper knowledge, improved capacity to innovate, faster advancement, and greater status and authority. Building and nurturing professional relationships also improves the quality of work and increases job satisfaction."[33]

I found that networking became easier after I started launching startups and had something innately interesting to talk about. Finally, *I* was the person excusing himself to converse with another group. I had become an accomplished networker! I also found that becoming an entrepreneur reshaped my objective. Instead of networking to collect a pocketful of business cards from strangers I never intended to contact, I had a purpose: to connect with potential customers, employees, advisors, and partners. I learned that networking was simply building, growing, and leveraging relationships, and realizing that changed everything.

Just like sales, networking is both an art and a science. The pillar of the art is, "It's a small world." The science's foundation is, "It takes a village."

It's a Small World —ZEFER

Because it's a small world, business leaders should make connections freely and frequently. Chance meetings can turn into business opportunities.

ZEFER didn't throw a massive launch party. Instead, we wanted the event to feel exclusive. We simply informed our friends and colleagues about our launch date, explained that it was a private event, and mentioned that a few people might drop by to wish our new team well. Our approach seemed to pique quite a bit of interest. It's a small world, and several hundred colleagues and friends, many of whom I hadn't seen in years, showed up at our offices that day to congratulate us and wish us luck.

I'm always a bit uncomfortable in situations like that because I have a mild case of prosopagnosia, or face blindness. I don't always recognize a familiar face—especially if it's out of context. And at this point, I was still trying to get more comfortable with networking.

Tony, the founder of the internet strategy company that we acquired, noticed my uneasiness. "Bill, there are a ton of people walking over to you to chat. Why aren't you introducing me to any of them?" Tony asked.

Embarrassed, I scoured the office desperately hoping to see someone I recognized so I could introduce Tony. And I found someone! I grabbed Tony by the arm, walked over to our newest visitor, and said, "Tony, meet Ray. Ray is my trash guy from Wellesley." Another small world encounter! I continued, "Small world, Ray. What are you doing here?"

Ray replied, "I'm sorry if I'm crashing your party, but I heard about your opening and didn't want to miss the opportunity to stop by and congratulate you on launching ZEFER. Coincidentally, I'm in the neighborhood because I just expanded my recycling business to the Leather District. In fact, it's my first day doing business here, and I'm meeting my new clients for the first time."

"Small world," I said. "It's also *my* first day here. And I'm meeting some of ZEFER's clients for the first time."

Ray went on, "I also have a new team, and I'm in the neighborhood to get to know them better."

"Me, too," I said. "I'm meeting new team members for the first time as well!" I continued, "Talk about a small world, here you are at my office, twelve miles from Wellesley. It's the first day that both you and I are launching a new company. And we're both here meeting our team and our clients for the first time." Pausing, I said, "I notice that you're wearing a Penn State sweatshirt. I received my undergraduate degree from Penn State. This could *really* be a small world story. Did you attend Penn State?"

Ray's face reddened. "No, Bill. I found this in your trash last week."

You know it's a small world when your trash collector finds out about your opening event and crashes it wearing a sweatshirt that he found in your trash. A week later, I received an email from Ray introducing me to the CEO of an e-commerce startup whom he met later that day. Ray's referral became one of ZEFER's earliest clients.

It's a Small World — Mobiquity

When launching Mobiquity, I would occasionally fly from Boston to New York or Philadelphia to test my ideas with several colleagues. One Friday, my evening return trip was delayed by severe thunderstorms. Facing a three-hour delay, I hurried to the closest airport bar and secured the last stool. It was next to an attractive woman, perhaps ten years younger than me. Kimberly broke the ice by telling me that she was flying home to Providence, Rhode Island, and also expected a long delay. We passed the time by chatting for the next three hours.

As my boarding call neared, she asked, "Where did you vacation growing up?"

I told her the truth. "Living in Pittsburgh, I vacationed at Lake Erie. What about you? Living in Rhode Island, I'd guess you spent your holidays in Newport."

"I do now," Kimberly replied. "But growing up, my boyfriend lived on Cape Cod, so I vacationed there."

I smiled and said, "Small world. I live on Cape Cod. What part?"

"The part that you get to by crossing the Bourne Bridge," she answered.

My smile turned into a grin. "Small world. That's the part of the Cape where I live. Tell me more."

"It's in the Falmouth area." And then she added, "in a town named North Falmouth."

"The small world is getting smaller," I replied. "I live in North Falmouth. What part?"

Now Kimberly began to smile. "It's on Old Silver Beach, near the Seacrest Hotel."

I was stunned. "I live on Old Silver Beach and near the Seacrest Hotel! Small world. Which house?"

"It was the first home built on Bay Shore Road, on a hill overlooking Buzzards Bay. It was owned by a doctor, and his son was my first boyfriend."

"Oh my God," I exclaimed! "Small world! That's my house!"

She paused, blushed, and said, "Oh my God! Small world! The first time that I had sex was in your bedroom!"

That's when I heard, "USAir Flight 243 boarding for Boston." I headed for my gate and never saw her again. Three months later, a fashion and jewelry retailer engaged Mobiquity to develop their mobile commerce app. When I asked how they heard of us, it was a referral from Kimberly.

It's a Small World — Everywhere

I could cite many other examples of landing early clients because of chance meetings. Mobiquity, for example, drove 80 percent of our first-year bookings of $5.3 million by leveraging contacts. Our largest client, Panera Bread, came from a venture partner who sat in on one of our pitches. And our second largest came from a round of drinks I bought for the patrons of the Fare' Hoa Beach Bar in Bora Bora to celebrate Mobiquity's funding.

For an entrepreneur, the art of networking is simple. Just tell your story. And if you're passionate about what you are doing, people will listen. And some of them will remember.

It Takes a Village

For the science of networking, I turned to my close friend Augusto (Gus) Vidaurreta. We once worked together after Cambridge Technology Partners (CTP) acquired Gus's company, Systems Consulting Group (SCG), twice named one of the five hundred fastest growing companies by *Inc. Magazine*. Gus ran CTP's US southeast and Latin America regions. Following that, his entrepreneurship track record included a variety of startups, from sports bars to hotels, manufacturing, nutrition, banking, internet of things consulting, and an artificial intelligence accelerator that helps global startups enter the US market. Don't get me wrong—Gus is a master of the art of networking. But he is also the coauthor of *Business Is a Contact Sport*,[34] where he does a great job of capturing the science of networking. I asked Gus, "What's the one thing that you'd tell an entrepreneur about networking?"

"It takes a village," Gus said. "Networking is about building and leveraging relationships. Not just with your clients. You should treat all your stakeholders like your clients. Business opportunities can originate from partners, investors, media, competitors, and ex-employees. Especially ex-employees."

I asked Gus to expand on that.

"When an employee resigns, it's easy to feel betrayed. But don't let that influence how you treat them on the way out. They may end up in a position that can help you in the future. It's even more important when you let them go. At SCG, we helped them find their next gig—one where we believed they could be successful. That trumps any resentment they might have felt."

"Tell me more about how you managed relationships across all your stakeholders," I asked.

"My partner and coauthor, Tom Richardson, and I went to Target and filled a shopping cart with large, plastic buckets—the kind that kids play with on the beach," Gus explained. "We labeled them: clients, ex-clients, ex-employees, partners, competitors, media, universities, service providers, and bankers/investors. After lining them up in a circle in a conference room, we asked our employees to toss in the business cards of all of their contacts. That helped us build a database of relationships and their owners. More importantly, it highlighted areas where our relationships were light and where they were abandoned. The media and banker/investor buckets had only a few cards. So, we knew we had to increase our efforts to network in those areas. We dubbed this 'Hunting.' Many of our existing relationships hadn't been touched for a long time. We named this reconnection effort 'Gathering.'"

I asked, "What then? How do you manage those relationships to provide value to your company?"

"That's the wrong question," Gus responded. "The right question is, 'How do you manage relationships to provide value to both companies?' It works best when you put yourself in the other party's shoes and think through both the long-term and short-term wins from the other person's perspective." A company needs to view relationships as valuable assets that require continuing investment so their value can grow even more.

Gus continued, "There are three types of business relationships. The first one is transactional. In school and in business we're taught to deliver transactional value. For example, if you order three thousand screws from me for delivery on the first of every month, I deliver, and you pay. We have just exchanged transactional value. Transactional value falls short of building strong and long-lasting relationships."

"I call the second type of business relationship 'creative transactional.' That's the next step, where both parties meet to discuss how they can improve the value each is obtaining from the transaction, maybe something as simple as larger production runs, prepayment, or cheaper delivery. These discussions go a long way toward building strong and long-lasting relationships."

"The third relationship is 'outside of the transaction.' When I teach a seminar, I like to ask the participants if they think it's a bad idea to do business with friends. More than 50 percent of the audience usually feels it is. However, I believe that we should only do business *with* friends, and that friendships are developed through the exchange of value outside the transaction. This exchange of value can be very simple: helping a colleague transition to a new job, introducing a potential client, sharing a doctor reference, and so on."

Gus summed up, "The key is to move from transactional to creative transactional to outside of the transaction by consciously moving the relationship down that path. People remember who their friends are. They rarely end a business relationship with a friend without discussing it and giving it a second chance."

I responded, "It seems like you are exploiting your relationships."

"It's only exploitation if it's one-sided," Gus explained. "Not if it's win-win."

"Any final thoughts?" I asked.

Gus responded, "Networking is about building relationships. Those relationships are assets that will grow in value if you invest in them. If managed properly, they can create significant opportunities for your business. One introduction is worth ten leads."

Parting Thoughts

- Networking is simply about building, growing, and leveraging relationships. It is a key skill that every startup CEO must learn.

- It's a small world, and any connection that you make may result in an introduction that leads to a potential customer, colleague, advisor, or partner. As Gus explained, the point isn't to collect as many contacts as you can. Instead, it's about investing in your network to strengthen and increase the value of your business relationships.

- Networking isn't exploitive. It's win-win. As the author and entrepreneur Keith Ferrazzi said, "The currency of real networking is not greed but generosity."

The next chapter explains how to continue to land and expand within your customer base.

• • •

CHAPTER ELEVEN

How Do You "Land and Expand?"

We do a lot of one-night stands in lead generation and not enough long-term relationships.

– Michael King, founder and managing director, iPullRank

Where Should a Successful Startup Look for New Sales?

MOST OF A successful startup's new sales should come from their existing customers. Make it clear to every member of your leadership team that they are, in essence, executive sponsors responsible for this strategy. It's not a ceremonial role. Executive sponsors provide a formal, bidirectional escalation point to intercept and resolve issues with existing customers before they become serious problems. Even when an engagement is on track, they should invest their time to strengthen their relationships and become a trusted advisor. Executive sponsors should aim to become a sounding board that clients turn to when they want to chat about their business and perhaps to explore new opportunities. By building a solid understanding of client businesses, your team will build stronger relationships—and that combination will drive a significant amount of repeat business. I'm surprised that so few startups make this a priority. It's actually more fun than it is hard work. And I find that personal relationships stay intact even after the professional associations fade.

How Can Executive Relationships Drive Current Customer Sales?

It was February 1994, and the executive team of Hoechst-Celanese had flown to Amsterdam to participate in Cambridge Technology Partners (CTP)–Europe's first Rapid Solutions Workshop (RSW). An RSW embodied CTP's secret sauce, a three-week workshop that achieved consensus on the subset of a solution's functionality that would drive the majority of its benefits, packaged with a fixed price for delivering it. I had been the executive sponsor for Hoechst before I left Boston for Europe, and I had developed them into our largest client worldwide. They knew that it was very important for me to build references in Europe—and what better way to help CTP than to bring their project to Amsterdam? In short, they were doing me a huge favor.

It was Thursday afternoon, the day before our final presentation, when we were tying up loose ends and crafting our fixed-price, fixed-timeframe commitment. When the client's executive team flew in that evening, we would host them for dinner and look for the best time to break the news about the price and schedule. Our executive team knew it was critical to avoid surprises and to get alignment in advance.

My team was worried. Our estimates were coming in at $1.6 million, much higher than we expected and no doubt exceeding Hoechst's budget. Our RSW team asked me to discount the price. They argued that it was more important to successfully execute our first RSW and win the follow-on project than it was to risk alienating Hoechst based on our higher-than-expected price. A discount, they argued, amounted to an investment in CTP–Europe's future.

I explained that I had an agreement with Joe, their chief information officer. When we began working together, I promised I would be honest and transparent whenever I presented a price. I would never adjust it based on what I believed his budget might be. If the price fit within Joe's budget, he wouldn't negotiate the price. If it didn't, he would tell me what he could afford, and I would reduce our price to match it. I told Joe, "That's what I believe good partners do. If we trust one another, it will all work out in the long run."

My team continued to push back. But I trusted the relationship I had built with Joe and planned to find a time that evening to chat with him.

I hosted our RSW dinner at my favorite restaurant, De Gouden Reael, a French restaurant on a houseboat in one of the canals, best reached by water taxi. The owners would close it for four weeks at the end of every quarter so that they could visit another province in France, where they would plan their menu and wine list for the following quarter. It was the perfect setting to establish the mood for the evening.

Afterward, I escorted the group on the obligatory stroll through the red-light district. Along the way, I put my arm on Joe's shoulder to pull him aside.

"Joe, I have your price, and I'd like to share it with you. I think it's higher than you expected, but I promised you that if you couldn't afford it, I'd reduce it to fit your budget." With that I slipped him a note with $1.6 million written on it.

Joe glanced at the note, tore it into little pieces, and tossed them in the air. "That number is bullshit." After pausing, he said, "I'm not willing to pay anything less than $2 million."

I wasn't sure I'd heard him correctly. But then I realized that his budget must be higher than we estimated, and he was compensating me for the price reductions that I had given him in the past. But I couldn't resist. "Don't be unreasonable. I'm not willing to do it for anything more than $1.7 million," I countered.

"I don't want to negotiate any further. I'll drop my price to $1.9 million." It was great to see that Joe was also enjoying our game.

I said firmly, "Let's split it down the middle—$1.8 million." Joe agreed, we shook hands and continued on our walk.

My team was still awake and waiting for me when I returned to our offices late that night. They asked, "Are we still going forward? And what price did you agree to?"

"Everything is a 'go.' And we agree on a price of $1.8 million."

My team was shocked. "You are a hell of a negotiator," they said as they packed up to go home to bed.

I smiled as I thought, "If they only knew..."

How to Grow Your Current Customers by Getting to Know Them

It was February 2000, and I was preparing for ZEFER's IPO. I had heard that roadshows are exhausting. Sure, they included amenities like private jets and luxury hotels, but they also required three jam-packed weeks away from home, usually with six to ten presentations in three to five cities each day. Unfortunately, I suffered from a chest cold that I just couldn't shake. That's when my marketing vice president told me that our newest client, one of the largest holistic health companies, wanted me to become their executive sponsor. In return, they offered me an afternoon of free treatments so I could learn more about their business. Interested in meeting a new client and simultaneously hoping they could help me shake my cough and cold in time for the IPO road trip, I scheduled my visit.

Of course, my treatment was appropriately located in the "People's Republic of Cambridge." When I arrived, I walked through beaded curtains and an incense-filled reception area to the front desk. The owner welcomed me, chatted about his business, explained my treatments, and escorted me to the office of Doctor Bon Jovi. I'm not kidding—I still have his card.

I've always had a strong admiration for people who are fluent in more than one language. For my part, I've learned foreign vocabularies but always get hampered by my Pittsburgh-based pronunciation, leading to many humorous stories. I am hopelessly monolingual. Doctor Bon Jovi was Eastern European, fluent in five languages, though he did speak English with a very strong accent.

"Vhatt wrong wit you?" he asked.

"I have a chest cold and a congestion problem that I need to fix in the next few weeks," I replied.

"A kahrecsion problem?"

I attempted to clarify, "A congestion problem."

"Hahrrecsion problem?"

I tried one more time, "A congestion problem."

"Oh, a rahrrectsion problem?"

Giving up, I said, "Yes. A rahrrectsion problem."

Dr. Bon Jovi went to the back of his office and returned with a vial filled with a dark liquid that he concocted. He handed it to me as he explained, "Take big swallow nighttime. Tastes very, very bad. But drink. You be very, very happy." He walked me to my next stop.

I met Dr. Ting (I remember his name because it rhymes with "sting"), the staff acupuncturist. Previously a highly regarded physician in China, he had fled to the US to escape prosecution for a political crime. Rather than take the training necessary to become a practicing doctor in the US, he chose acupuncture as a quicker path to drawing a paycheck. Dr. Ting's procedure improved my congestion, and I looked forward to my last stop.

I don't remember the third doctor's name. He specialized in improving blood circulation. Asking me to take off my shirt and lie on my stomach, he brought in a bucket of wet stones that he wrapped in a cloth and rolled across my back. It hurt like hell. He explained that the treatment was intended to bruise my back. And it did. His theory was that my body would respond by pumping more blood to the injured area. The increased blood flow from my lungs to my back would improve my congestion.

Before I left, he prescribed another treatment. "Put on white athletic socks and soak your feet in ice-cold water, for as long as you can, just before bedtime. When you are done, cover them with a pair of black socks and get into bed. When you wake, you'll find that the blood circulating from your lungs to your feet will have made your socks bone dry. That circulation will help your cough and chest congestion."

I arrived home a few hours later. Carol was waiting for me and asked how my treatments had gone. "I'm not sure," I replied. "I think I'll know more tomorrow morning." We had a glass of wine and retired early.

"What are you doing in the bathroom?" Carol called from bed.

"I'm soaking my feet in ice water."

"Why?" Carol asked.

"To increase the circulation from my chest to my feet. It'll help my cough and congestion." I heard her begin to chuckle. Fifteen minutes later, I walked into the bedroom wearing only sopping wet white athletic socks partially covered by black dress socks. Carol's chuckle progressed to hysterical laughter. When I turned to put on my pajamas, she saw my back and screamed. "It looks like you were run over by a car! What happened to you?"

Too tired to explain, I took my "big swallow" of Doctor Bon Jovi's herbal potion and jumped into bed.

In the middle of the night, the strangest thing happened. I woke with a huge erection. And my feet were bone dry. As the week went on, my congestion improved. But I continued to wake up in the middle of the night with an erection.

Eventually I realized why. Doctor Bon Jovi didn't understand that I was complaining about a "congestion" problem. He must have thought I was complaining of an "erection" problem. I had never expected to be an "executive sponsor with benefits."

How Do You "Land and Expand" to Grow Your Current Customer Business?

Fortune 1000 enterprises span many companies, divisions, brands, and countries. Unilever, for example, encompasses more than four hundred brands across one hundred ninety countries. To grow business with your existing customers, think beyond opportunities where you first land. Find ways to expand into other areas of their companies. How do you do that?

- Stop spending all of your marketing budget on new prospects. Allocate some of it to your existing customers. Use it to cultivate recommendations and to create opportunities for you to broadcast the great work that you're doing across their company. It's likely your client will proudly showcase the initiative that he is funding. Convince him to sponsor an event and invite his colleagues.

- Quite often, clients are reluctant to provide a formal recommendation because they require corporate approval. Instead, ask for word-of-mouth recommendations early and often. Conventional wisdom says that a customer's enthusiasm peaks when you successfully implement your project or product—that's the time to ask for introductions. But it may take three years to get to that point. A customer's enthusiasm also peaks within the first few weeks after a project begins—before anything goes wrong. I believe that's the best time to look for opportunities to expand business with a client.

- Give your customers something to remember you by. At the end of a successful project, a CEO that I advised would deliver champagne to the client's executive team. The bottle came with a custom-designed label including the name of the project, the logos of both his company and his client's, and the client's name. No one ever drank the champagne. Everyone kept it as a trophy, and years later you could still see it displayed on their office bookshelves—a long-lasting advertisement.

- Invite clients to your exclusive events. I asked all of Mobiquity's clients to join the company's five-year birthday party. In my invitation, I asked them to send their congratulations and good wishes to the project team that they worked with, and I explained that I would assemble the notes that I received into a slide show that would continuously play at the party. More than fifty clients attended, and close to one hundred sent a congratulatory letter. Clients that would never permit us to mention their names on our website sent effusive notes for our slide show singing our praises. For example:

  - "Mobiquity is the most talented professional services firm that we have ever worked with."

  - "Mobiquity's work was instrumental in making our new business unit successful."

  - "Mobiquity promised that they would never let us down. And although our project was complex and difficult, they were true to their word."

  All of the clients included the names of the Mobsters who worked with them and the name of their company. As a result, we had a gold mine of informal references. We never used them on our website or included them in a pitch deck. But we did run the slide show continuously on lobby screens in every one of our offices. We made certain to park prospective clients visiting our offices in front of that streaming video for several minutes before ushering them into a conference room in order to subliminally reinforce our credentials.

- Incentivize your sales team to become embedded within your clients. Remind them that they aren't there just to close a deal. They're also there to walk the halls and cultivate new relationships. Publicly reward an account executive when they earn their own security badge (instead of a visitor's badge), or if six vice presidents from other client divisions know their name. Expect them to develop and review their client expansion plan. Offer commissions for follow-on sales.

Parting Thoughts

- Existing customers represent important relationships. Focusing on them can drive much of your growth. Bain & Company reports, "It costs six to seven times more to acquire a new customer than retain an existing one." Over-deliver. Do whatever it takes to get to know them and to build relationships with them. You never know what unexpected benefits your efforts might bring!

- Apply the life lessons you've learned about growing personal relationships to your clients. Follow through on your commitments. Never break a promise. Be transparent and honest about any mistakes that you've made. Go the extra mile. Always be responsive. Make time for your clients even if they call you at 2:00 a.m. Make them feel special.

Next, I introduce what I believe is the most important determinant of a startup's success: "How good is your team at executing Plan B?"

• • •

Part 3

Scaling

There are people who make things happen, there are people who watch things happen, and there are people who wonder what happened. To be successful, you need to be a person who makes things happen.

– Jim Lovell, American astronaut

CHAPTER TWELVE

How Good Are You at Executing Plan B?

Everybody has a plan until they get punched in the mouth.

– Mike Tyson, world heavyweight champion boxer

Every Successful Startup Pivots at Least Five Times

BUSINESS PLANS NEVER survive their first contact with the customer. I've heard that every successful startup will pivot at least five times. Sometimes the founders have to tweak the technology. Perhaps they need to fundamentally rethink their business model or use cases. Often their go-to-market strategy has to evolve. Every one of these scenarios will most likely occur at some point in a startup's life. Plan A will not always happen. That's why it is so important to excel at executing Plan B.

A startup is an organization in search of a scalable business model. The path to that discovery is never a straight line. Paul Graham—a computer scientist, entrepreneur, venture capitalist, author, and essayist— agrees. "Startups are inherently chaotic. The rapid shifts in the business model is what differentiates a startup from an established company. Pivots are the essence of entrepreneurship and the key to startup success. If you can't pivot or pivot quickly, chances are you will fail."

Examples are easy to find.

- Instagram began as Burbn, a location-based social network with an *optional* photo sharing feature.

- PayPal started as Confinity, a cryptography company that provided security for handheld devices.

- Facebook began as FaceMash, a "hot-or-not" game that allowed Harvard students to compare pictures of two female students and vote on who was more attractive.

And pivoting doesn't just apply to tech startups.

- Shell Oil Company began as a small antique shop that imported decorative shells from the Far East.

- Nintendo started as a playing card company.

- Nokia's first break-out success was manufacturing rubber boots.

- Remember Wipro from Chapter 3? One of the world's largest IT companies began by manufacturing and selling vegetable oil to Indian housewives. In fact, Wipro is short for "Western India Palm Refined Oil Limited."

Launching Cambridge Technology Partners–Europe

I knew nothing about pivoting when I relocated from Boston to Amsterdam in the spring of 1993 to launch the European division of Cambridge Technology Partners (CTP). Nor did I know anything about doing business in Europe.

With one hundred employees in two locations (if you count the basement of the Hughes Aircraft headquarters), CTP was much too small to expand internationally. But we didn't know enough to let that slow us down. CTP assembled a team of two of our experienced

consultants, led by me, to relocate to Amsterdam to launch a
joint venture (JV) with the largest IT consulting company in the
Netherlands. Six of their consultants transferred to the US for six months
of training in our technology, tools, and methodology. They would join
us after the business was running. And as I mentioned earlier, Carol
and I married two days before departing Boston for Europe. With her
background as a senior project manager, I benefited from another talented
resource in the wings.

It seemed like a well-thought-out Plan A. Amsterdam is a gem of a city, the
perfect location for a US company to launch its European operations. It
combines a pro-business tax structure with a highly talented, multilingual
workforce; a superior infrastructure; and easy access to Belgium, Germany,
and France. It's also an exciting place to live—the '60s frozen in time—
both 1660s *and* 1960s. And the JV was a perfect match. It leveraged
CTP's differentiators—Rapid Application Development and Fixed Price/
Fixed Timeframe—factors which were unique at that time. Our JV partner
backed up our strengths with their infrastructure, name recognition, client
base, financial strength, sales team, and vast army of consultants. With
an operation staffed by an experienced CTP consultant (Howard), a
solid CTP sales executive (Fergal), a senior project manager (Carol), and
six fully trained senior European consultants, led by me, what could go
wrong? Let me tell you.

Carol and I arrived in Amsterdam to begin our adventure late on a Friday
afternoon. Our fourth-floor apartment's tall, wide, and uncurtained
windows overlooked the houseboats on the Keizersgracht, the "Emperor's"
canal. After settling in, we began preparing for Monday—our first day
with the JV. Having traveled by train on our honeymoon for the prior
two weeks, we badly needed to launder our clothes. Relieved to find a
combination washer/dryer in our bathroom, I located the user manual
in a nearby drawer. It was in Dutch. But that didn't stop me. I'm a blue-
collar guy from Pittsburgh. We don't really have to read user manuals.
We're handy. So, I tossed my business shirts into the washer, set the dryer's
temperature to eighty degrees to avoid the risk of shrinking anything,
and took a short walk with Carol to explore the neighborhood. After
we returned, I opened the door to find that all of my shirts had shrunk

to a size I had outgrown thirty years earlier. That's when I recalled the difference between Fahrenheit and Celsius. We added new shirts and a Dutch-English dictionary to our shopping list.

Without curtains or blinds, the sunrise awakened us at 5:20 a.m. on Monday, so we had an early start. Our offices were just off the A10 highway that circles Amsterdam, and I had the name of the exit. In order to find our way home at the end of the day, I asked Carol to write down the name of our apartment's exit as we merged onto the highway. "The sign says 'Afrit,'" she said, and wrote the name in her notebook.

Our partner's executive team arrived shortly after we did. After introductions, they explained our "rules of engagement." The JV's parent would bring us our leads, manage our involvement throughout the sales process, set pricing, close the deal, and own the client relationship. That seemed like more help than we needed—or wanted. An uncomfortable feeling gnawed at me, and I hoped it was the Haring Hollandse Nieuwe I had eaten the night before. On our way home that evening, I asked Carol to remind me of the name of our exit. She checked her notebook and said, "Afrit." Before long we realized that "Afrit" was the Dutch word for exit, and we had no idea how to find our way home.

My uneasy feeling had nothing to do with my Dutch New Herring dinner. It soon became clear that our JV partner didn't believe in CTP's value proposition. They just wanted to parade us in front of their prospects to pitch Rapid Application Development and Fixed Price/Fixed Timeframe as a way for them to create more sales opportunities for their own service offerings, not the JV. I realized that I was nothing more than bait. Nothing that I said or did had any impact on their strategy.

Frustrated, I called Jim Sims, our CEO. With his backing, I planned to walk into our partner's European managing director's office and announce that I was dissolving the JV. My team of CTP consultants would remain in Amsterdam, build a business without their help and support, and compete with them.

The thought of having that conversation kept me awake for several nights. I wondered what to expect. Would he be angry? Would he realize that he needed CTP and try to convince me to stay? I anticipated a wide range of possible reactions—but I didn't expect the managing director to burst into wild laughter. He controlled it long enough to say, "You have no market presence, no offices, no infrastructure, no partners, no clients, and no prospects. Your entire team is four people, none of whom has ever done business in Europe before, and no one who speaks our language. You obviously haven't clearly thought this out."

"If you put it that way," I thought to myself, "you may have a point." But I didn't say anything. I reflected on the question that all of my European prospects had asked me. "When things become difficult, will you pack up and return home?" I knew that if we did, we would lose all credibility, and it would be much more difficult for us to return to Europe in the future. We would not, and could not, allow ourselves to fail.

My team was waiting in our ex-partner's lobby, looking very nervous. Carol asked, "Why are all of our partners laughing?" I dodged the question and asked everyone to pack our belongings in the trunk of my leased car. As I exited the parking lot, I reported that I had canceled the JV and that the four of us would build CTP–Europe on our own. Everyone looked nervous, but there was no going back. They appeared to trust my judgment and seemed to buy in. Then Howard, our senior consultant, asked, "So what's Plan B?"

Plan B

I didn't have an answer, so we collaborated on Plan B as we drove the A10. Fortunately, we had a full tank of gas. First, we needed an office—not just any office, but one that symbolized a startup. Howard suggested using a garage, not realizing that garages don't exist in Amsterdam. The next idea, a basement, fell to the same fate. "What about an attic?" Carol asked from the back seat. "There are a million attics in Amsterdam." Plan B was starting to take shape.

Office infrastructure was the next hurdle. Carol found an office supply store that would accept our credit card, but because we didn't have a

Dutch bank account, we were required to leave our passports with them as collateral. No big deal—we weren't going anywhere.

Next on the list: someone technical who could actually speak Dutch. Howard visited Eindhoven University and hired a student scheduled to graduate in eight weeks.

Now all we needed were clients, so we began our cold-calling campaign. If you think that cold calling "sucks," try doing it when you don't speak the language.

Carol and I had been able to get through our daily routines without learning Dutch. We knew a few of the "important" words. And we could point to items in stores and restaurants. Occasionally, we'd notice a new sign, written in Dutch, posted in our apartment building's elevator. If the sign was still there a week later, we assumed it was intended for us, and we would bring it to our office for someone to translate. But cold calling requires more advanced language proficiency. So, we decided to take Dutch lessons. We quickly reached the point where I knew simple vocabulary and grammar. But my Pittsburgh accent made it difficult for others to understand me. Carol, on the other hand, struggled to remember the words, but quickly mastered the Dutch accent. For example, at dinner with a prospect, I once said, "eet smakelijk" (which is Dutch for "bon appetit"). Our guest looked at me and responded, "I didn't know that you were a realtor" (een makelaar). Carol repeated what I had attempted to say, and then our prospect understood perfectly. As long as we were together, we were okay. But if Carol went to the lady's *badkamer*, or if I stopped at the *bar*, we were lost. As individuals, we were hopelessly monolingual.

At the same time, we were stumbling our way through learning the Dutch culture. The Netherlands appears to be a very free country with few restrictions, much less conservative than the US. But at the same time, they intentionally make it difficult for foreigners to do things they don't want them to do—immigrating, for example.

Soon after arriving in Amsterdam, Carol and I made our way to Rabobank to open a checking account and deposit our traveler's checks. Sounds easy, right? The teller gave us a stack of forms to complete. After that, the bank manager required an interview. He asked us a number of questions, recorded our answers on another form, and inserted the entire bundle into a pneumatic tube that whisked it away to God-knows-where. He shook our hands, explained that the process was almost complete, and asked us to wait in the lobby.

Forty-five minutes later, the bank president called us back to his desk and asked, "Can I see your residency permit?"

"What's a residency permit?" I replied.

He shook his head and said, "You cannot open a bank account unless you are a legal resident."

"But I don't want to borrow any money," I explained. "I just want to leave my money with you! Are you worried that after I give you my money, I'll sneak out of the country and leave all of it with you?" He politely asked us to leave.

Occasionally, on a rainy Saturday morning, Carol and I would return to the Rabobank and sit in the lobby to watch naïve, unsophisticated Americans attempt to open an account. After sixty minutes of filling out forms, a thirty-minute meeting with the bank president, and several launches of the pneumatic tube, we would watch as they confidently walked back to the lobby to wait for their new checkbook. Carol would nudge me and say, "Look at them. They really think they will be able to open an account. Ha! Little do they know!" The results were always the same.

After six months, we decided it was time to become *official* residents. With forms filled out and passports in hand, we made our way to the immigration office. No appointments were allowed; it was first come, first serve. The office opened at 9:00 a.m., but we were advised to be in line by 5:00 a.m. if we wanted to be processed before the office closed in the midafternoon. We arrived at 4:30 a.m., and the line was already a mile long. It wasn't that we had selected a busy day. Apparently, this was normal every day. In fact, businesses were built around it. Street vendors were already set up, hawking food, drinks, sweaters, rain gear, and everything else that you can imagine.

We slowly made our way to the entry and were next in line when they closed for their lunch break. Finally, at 1:15 p.m., Carol and I reached the desk of an immigration official. He quickly checked our passports, stamped our forms, asked us to return in six weeks to receive our residency and work permits, and explained that we couldn't leave the country until then. We had waited for almost nine hours for a five-minute transaction. And I thought the Massachusetts Registry of Motor Vehicles was bad!

When we returned six weeks later, we joined the same line at 3:45 a.m., which enabled us to reach the immigration desk by 10:45 a.m. The agent found our file and said, "I see that you have applied for both a Residency Permit and a Work Permit?"

"Correct," I replied.

He left and returned after a few minutes with a large manilla envelope that contained two white envelopes. He opened one of them, stared at the contents for several minutes, and said, "This is the application for your work permit. I cannot grant that to you because you do not yet have a residency permit." Our jaws dropped as we watched him stamp "DENIED" on our application. Carol and I were stunned and didn't know what to say. Next, he opened the other envelope. "Aah," he said. "This is the application for your residency permit. I cannot grant that to you because apparently you were turned down for a work permit. As before, he stamped "DENIED" on the application.

"Wait! This is crazy," I said. "You had both applications in front of you at the same time. You rejected us because you randomly opened the work permit first. What if you had opened the residency permit first?"

"But I didn't," he replied. "You will have to wait another six weeks and repeat the process."

This system was Kafkaesque. But it was a perversely effective way to control immigration. Carol and I never returned. Instead, we decided to stay and work in the Netherlands illegally. If the authorities caught us and sent us back to Boston, so be it. But they never did.

As difficult as all of this must sound, I cannot remember a day that felt like a bad day. We must have had some, but I don't recall any. Our time in Amsterdam felt more like a quest, and Carol and I still look back at those years as the best of our lives. Through perseverance, hard work, strong support from Jim, an uncontrollable fear of failure, and more than our share of good luck, we pulled it off. Six years later, CTP–Europe hit $100 million in revenue, was highly profitable, and had thirteen offices in nine countries. Now that CTP–Europe was a substantial business with solid performance, Carol and I could plan our return to Boston so I could launch operations in Asia and Latin America.

Before we left, I reconnected with the first prospect I had pitched to six years earlier, a senior executive from KLM, to say goodbye. He was also the first prospect to turn us down. After I updated him on our progress and plans, he smiled.

"Remember our first meeting, when you shared your plans for building a business in Europe? I explained the difference between American and European businesses. The European model is the cathedral. It's there for all time and defines the culture and social structure of the towns that surround it. Masses are held on the same schedule as they were one hundred years ago, and the celebrants sit in the same pews where their great grandparents once sat. Europe is about structure—and the individual's place within it."

He went on. "The American business model is the wagon train. An assembly of strangers, sharing a common vision to 'go West to find gold,' come together to achieve it. Along the way, they face many dangerous unknowns—Indians, mountains, raging rivers, bandits. They survive by banding together and refusing to turn back. If they survive the journey, they settle in farms miles apart and may never see each other again. The US is about the mission and the teamwork and persistence that are necessary to accomplish it."

He paused to smile before he finished. "That's why I turned you down six years ago. I didn't believe you could ever be successful here. Our business, political, and cultural models are so different, and you didn't understand that. Now after six years, you have accomplished what I, and many of my colleagues, believed was not possible. You hitched your horses to a cathedral, dragged that over the mountains and through the rivers, past the Indians and bandits—and arrived at the promised land."

Why Is Simpler Better?

When you pivot, make both your new business model and your buying experience as simple as possible. As Albert Einstein said, "Everything should be made as simple as possible, but not simpler."

Big ideas are often complicated, and, therefore, are more difficult to successfully execute. I like to apply the "Leif Rule." Leif once built a successful company using a very simple business model and sold it to CTP a few years later for a small fortune.

Many of his colleagues were jealous. "How can someone as dumb as Leif be so successful?" I began to use that question as the litmus test for new business ideas that CTP alumni pitched to me. Very often, their concept was compelling, but their business model was unnecessarily complex. If I liked their idea, I'd ask, "Could Leif run this business?" Many would respond, "Leif? Hah! Of course not. He isn't close to being smart enough." I'd respond, "If you can simplify the business model to the point where Leif could be CEO, come back and I'll help you take it to the next step." I believe that most often companies don't fail because their idea isn't big enough; rather, they fail because their idea is too big.

Poorly thought-out use cases can unnecessarily complicate a business model. One of Mobiquity's investors called me to share his excitement about a new mobile startup. "It's a custom-fit earbud company," he said. "It's named 'Normal hEar' because everybody's ears are different. That's why custom-fitted earbuds are so important. But they're also damn expensive. With the Normal hEar app, you use your phone to take pictures of both ears. Their artificial intelligence software analyzes the images and sends the results to a 3D printer that fabricates the earbuds. They mail the final product to the customer, and the entire process takes only five days. And it's 90 percent less expensive than a fitting by an audiologist. Their team is solid, and their revenue forecasts are off the charts. Should I invest?"

"Not until you buy a pair and try them out," I said. "Make certain the experience works first."

When we reconnected at our next board meeting, I inquired about his investment. "I decided to pass. Their buying experience was much too difficult. Did you ever try to take a picture of your ear canal? It's more difficult than it sounds. I kept getting blurry selfie shots of my earlobe or neck, so I was forced to ask my admin to take the picture for me. And do you know how creepy it sounds when you ask someone to take a close-up of your inner ear? But then I realized the photos wouldn't show whether I had big ears or small ears. So, I laid down on the floor on my right side, balanced a dime on my cheek for scale, and had my admin take a picture of my left ear. That was even more creepy. And then it occurred to me that their AI software might not be able to recognize which ear was which. I asked my admin to identify each ear by marking it with an 'R' or an 'L'. Then I got back on the floor so he could reshoot both ears. I received the earbuds in three days, they fit perfectly, and the audio was fantastic. But the buying experience was unworkable."

Can You Muster the Courage to Pivot?

Markets change. Even if you have been operating successfully, most likely you'll reach a time when you need to pivot. And the more successful you are, the harder it is to pivot. As Marshall McLuhan said, "We become what we behold. We shape our tools, and then our tools shape us." In other words, first we define our business model. If we are successful, our business model then defines us.

It takes courage to pivot, even when it's crystal clear that your business is headed in the wrong direction. If your company is already feeling a financial impact, it's difficult to find the resources you need for reinventing yourself.

Let's say you are the CEO of a company that is currently performing very well, but you believe you need to make a fundamental change to your business model to sustain that performance three years from now. Committing to that change requires superhuman courage. Do you gamble everything and steer away from what appears to be a successful course in order to prepare for a future that may or may not await you? If you're wrong, everyone knows you are the one who derailed a successful company, and you'll carry that on your rap sheet forever. If you're right, it won't be obvious for years and your successor will get most of the credit. These decisions are very scary to make.

Parting Thoughts

- Both in startups and in life, the simpler plan is often better.

- The real measure of a startup team's ability to succeed is how good they are at executing Plan B—because Plan A seldom happens.

- Plan B isn't a document. It's more of a mindset that constantly monitors Plan A's trajectory. It's a frame of mind that attempts to anticipate future bumps in the road. Mostly it's an attitude that responds to setbacks by turning one step backward into two steps forward.

- If Plan A works in a selected vertical or geographic market, do not assume it will work everywhere. You have to treat a new vertical or geographic strategy like a new startup business. When you pivot, make sure you create a business model and buying experience that are as simple as possible.

- It takes courage to pivot, especially when everything seems to be going well. That's as true in life as it is in business. When you decide to pursue Plan B, don't straddle the fence. Once you make a decision to pivot, there is no return. Fully commit to Plan B and make it happen.

- And what happens if Plan B doesn't work? There's always Plan C...

Some startups raise money before they earn any revenue. Others wait until they have traction. And some never raise any money at all. Next, I'll discuss when and how to raise money.

• • •

CHAPTER THIRTEEN

What Are the Secrets to Raising Money?

Venture Capital is a hell of a drug. Used properly, it's like adrenaline energizing many of the greatest companies of the last fifty years. Used incorrectly, it creates toxic dependencies.

– Eric Paley, managing partner, Founder Collective

– Joseph Flaherty, director of Content & Community, Founder Collective

Boston Business Journal

FEBRUARY 27-MARCH 4, 2004

Closing the deal: The art of funding and getting to yes

For private companies seeking *financing, deals take planning, research and, most of all, patience*

When Should You Raise Money?

DON'T RAISE MONEY unless you have to. If you do have to, don't raise it until you need to. And when you do raise money, make sure you raise more than you think you need.

Sometimes raising money is easy. Within six weeks, ZEFER received a commitment for $100 million based on a fourteen-slide PowerPoint deck. I wonder how much more I could have raised if I'd presented a deck with twenty slides.

In retrospect, $100 million proved to be too much money, but our investor's business model required us to raise as much as possible. Venture capitalists (VC) are paid a percentage of the money that they manage, creating an incentive for them to raise increasingly larger funds—which requires them to write increasingly bigger checks, whether or not the startups need all of the money.

We didn't ask for $100 million. We didn't need it. We had no idea what to do with it. But we sure the hell weren't turning it down, and eventually we figured out how to spend all of it.

We rationalized the $100 million investment because it created a number of advantages. The funding:

- provided capital to make the investments necessary to rapidly scale the business;

- generated publicity that created instant credibility with prospects and prospective employees; and

- enabled the management team to focus on running the business without being distracted by the effort to raise additional capital.

It seemed like an obvious choice to accept all the money we could get.

The Notorious B.I.G. released his hit single, "Mo Money Mo Problems," a few months before we closed our funding round. I should have paid more attention to the lyrics.

- Mo' Problem #1: Too much capital can create bad habits that are difficult to break. Raising $100 million encouraged me to set a high burn rate. That enabled ZEFER to scale to revenue of $134 million in only eighteen months. I believe I spent the money wisely. But when the dot-com crash hit, our larger budget required more radical cutbacks in order to survive the ensuing cash crunch.

- Mo' Problem #2: Huge investments create huge valuation expectations. At the start of the dot-com downturn, we received an offer to sell the company for a high nine-digit number. Our board rejected the offer, but ultimately sold a sizable stake in ZEFER one year later for a fraction of that price following a market downturn.

- Mo' Problem #3: Unusual investor requirements can skew spending. The terms of our investment required us to return all unspent money to our investor—without impacting their ownership percentage—in the event of an exit. That caveat created a perverse incentive for us to spend rather than save.

Raising Money Will Always Be More Difficult Than You Expect

Most of the time, raising money is difficult, frustrating, stressful, and taxing. According to a study conducted by Stanford University,[35] only 0.19 percent of the new businesses started in the US each year receive funding from VCs.

I'm often asked to help startups understand how "seed investors" decide to buy in. First, they look at the size of the market opportunity to determine if the exit scenario is sufficiently large to yield their expected returns. If the startup passes that test, the investors progress to assessing three categories of risk.

- Market risk assesses the growth potential of the opportunity that the startup is targeting. Will the market accept a new entry? How embedded are the competitors? What are the market trends? Is the market timing right? If the startup's product doesn't have any customers, the market risk is high.

If there are several non-paying users, the risk is lower. If there are a number of paying customers, that further reduces the market risk.

- Intellectual property risk evaluates the technology, the likelihood of developing a differentiated and defensible product, and legal ownership concerns.

- Operating risk assesses the business model and the assumptions that drive profitability. It also evaluates the startup's ability to execute. Does the team have the necessary skills and experience? Do they have a track record of successfully scaling startups? Is the investment that they are seeking sufficient to get them to their next funding round? Is their business model capital efficient, or will it require additional significant investments in the future? Investors believe that most business models are viable, but few management teams are viable. A great team with a mediocre idea trumps a mediocre team with a great idea. As a result, seed investors often place more value on the team than on the idea.

The reality is that most ventures will never qualify for venture capital. Even when invited to pitch, a startup has a very small chance of getting funded. And even when a new venture receives funding, there is a 90 percent chance that they will fail within the first three years.[36]

The takeaway? Expect that raising capital will be more difficult and take longer than you expect. Don't let that reality disillusion you or your team.

Raising Money at Demantra

Raising money for Demantra, a forecasting software product company founded in Israel, wasn't easy. I joined as CEO in October 2001, twenty days after the 9/11 terrorist attack and nine days after the largest one-week drop in New York Stock Exchange history. Not my best timing. But not my worst.

I knew from the very beginning that Demantra was a restart. The six-year-old company had $6.3 million in revenue in 2000—$6.3 million the year before that—and $6.3 million the year before that. So, it was a $6.3 million company on the way to becoming a $6.3 million company. Almost all of that revenue came from two of our partners, JD Edwards and Baan, who packaged our product as a forecasting add-on to their Enterprise Requirements Planning (ERP) software suite.

I accepted the CEO role because I believed that Demantra's technology would enable us to pivot to lead a new category of demand planning. No other company was focused on that opportunity. The concept sounded both simple and obvious: an enterprise's supply chain forecast must match its sales and marketing forecast. Burt, one of Demantra's founders, told me the green Volvo story to explain what can happen when they are not aligned.

Demantra's Pivot

Several years earlier, Volvo manufactured more green sedans than they could possibly sell. According to Burt, their sales and marketing teams kicked into action to launch dealer incentives, rebates, and TV promotions featuring attractive men and women driving green Volvos. The campaign, although expensive, was expertly designed and executed, and it produced the desired result. Customers began to buy more and more green Volvos.

However, Volvo's supply chain team saw the dramatic increase in green sedan sales and believed they needed to get ahead of it. They raised their forecasts and spared no expense to increase inventories and authorize overtime. You guessed it—Volvo spent a significant amount of money, but ultimately, by December the lots were full of more unsold green sedans than ever.

I believed we could retool our forecasting technology to enable Demantra to become the leading provider of sales and operations planning software. But we needed to raise money to get there. We revised our product roadmap and operating plan, developed our pitch deck, and hoped to begin meetings with potential investors in mid-2002.

We had an easier time landing meetings than I expected. But as a result, our leadership team spent too much time on airplanes and in meetings with potential investors. Although most of our pitches were in Boston and Silicon Valley, we also met with investors in New York, Chicago, London, and Israel. With offices in Boston and London, R&D in Tel Aviv, and customers across the world, I was already traveling constantly. On one of my trips to Israel, I discovered an antique Roman tear vial in a shop in Jaffa. The shopkeeper explained that during the Roman occupation, the legionaries left home for many months, sometimes years. Before they departed, they gave their wives and mistresses a glass blown vial to collect their tears. They showed it to the legionaries upon their return. The more tears in the vial, the more the legionary was missed. Given my lengthy absences, I thought that an antique tear vial would be a fun present for Carol. I purchased one—remembered Plan B—and wrapped it in a box with a bottle of Visine, just in case!

Most of our meetings with VCs ended with our team high-fiving one another. The investors voiced their respect for our team, were impressed by the blue-chip customers that we were winning, and consistently said that our business concept was visionary. But every one of them passed, and our team grew more discouraged.

It seemed like every rejection was followed by calls from two new VCs. On a Wednesday in March, I was contacted by someone who described himself as "a senior Analyst at a Silicon Valley VC firm." He followed the same script. "We are well aware of Demantra and have been following your progress for quite some time. Our entire investment team is very impressed with Demantra's vision and the team you have assembled to achieve it. We would like to invite you to pitch to our partners next Monday."

Typically, I would thank him profusely for the offer and book the next flight to San Francisco. Not this time!

"Thank you for your invitation and your interest in Demantra," I replied. "I appreciate your comments about the potential of our vision and the strength of our team. As you learn more about us, you'll only find three reasons not to invest. No matter how hard you look, you won't find more. I'm going to save you the time and tell you what they are."

"First, we began as an Israeli company, and our R&D team is still based there. Given today's international climate, that might make some of your partners uncomfortable. Second, our software addresses efficiency in an enterprise's supply chain. We're aiming at a crowded market, and we don't have enough clients at this point to confirm that our 'demand management' platform will differentiate us. And third, we sell to retail and consumer goods companies, and many investors believe that those sectors lag others in investing in technology."

"That's it?" the senior analyst asked.

"That's it," I responded. "I'd like you to share these three objections with your partners at Monday's meeting. Call me if they are okay with them, and my team and I will be there to pitch the following Monday."

He pushed back. "But we already know all of that. We've been following and researching Demantra for quite some time. You're wasting time for absolutely no reason."

"Humor me," I replied. "I'm not willing to spend the time and money for another trip to the West Coast until it's clear that the three issues that I have consistently heard from a number of other venture capitalists will not factor into your firm's decision."

He was clearly annoyed, but he begrudgingly agreed, and hung up without saying goodbye.

To my surprise, he called late Monday afternoon. "I did as you asked and reviewed the issues that you raised with my team. As I told you, they were already aware of them, and have absolutely no concerns."

We scheduled our pitch for the following Monday. Our meeting was scheduled to last forty-five minutes, beginning at 11:00 a.m., but continued through lunch until 1:00 p.m., a positive sign. Elated, we high-fived all the way to the airport. We nailed it!

The analyst from the VC firm called the next day. "Thank you for investing your time yesterday. We were all very impressed with Demantra. However, we've decided to pass."

I was stunned and asked, "Why?"

He responded, "They had three concerns..." You guessed it—precisely the three issues that I had called to their attention.

Before I ended the call, I asked, "How many startups do you invite to your Monday meetings?"

"We met with more than four hundred last year," he replied.

"How many of those did you invest in?" I asked,

"Only two. We have a very high bar for investing."

"Then why do you invite so many companies?"

"Because my job is to fill our Mondays with meetings. That's the day all of our partners are in the office. We use the day to increase our awareness of what's going on in the industry," he said. "Thanks again for investing your time."

A few weeks later, I received a call from a VC who had heard our pitch two months earlier. At the time, I didn't think it was well received, so I was surprised to hear from him. He told me to expect a term sheet the next day. Our funding closed thirty days later. Go figure.

Soon after Demantra completed our funding round, I received a call from our contact at JD Edwards. "I'm calling to notify you that one of our competitors is acquiring us. Unfortunately, they have their own forecasting module, so effective Monday we will have to cancel our partnership with you."

That was a huge blow. JD Edwards' vast salesforce generated 72 percent of our product sales. We spent the weekend working around the clock to move as much of our sales pipeline as we could to our three account executives. That Monday, I received a call from our contact at Baan, which generated 22 percent of our product sales. "I'm calling to notify you we are being acquired," he said. "Unfortunately, they have their own forecasting module. Effective Friday we will be canceling our partnership with you."

I've had good weeks and bad weeks as a CEO. But losing 94 percent of my revenue in one week is way up there among the bad weeks. If we hadn't added a sizable reserve to our funding request, Demantra would not have survived. Instead, we had the capital to recover from this setback and accelerate our move to sales and operations planning.

What Can You Learn from Featherbone?

A few months later, I engaged Gus Whalen as the keynote speaker at Demantra's user conference. Gus was the fourth-generation CEO of Warren Featherbone, a company his great-grandfather founded in 1883. He was a quiet, ordinary looking man of small stature—that is, until he walked on stage to tell his story about how Warren Featherbone continued to reinvent itself every time it faced adversity.

Gus mesmerized the audience with his story.

> In the late 1800s, women's corsets used whalebone as a stiffener. As a result, corsets were heavy to wear and expensive to buy. After years of research, my great-grandfather patented a process to stiffen corsets with featherbone, a lighter and more durable component than whalebone. Because it was made from discarded turkey quills, featherbone was also less expensive. In 1901, famous actress Sarah Bernhardt commented that she always used Warren's featherbone to create her costumes, and it was the best dress boning material in existence. Warren Featherbone quickly grew to become the market leader in corset stiffeners with offices across the world. Featherbone was here to stay forever!

Everything changed in the autumn of 1931, after plastic was invented. That made the two-way stretch girdle possible. And that made corsets obsolete. Almost overnight, Warren Featherbone's sales plummeted. Even worse, we owned the world's largest inventory of discarded turkey quills, which had no application in any other product and absolutely no value.

Gus went on to describe the attitude that a company needs to adopt in order to reinvent itself. That mindset shaped Warren Featherbone's culture and enabled it to overcome additional adversities over the years. They currently had 2,600 wholesale customers for their infant apparel line, including most of the large department store chains in the US, Canada, Europe, and Japan. This was the message we needed to hear. Gus made us believe it was possible to reinvent Demantra. And believing that something is possible is the first step toward getting it done.

A few years later, Demantra placed second at the American Business Award's "Best Business Turnaround" ceremony that was broadcasted on

STEVIE FINALIST

THE STEVIES

2003 American Business Awards[SM]

Presented to

Demantra

for

Best Business Turnaround

THIS AWARD IS PRESENTED IN RECOGNITION OF AN OUTSTANDING ACHIEVEMENT IN BUSINESS, AS NOMINATED IN A COMPETITION ORGANIZED BY THE STEVIE AWARDS.

Michael Gallagher
President, The Stevie Awards

NPR. Caught by surprise when the master of ceremonies announced Demantra's name, I made my way across the Manhattan ballroom to accept the award and say a few words. I hadn't expected to win, so I hadn't prepared any comments. What can one say when his company is selected as one of the world's top business turnarounds?

The best I could come up with in the brief time that it took me to reach the podium was, "I would like to thank my predecessors, without whose incompetence this moment wouldn't be possible."

In June 2006, Oracle acquired Demantra. Their strategic rationale included Demantra's leadership in demand management and sales and operations planning, driven by our strong data analytics capabilities. Demantra's Spectrum suite of products became a key component of Oracle's Fusion platform.

Parting Thoughts

As you consider the following takeaways, recognize that Demantra attempted to raise money for a restart when the financial markets were going through extreme turmoil. Our situation was unique, and your experience might proceed much more smoothly. But don't expect that it will.

- It's not the money that you raise, but the money that you spend, that creates dilution. Don't raise more money than you need. Capital is like food. You need enough of it to survive—but too much of it is bad for you. If you have too much money, you aren't forced to solve the real problems your startup faces. But you do need to plan for the unexpected. My rule of thumb is to calculate, as precisely as you can, the exact amount of money that you will need. And then double it.

- Anticipate that the process of raising money will take much longer than you expect and consume a significant amount of your management team's time. Don't be deceived when it's easy to set up pitch meetings and you receive lots of positive feedback. Only a small fraction of those meetings will lead to an actual check.

- It's difficult to keep your team positive throughout the process. Investors will pursue you and ask you to meet with them. But odds are that they won't actually invest in your company. Don't let rejection disillusion you or demotivate your team. Many unicorns were dismissed by some of the top-rated VCs. You will reach low points. I hit mine while negotiating with a potential investor while driving in a downpour near Atlanta. Instead of hanging up my phone, I angrily tossed it out the car window. When I realized what I had done, I pulled to the side of the road—but never found it.

- Raising money is similar to fishing. Throw as many lines as possible into the pond. You can't predict which lines will attract your fish, or when they will bite. Your ultimate success requires both patience and an unwavering belief that your fish are out there somewhere.

- Don't waste time cold calling investors. Identify VCs who invest in businesses like yours and fit your financial goals. Find a connection who can introduce you. The chances that a cold call will lead to an investment are miniscule.

- Try to find investors whose value is greater than just the money they give you. Don't necessarily select the VC that offers you the best terms. Pick the firm that you think will stand by your side as a long-term partner even when things are not going well. Times will get tough at some point. Talk to an investor's portfolio companies to learn what it's like to work with them when the going gets rough.

- VCs will study the market potential of your idea. Then they will look at market, intellectual property, and operating risk.

- Learn the calculus and lingo of investors. Understand convertible debt, bridge loans, the differences between common stock (what you get) and preferred stock (what the investors get), drag-along rights, anti-dilution provisions, liquidation preferences, participating preferred stock, post-money valuation, and vesting.

- Keep in mind that CEOs are sometimes replaced after a funding round. When I heard a VC discuss his firm's recent funding and introduce the *new* CEO, I raised my hand and asked, "How often do you replace the CEO after you make an investment?" He replied, "Almost always —it just depends on how quickly." Maybe this happens less often now, but it still happens.

- And finally, some tips on your pitch deck:

  - Your deck should have no more than ten to fifteen slides. Send it to the investors ahead of time. Bring hand-outs so that it's easier for them to take notes.

  - Your first slide is your most important slide. Don't waste it. It should tell the investors about the problem that your startup solves, who has it and how much pain it's causing, how you will solve it, why your solution is differentiated, and who will pay for it.

  - Your last slide is the second most important. It's the one that remains on the screen during the questions and discussion that follow. Because it's in front of the investors for the longest time, make certain that it does a compelling job of capturing and reinforcing the opportunity that you are pitching.

  - Your "team slide" is next in importance. For most investors, a great team trumps a great idea.

  - Your "customer slide" is fourth. How real are your customers? Are they using your solution or just piloting it? Are they paying you or using it for free? Do they genuinely believe that you have the solution that they need and have been looking for?

  - Invest time preparing your deck. Don't just slap together slides from other presentations. Engage your audience. Excite them about the opportunity and your ability to capitalize on it.

What does the future of venture capital and private equity look like? How might fundraising change? I share my point of view in the next chapter.

• • •

CHAPTER FOURTEEN

What Is the Future of Venture Capital and Private Equity?

Lately I've been learning more about how the VC world works, and a few days ago it hit me that there's a reason VCs are the way they are. It's not so much that the business attracts jerks, or even that the power they wield corrupts them. The real problem is the way they're paid... This turns out to explain nearly all the characteristics of VCs that founders hate.

— **Paul Graham, author, "A Unified Theory of VC Suckage"**

ALL OF TODAY'S venture capital firms employ the same investment model that American Research and Development Corporation (ARDC) and J.H. Whitney & Company created in 1946. It continues full speed ahead without blinking, even though the road has become much bumpier.

Returns are decreasing. Alex Graham reports that ten-year venture capital returns, which historically exceed 20 percent, have fallen below 15 percent,[41] largely underperforming public markets and private equity.

The venture capital model is not entrepreneur-friendly. The disparity between the top funds and all of the others is widening as venture capitalists (VC) attempt to maximize returns by chasing unicorns. On average, only 1 percent of venture-backed startups reach unicorn status. That creates a misalignment with the other 99 percent of startup CEOs who have all of their potential wealth tied up in only one company and would be delighted to reach a $10 million exit. Chasing unicorns leaves many good companies behind.

In addition, exits are taking longer than they used to. Alex Graham also points out that the median time for a venture-backed startup to exit by IPO is now 8.2 years.[41]

And finally, funds are growing too large. According to CrunchBase data, roughly 84 percent of the capital raised by US venture investors in 2018 went into funds raising $250 million or more. That total includes the massive $1.85 billion raised by Bessemer Venture Partners for its tenth flagship venture fund.[42] VCs are paid a percentage of the money they manage, typically 2 percent annually, creating an incentive to raise increasingly larger funds. As a result, investments are much larger than a startup requires, valuations are much higher than they should be, and partners have less time to spend on each investment.

What Is the Future of Venture Capital?

If you Google "the future of healthcare" or transportation or almost any industry, you'll see that experts predict remarkable change. Try searching "the future of venture capital." The experts mostly foresee business as usual—with a single exception. Supposed visionaries predict that "smart money," where investors add value through their operating experience, will gain importance. That "new idea" has existed for more than twenty years. It's listed as a "differentiator" on the website of every venture capital firm that I've ever pitched to. But the concept rarely succeeds because the challenge remains the same. Not all VCs have the skills and experience that a startup needs. How much operating value can a VC provide if the ink on their MBA diploma hasn't dried? Or if the partner assigned to the job has never held an executive role in a successful startup? Or if they haven't led a company in decades? As funds get larger and each partner's attention is divided among an increasing number of investments, that challenge becomes even more difficult.

I see the future of venture capital quite differently. Perhaps, because I'm an outsider, it's easier for me to foresee the changes that will occur. New models are beginning to be introduced. Perhaps it's time for the venture capital model to be disrupted.

What Can Corporate Venture Capital Do for Your Startup?

Corporate venture capital (CVC) is an investment alternative where corporations directly invest in private companies. The model is not new. My first experience dates back to 2002 when Cargill invested in Demantra. CVCs began to take off after 2010. Between 2013 and 2018, they increased their capital expenditures by more than 400 percent, and, in 2018 alone, 429 CVCs invested more than $50 billion in startups.[38] That's fueled because large enterprises seek ways to innovate more quickly and to increase their odds of success.

In today's global, complex, diverse, and fast-moving business world, it's difficult to find any one thing that a majority of CEOs agree on. And yet, a Dell survey of four thousand senior business leaders succeeded.[39] Their research found that 78 percent of C-level decision makers believe digital startups will pose a threat to their organization now or in the near future. That fear is well founded. Business disruption is real and it's accelerating. It seldom comes hard and fast, like Uber. Instead, it targets specific segments of a company's products and services, and presents itself as death by a thousand cuts. More than 90 percent of CEOs respond to that threat (or opportunity) by launching a formal digital disruption program, and appointing a VP of Innovation to lead it.[40] But 84 percent of these initiatives fall short of delivering any meaningful business impact.

Large companies can provide an intrapreneur with capital, customers, distribution, management, talent, market presence, global coverage, facilities, and much more. With all of the resources available within a large company, why aren't the odds better? Shouldn't these pre-established advantages make things easier?

It's just the opposite. Rubicon Intelligence reports that the success of a new venture is inversely proportional to the amount of corporate help it receives.[37] Only 4 percent of such ventures will ever reach $1 million in yearly sales. And only 0.4 percent will ever reach $10 million. That doesn't even begin to move the bar for a large corporation.

Startups must deal with uncertainty for a very long time. Successful startups embrace this uncertainty. They have an intense sense of urgency and can pivot quickly. They are skilled at executing Plan B—because Plan A seldom occurs. They don't have to follow a lot of rules. Startups have no market share or existing revenue stream to defend. They don't have to worry about upsetting existing customers, partners, or distribution channels. Successful startups have an experienced team with an unwavering commitment. They don't "celebrate" failure. Instead, they believe failure is not an option.

Startups within large enterprises have none of these advantages. In addition, they must battle the corporate antibodies that have been genetically engineered to kill new ideas prematurely. Making it more difficult, the management team for the new venture is customarily selected from within the existing enterprise's own ranks—typically without startup experience. No wonder most of them fail.

As a result, CVC investments have been booming. Large enterprises are investing in startups to gain access to innovation and to increase their odds of successfully launching new products. Some corporations are investing "off-balance sheet" while others form dedicated venture capital funds to invest in startups.

In addition to capital, what advantages does a CVC provide for a startup? A direct connection to a leading market player can:

- validate business plans, go-to-market strategy, and assumptions;

- contribute valuable resources;

- provide introductions to the corporation's network;

- add to the startup's credibility;

- test the startups solution in a live business environment;

- become an important distribution channel; and

- perhaps, ultimately, lead to the corporation acquiring the startup.

There are disadvantages that an entrepreneur should be aware of.

- Corporate investors can be bureaucratic and move much more slowly than VCs.

- CVCs may block financing rounds and acquisitions that they believe are inconsistent with their strategic interests.

- If the CVC receives its funding annually, follow-on investments may depend on how well the parent's business is performing.

- Corporate investors may require right of first refusal. That preempts anyone from acquiring your company and scares away other potential buyers that fear wasting their time on due diligence.

Strategic investors have become an important value-added source of venture capital that most entrepreneurs overlook. No investment comes without risks. But the relationship that a startup can form with its strategic investor often can create a win-win opportunity that can't be found with traditional investment models.

What About Revenue-Based Financing?

Revenue-based financing (RBF) originated as a funding mechanism for wildcatters searching for oil more than one hundred years ago. The model evolved as it expanded into Hollywood productions, then into pharmaceuticals, and more recently into startups. Arthur Fox is credited with pioneering it for early-stage businesses in New England in 1992. RBF has invested billions of dollars in startups since then. Given that long history, I'm surprised that most entrepreneurs don't know very much about it.

RBF is an alternative to equity funding and debt financing. Firms can raise capital by pledging a percentage of future revenues in exchange for money invested.

Unlike equity funding, the entrepreneur isn't selling a stake in their company. Although there are many well-known funds that combine revenue with equity, RBF typically doesn't create dilution, doesn't come with restrictive financial covenants, and doesn't require board seats. Moreover, revenue-based investments aren't focused on a company having an exit.

Unlike debt, where a company makes fixed payments over a fixed period of time, RBF payments and time period are typically variable. They are based on the startup's future revenue performance. Generally, payments are made until the lender receives a predetermined multiple of the original loan or achieves a predetermined internal rate of return. And there are no personal guarantees.

I spoke with several successful equity investors who shifted their model to revenue-based investing so that I could understand their motivation. They all were frustrated by the constraints of the equity-only model and its dependency on exits as the only way to generate returns. The managing partner of a successful RBF firm summed it up the best: "The myopic obsession with unicorns as the only kind of company worth my time and attention isn't just bad for investors, it's bad for entrepreneurs. Believing that value is only created through exits just isn't true—and it drives bad behavior. With the equity model, founders can easily become more focused on raising their next round than on building customer-facing companies that deliver products and services that the market really wants and will pay for. So, I began looking for an 'exit-agnostic' investment alternative for early-stage companies."

Because RBF doesn't follow the monolithic model that most venture capital funds stem from, there are many "flavors." The specific structure of a deal varies considerably based on the investor—and there are many today. Melissa Withers, managing partner of RevUp Capital, explains, "The incredible variation across deals is a good thing. That means that you can find a deal that is customized to your needs. But all this variation makes evaluating deals and the differences between them real work with real effort."

What typically matters most to deal structure is a company's current revenue, projections for growth, growth margin and, often, overall profitability. As for terms, founders should carefully evaluate the total return expected and how it's structured: the percentage of revenue that goes back to the investor; is it variable or fixed; how is it paid; the timeline for returns; what the contract defines as revenue; and what happens if the company doesn't grow as expected.

To build a company, an entrepreneur needs the right capital at the right time. There are many times that equity is the best choice, especially when it comes to funding companies that have a heavy R&D dependency and that don't produce revenue quickly. However, the advancement of RBF has substantially broadened the capital toolkit that founders can use to build their business. It fits companies that have never raised venture capital, as well as those that have or plan to. For companies that have pursued venture capital, RBF sits nicely in between a seed round and Series A. It won't impact a startup's ability to raise additional capital in the future. And it's a way to build traction and momentum that can lead to much more attractive Series A terms.

Funding is no longer a one-size-fits-all proposition. Entrepreneurs—especially early-stage entrepreneurs—need to develop a deeper understanding of the different funding alternatives that are now available. The opportunity comes with the pressure of becoming knowledgeable about the advantages and disadvantages of an equity investment, and the dozens of variations of RBF. Founders can benefit from an advisor that has experience with the different funding alternatives and can help them select the best fit for their business. In any case, choose carefully—it can be a game changer.

Will New Venture Models Emerge?

Envision a new venture model that provides the upside of venture capital while reducing investor risk. Returns are driven by "airlifting" proven business models and technology platforms into adjacent but untapped markets to create new companies. It's a model that focuses on quick wins, while everyone else chases unicorns. I call the model "Untapped." It reduces venture risk (market, intellectual property, and operational), capital required, dilution, and time to exit.

I tested the concept with a number of CEOs, including the founder of a startup that focused on technology for dogs—tracking, feeding, exercising, and health monitoring. By their sixth year of business, they pivoted three times, raised $35 million in capital, reached revenue of $15 million, and were profitable and growing rapidly. Their startup met all of my criteria for a "proven business model."

I asked their CEO, "Will your solution work for cats?"

"Of course," he replied. "There are 370 million pet cats. Not quite as many as dogs, but still a lot. Cats get lost, have to eat, need their exercise, and have owners who want to make certain they stay healthy."

"So, when are you going to pursue the cat market?" I asked.

"Cats?" he barked, almost looking like he was about to spit on the ground. "Cats? We're dog people. We don't do cats." I knew that even if he didn't have a strong bias against cats, a wise CEO, growing rapidly in one market, would never dilute his attention or capital by jumping into another. His value gained per dollar of investment in the dog market would dwarf the potential outcome for cats. At this point in a startup's lifecycle, a CEO needs to focus.

I continued, "What if I give you $1 million to acquire an instance of your technology and business model exclusively for the cat market? I would have to bring in a 'market maker,' sort of a big dog in the cat world, to confirm that the business model is transferable and that the demand exists. And I would have to go through technical due diligence. Assuming that all checks out, I'll invest a minimum of $5 million to airlift your solution to the new market and fuel growth marketing. I won't need any of your support after due diligence, and I'm not interested in any of your future releases. Since I'm getting a huge head start, I believe I can exit in three to five years. At that time, I'll carve out 5 percent of the proceeds for you. And if, before then, you decide that you do want to pursue the cat market, I'll sell the business back to you at fair market value. I can do that because I'm not chasing unicorns. I'm looking for quick wins."

The CEO tilted his head and stared at me, perhaps wondering if I was joking. Then he said, "Let me get this right. You want to pay me $1 million to *not* do something I have *no* intention of ever doing. And you are going to invest *your* money and *your* resources to build the business instead. If you're successful, I'll receive another 5 percent at the end. And if I change my mind, I can buy it back. That's the best deal I've ever seen! Where do I sign?"

Untapped—What's Behind the Curtain?

How would the Untapped model work?

- By reducing risk.

  - The market maker's deep knowledge of a targeted vertical, combined with a growth-market focus for the majority of capital, mitigates market risk.

  - Repurposing proven business models and technology platforms reduces intellectual property risk.

  - Operating risk declines because the new business is led by operators with an exceptional track record in scaling technology companies. They are supported by an experienced operations team shared across the portfolio of investments.

- By reducing required capital and the ensuing dilution of equity.

  - The airlifted solution, built on a proven business model, is already developed and operational, decreasing the likelihood of a need to pivot. Any follow-up investment rounds can be significantly smaller.

- Owning 100 percent of the new businesses enables Untapped to leverage a team of shared, experienced operating resources across the portfolio, providing economies of scale.

- Sixty percent of the ownership does not have to be allocated to the founding team—because there is no founding team. Experienced operators can be hired with lower equity incentives that are typical for a later stage company.

- By accelerating time to market and time to exit.

  - Airlifting a proven solution to a new market opportunity creates a three-to-five-year head start.

  - A much higher success rate, combined with lower capital requirements, creates economics that enables Untapped to generate stronger returns by focusing on quick wins instead of chasing unicorns.

Surprisingly, a high percentage of VCs are supportive of the model. But, as you can imagine, most are trapped by inertia. As a consultant pitching business disruption to large enterprises, I've watched that movie replay many times. Business executives immediately look for flaws in new ideas rather than teasing out their potential. I've frequently heard the questions and assertions that unintentionally—or perhaps intentionally—kill an innovative idea. This instinctive resistance acts like corporate antibodies designed to reject innovation, and the tendency applies to VCs as well.

Parting Thoughts

- As technology evolves and creates new opportunities, corporations will be driven to find ways to innovate more quickly and more successfully than they can accomplish internally. That will continue to fuel the growth of CVC.

- RBF is an alternative source for growth capital that may improve a startup's positioning in preparation for its next round of venture capital.

- New investment models will begin to emerge. Perhaps Untapped will be able to overcome the inertia of investors. Perhaps other models will surface. In any case, someday, new and better models will disrupt the traditional venture capital model, benefiting both investors and entrepreneurs. I'd bet my "smart money" on it.

In the next chapter, I discuss how to build and manage both fiduciary and advisory boards and explain what you should expect from each.

• • •

CHAPTER FIFTEEN

How Should You Build Your Fiduciary and Advisory Boards?

One of the advantages of being a captain, Doctor, is being able to ask for advice without necessarily having to take it.

– Captain Kirk, Starship Enterprise Commander, Star Trek

How Do You Choose Members for Your Fiduciary Board of Directors?

I'VE SERVED ON the boards of ten nonprofits and twenty-seven companies. To be clear, a nonprofit is an organization that has been granted tax-exempt status because it furthers a social cause and provides a public benefit. It's not a startup that loses money.

In every case, the composition of the board had a significant impact on the success of the company. Choose your board members the same way you construct your leadership team. Chemistry, relevant experience, skill sets, and motivation are key selection criteria for both. Great board members can provide impactful advice, introduce you to potential customers and partners, and constructively challenge your thinking. Note, however, that after you raise money from a venture capitalist (VC), you can no longer unilaterally choose your board. Much of its composition will be determined by your investors. The terms of their funding will define the number of board seats and how many of those they will occupy. Unfortunately, their choices trump the No Asshole

Rule that I discussed in Chapter 5. And bad board members can make business very unpleasant.

Find board members who have successfully worked together before. Even though there are more than one thousand venture capital firms in the US, it's a small world. And it becomes smaller when you target investors within a particular geographic location or a specific vertical or technology. You'll find that most firms have previously coinvested and sat on boards together. Chemistry between board members is extremely important. Without it, you'll spend too much time trying to get them to work together effectively.

One of my companies had three VC board members. Surprisingly, none of them had ever met before. Making the situation more difficult, all of them had quite different styles and personalities. If Hollywood had produced that movie, it would have been titled, *The Odd Trio*. Felix was an anal, button-down conservative who delved into every operational detail. Oscar was a free spirit who made all of his decisions by gut feel. And Rain Man was a businessman who based his decisions on nothing but the numbers. We held board meetings every month. After the first few, it was clear that each of the directors annoyed all of the others. As a result, I had to hold a secret pre-board meeting with Oscar, followed by another where Rain Man would join us. After the full board meeting, I would privately meet again with Oscar and Rain Man, followed by a lengthy debrief with Felix. My one monthly board meeting effectively turned into five.

If your board is dysfunctional from the beginning, there's not much you can do to fix it. Just try to survive for as long as you can.

What Can You Expect a Fiduciary Board to Do?

The fiduciary board's primary responsibility is to govern. They review your business performance and approve stock options and major expenditures. A board meeting is a healthy exercise, especially when business is good. It forces you to think strategically about where your company is heading. Good board members can serve as sparring partners. By challenging you, they force you to think more clearly about the direction that you're setting.

But don't expect a fiduciary board to do much more than that. Your directors may sit on as many as ten other boards, not leaving them much time to actively support your company. Most importantly, they're wary of getting too involved in your operations—even if they have the time. If they cross that line and then something goes wrong, it will be difficult for them to hold you accountable. The adage is "noses in, fingers out." And that 26-year-old VC who has never run a business that I described in my last chapter may be assigned to your board. That's where independent board members come in.

What Makes a Great Independent Director?

The terms of your funding round will probably require one or two outside or independent directors. Select directors with the skills, experience, and time to help you. Make certain that they "get" what you do and buy into your long-term direction. Confirm their motivation, commitment, and fit. The No Asshole Rule does apply here.

David was the best independent director at ZEFER. He popped into my office several times a week to chat about the business. Regardless of how well ZEFER was performing, David would find something new for me to worry about—a potential problem to avert or a new opportunity to harvest. I'd argue that I could identify dozens of other things that were more important, and I just didn't have time to grow my to-do list. He would persist with his unobtrusively aggressive style until I became visibly annoyed. That's when his work was done. He knew that I would spend the night thinking about the issues he discussed and not be able to sleep until I figured them out. David provided tremendous value in many areas. But by pushing me to think three or four steps ahead, instead of just two, he made me a better CEO.

Jon was the best independent director at Cambridge Technology Partners (CTP). At the beginning of every month, he would fly from New York to Boston to meet with me. Jon would open his notebook, take out his pen, and ask, "Which CEOs would you like to meet this month? I'll make a personal introduction." As a very successful former CEO of several Fortune 100 companies, Jon knew everyone. After agreeing on our list of targets, we would brainstorm the message that Jon would take to each.

Never having seen other board members invest that much time and energy, I asked our CFO why Jon was so different. "We created a separate contract for Jon, paying him $5,000 each month for business development support that's outside traditional board responsibilities."

"$5,000 a month?" I questioned. "Jon is a billionaire. Why would he fly to Boston every month, work with me to identify prospects and develop messaging, and then personally contact those CEOs for only $5,000 a month? His time is much more valuable than that. And he certainly doesn't need the money."

"First," the CFO replied, "Jon believes in us and is committed to our success. Second, it's not *how much* we pay him. It's *how* we pay him. At the end of every month, I send a check to Jon's home address. I do that, instead of direct deposit or mailing it to his office, to make sure he personally opens the envelope. I know Jon, and as soon as he sees that check, he'll reflect on what he's done during the past month to earn it. If he feels like he fell short, his 'Catholic guilt' forces him to jump on a plane and fly to Boston to meet with you."

I've found the power of guilt to be cross-denominational. Select independent board members with the commitment, skill sets, experience, and contacts that can help you be successful. Define, in a separate contract, what you need them to do. Remember, it's not about how much you pay, it's about what makes them committed to your success.

How Can You Manage "BBV"—Boards Behaving Badly

- Choose your board using the same criteria you use to construct your leadership team.

- Find board members who have previously worked together successfully.

- Manage your board. Make sure you know where each director stands on key topics before a board meeting. Figure out what your board knows and wants and provide that for them. If one board member seeks more details than the others do, provide information one-on-one in a pre-board meeting, or create a report and distribute it in advance.

- Always be honest and transparent when sharing information.

- Value customer feedback more than your board's advice. Board members, even if they have deep business experience, can't invest the time necessary to get close to your business. Ignoring customers is the ninth biggest reason why startups fail.[23] Follow the old adage, "The customer is always right."

- It's okay to disagree with a board member's advice but explain your reasoning. There's a Pittsburgh phrase called "Yes-F***ing." That's when you pretend that you like the advice, but you have no intention of following it. That's a pet peeve of many board members. Do what you say.

- Independent board members should provide more support than investors. Select independent members who understand what you do and have the commitment, skill sets, experience, and contacts that your company needs to be successful. Define your expectations in a separate contract.

- Startups will experience ups and downs. Expect to enter the zone of BBV during times of volatility. When that happens, it's even more important to be honest and transparent with the information that you share.

Why Build an Advisory Board?

CEOs have a lonely job. There isn't an obvious go-to person whom they can call and ask, "What the hell should I do?" A CEO is supposed to *know* what to do. If they ask for help from their team or their board, they worry that will damage their credibility and make them look weak.

I'm often engaged to assemble an advisory board to provide a support structure that addresses that need. Your advisor is your "swim buddy" when you find yourself in the deep end of the pool.

Advisory boards have nothing to do with governance. They don't overlap or have a relationship with the board of directors. I've formed them to engage a diverse group of exceptionally smart and experienced people to both advise me and to actively help me with my business. Because advisory boards do not need to govern, they can provide advice more freely. And because they can't terminate me, I'm free to take their advice or leave it.

I organized my first board of advisors while leading CTP–Europe. As you may recall from Chapter 6, our customer value proposition, "Rapid Application Development and Fixed Price/Fixed Timeframe," wasn't resonating. European business executives, more risk-averse than their US counterparts, placed a higher premium on fixed-price than rapid development. Jim Sims, our CEO, frequently traveled to Europe to provide me with his support. On every visit, I'd argue that we needed to flip-flop our value proposition for Europe. Jim wouldn't hear of it.

Finally, I invited four Europeans to form my advisory board—two senior business executives from the Netherlands, one from London, and a well-known business educator from the IMD Business School in Lausanne, Switzerland.

I scheduled our first advisory board meeting to coincide with Jim's next visit. At that meeting, the board began to discuss the actions that CTP could take to become more successful in Europe. One of the Dutch business executives said, "Reverse the order of your value proposition. It should begin with fixed-price." All three of the other members enthusiastically agreed. I hadn't discussed the topic with them previously, and I was uncomfortable that it surfaced. I hoped Jim didn't think I was sandbagging him.

Jim sat back in his chair and said, "Wow! That's a great idea. Bill, I'm surprised you hadn't thought of that. I'm delighted that you've brought together this talented group of directors who can help you set the best direction for our business."

That's when I learned the power of a board of advisors. If one person makes a statement, it's an opinion. If a few people support the same statement, it's a bias. If a diverse group of smart, experienced leaders all concur, then it's wisdom. And there's magic in that.

What Are the Rules of Engagement for an Advisory Board?

Advisory boards, simply said, are there to actively support you and your company. Advisors don't have to worry about crossing the line between governing and operating. When a director tells me to do something, I take that as an order. If an advisor says the same thing, I can say, "Go to hell. This is my company and I can do whatever I want." That difference enables advisors to be more proactively engaged and more open to sharing their thoughts and providing guidance.

I expect advisory board members to:

- attend four meetings per year in person and stay connected and engaged between the meetings;

- provide business advice on growth challenges and opportunities, funding strategy, organization and people issues, partnerships, customer value proposition, go-to-market, positioning, marketing investments, and new services;

- make introductions to prospects, partners, and prospective employees;

- provide the perspective of a potential customer by reviewing sales decks for industries with which they are familiar, giving feedback, and helping with pitch strategy;

- mentor key employees; and

- allow me to leverage their credentials on the company's website and in press releases.

What startup CEO wouldn't find that support immensely valuable?

What Makes a Great Advisory Board Member?

The ideal size for a board of advisors ranges from six to ten members. With fewer than six members, if someone misses a meeting, the meeting dynamics will change. It's hard to manage more than ten advisors.

It's not difficult to find smart, successful candidates who have the time and motivation to engage and will "play together nicely." It's more challenging to build a team that combines the necessary skill sets and credentials with a diversity of experiences and perspectives.

Why are advisors willing to invest their time to provide that wealth of advice and support? They don't do it for the money. They join because they:

- receive a token amount of stock options to make them feel like they have skin in the game and are a key part of the team;

- enjoy the pace and energy of a startup, believe they can have a big impact, and value being part of a team that is attempting to build something special—a refreshing change from the large enterprises where they work;

- value the relationships they develop with the other advisory board members; and

- find the meetings to be intellectually stimulating and just plain fun, especially with the right (diverse) membership, and the right agenda. The half-life of a typical advisory board is two meetings. But if it's built around a company that they are proud to be a part of, with the right (diverse) membership and the right agenda, it becomes something that they very much look forward to.

How Important Is Diversity?

Always remember that diversity is one of the key design points for the advisory board. It's not easy for CEOs to get out of their comfort zones. My daughter, Stacey, taught me how to venture away from mine.

I wasn't surprised when my Stacey announced that she was marrying her partner, Julia. They had been living together in Minneapolis since she received her PhD in clinical psychology. Stacey chose to specialize in the field of sexual dysfunction. I was very proud of her. But that made it uncomfortable for me to ask questions like, "What did you do at work today?" A father just doesn't want to hear those details.

Carol and I looked forward to attending the ceremony, but we didn't know what to expect. At that time, same-sex marriages were still uncommon and not yet legalized in Minnesota. That meant a ceremony that would take place in a city garden instead of a church, be officiated by a friend instead of a priest, and vows that came from children's books instead of scripture. It was, by far, the most beautiful wedding that Carol and I had ever experienced.

But both of us were apprehensive about the reception, and it wasn't just because my ex-wife would be there. We wondered who we would sit with and what we would talk about. That uneasiness opened my eyes to something that I didn't like about myself. I realized that at a given event, I tend to seek out people who are just like me. I'm more comfortable meeting someone new when we have a lot in common. With a guest list comprised of university professors who taught courses in sexual dysfunction, fellow practitioners, and friends from the Minneapolis gay community, I didn't expect to find any other middle-aged technology entrepreneurs from Wellesley, Massachusetts.

As we looked for our table, I mentally reviewed my checklist of standard opening questions. If I asked, "What do you do for a living?" and our tablemate responded, "I'm a clinician who specializes in sexual dysfunction," how would I continue that conversation? Everything felt a little weird—until we sat down and met our tablemates.

A tall, handsome woman in her forties, who was a realtor in Nantucket, sat on our right. She was accompanied by a strikingly beautiful woman in her late sixties. They dominated the dance floor from the moment the music started, so we didn't get to hear their story until the band's first break. It turns out that the older woman was previously married and had several children. After becoming a grandmother, she realized that something was missing in her life and decided to end her marriage to become a nun. But the convent didn't provide the missing piece that she was looking for, and she found her current partner on a visit to Nantucket. I was fascinated and said, "You should write a book." "I have," she replied, and gave me the title. And I had been worried about finding someone I could talk to! Carol and I were having a blast.

The man seated on our left was accompanied by a rough looking woman. They met in prison. She was an inmate, and he was a guard. Our table had become a conversational gold mine!

"I didn't know that women's prisons are staffed by male guards," I said.

"Some are, some aren't," he replied. "But it didn't matter for us. At the time I was a woman." He continued with their story. "In prison, we knew that we were attracted to one another. When she was released, we began dating and fell in love. But she was not comfortable marrying a woman, so I had a sex change operation as a condition of our marriage."

After we finished our meal, the first couple headed back to the dance floor while the ex-inmate excused herself to use the facilities. Carol and I were alone with the ex-guard. He said, "You and Carol look like you're very much in love. Can I ask you a personal question?" At that point in the evening, how could I say no? "My wife has changed her mind and decided that now she wants to be with a woman. She's asked me to have another operation to reverse my last one. I love her very much and don't want to lose her. What should I do?"

As a long-time consultant, I've learned how to bullshit my way through any tough question. But all I could do was say, "Well, let me tell you about Plan C..."

That fascinating and enjoyable evening taught me the limitations of a comfort zone. Diversity drives interesting discussions and leads to innovative alternatives and better decisions. If all of your advisors agreed with each other on everything, you'd need only one advisor, not eight. "I don't need a friend who changes when I change and who nods when I nod; my shadow does that much better," said Plutarch. My advisory boards have included authors, artists, inventors, educators, politicians, futurists, a physician who ran a hospital emergency room and another who is a thoracic surgeon, many experienced business leaders, and even a venture capitalist!

If you surround yourself with smart people who will argue with you and put enough of them together in one space, good things happen.

How Do You Get the Feedback that You Need?

Suzanne, a recently retired CIO from a Fortune 500 company, had accepted a position on an advisory board that I was forming. Before our first meeting, she called to get some tips to guide her participation. "I'm wondering," she asked, "should I think about engaging with the advisory board the same way I take part in executive meetings at large companies?" I asked Suzanne to explain. "When I attend an executive-level meeting for the first time, I mostly listen and avoid contributing much. At the second meeting, I feel okay about asking questions. And by the third meeting, I'm comfortable expressing my opinions. Is that the protocol for an advisory board?"

I told Suzanne that we would value her point of view from the moment she walked into our conference room, and I encouraged her to jump in with both feet. I said, "We follow Dutch feedback protocol at our meetings. I lived in Holland for four years," I explained, "and learned about the Dutch communication style. It's a bit uncomfortable at first, but after you get accustomed to it, it's much easier to get your point across in a new group that might otherwise miss the subtleties of what you are trying to say."

Dutch feedback enables advisors to present their opinions without fear of offending a leadership team. I outlined three principles that I follow.

- Expect directness. The Dutch speak to the point. They do not mince words, nor do they beat around the bush. At first, you might think the Dutch are actually rude.

- Keep it simple. The Dutch value plain speaking over subtlety, diplomacy, and coded speech. You don't have to wonder what they are thinking. The Dutch will tell you clearly.

- Don't take things personally. Disagreement signals nothing more than an opinion of your idea, not a judgment of your character.

How Do You Manage an Advisory Board?

To do their job correctly, a board of advisors provides a lens that enables you to see your world from an outside-in perspective, and that leads to new ways for you to think about the problems and opportunities you're facing. Some of their observations won't be accurate, and some of their ideas will not be sound. It's up to you to sort that out.

Many of the advisors will bring perspectives from large, successful companies to the board. That's a huge part of their value. But because of their backgrounds, they can fall into the trap of applying the lens of an IBM or an AT&T to a small startup. When they do that, you will leave the advisory board meeting feeling like you were clobbered with a thousand questions and suggestions that you can't possibly process, much less implement. "Good advice" isn't good if it's theoretical and cannot be followed.

As a best practice to avoid this trap, set clear expectations for every topic that's on the meeting's agenda. Open every discussion with three questions highlighting the areas where you need their help. That will keep your advisors focused. Follow your opening with a few slides to set the context. Remember, you have a diverse advisory board, and by helping them understand why you are wrestling with a problem and the kind of constraints you're facing you can generate valuable input. Encourage questions along the way but try to stay focused until the presentation concludes. End by restating your original set of questions, and let the real discussion begin. Remember that Dutch feedback is bidirectional. It's okay for you to say, "Thanks for your idea, but that's not a priority for us right now." One of your many jobs as CEO is to decide which advice to take. Your board will do a better job of advising you if they understand not only which suggestions you followed, but also what you decided you wouldn't do, and why.

Where Do Advisory Boards Help?

Advisory board members can provide help wherever and whenever you need it. You should think of them as key members of your team. They think of themselves that way.

Here are some questions you might include in your agenda.

- Is our customer value proposition engaging and compelling? What changes should we make?

- What is your reaction to our pitch decks? Do they need to be modified for ABC or XYZ industries?

- What's your reaction to our website?

- Should we raise money? If we should, do you have suggestions for our fundraising strategy? And how can we improve our investor presentation?

- What type of acquisitions should we consider and explore? What should we be cautious about?

- Is it time to increase our marketing spend? How do we better represent what we do? Where should we target our marketing investments?

- We're considering investing in a lab to drive innovation. What do you think of that idea?

- What are your thoughts on next year's financial plan? What are the best incentives to encourage my team to make that happen?

Remember, they are your sounding board for any decisions you are facing.

If you are not sold on the concept, think of it this way. Your advisory board is a team of business executives, thought leaders, industry experts, serial entrepreneurs, strategists, marketing gurus, and individuals with any other expertise or perspective that you believe would be helpful. They are committed to your success. Their advice is hugely valuable—but you don't have to follow it if you don't want to. Their extensive network is populated with potential customers, employees, and partners. And their credentials add to the credibility of your company.

If you hired them as consultants at their daily rate, they would typically cost you between $60,000 and $200,000 for a two-day board meeting. But, as advisors, all they expect is a token amount of stock options and their travel expenses covered. My bet is that you won't find many deals better than that.

Tips for Building and Managing Your Advisory Board

- Consider creating an advisory board to actively help you with your business challenges. Because advisors operate separately from the board of directors, they can provide advice and support more freely.

- To build an impactful advisory board, choose members with the skill sets and credentials that will help you the most, incorporate diverse experiences and perspectives, and bring a chemistry that promotes working together.

- Be clear about what kind of feedback you need. Encourage your advisors to use the appropriate lens and to provide Dutch feedback when doing so.

Parting Thoughts

- Fiduciary and advisory boards both play important roles in guiding a startup. A fiduciary board's primary role is to govern. However, great board members will also provide impactful advice, introduce you to potential customers and partners, and constructively challenge your thinking.

- Advisory boards, when carefully crafted, will help you think through growth challenges and opportunities, funding strategies, people issues, customer value proposition, new services, and go-to-market strategies. They are more open to providing advice because they understand that you can decide to follow it or not.

- The best advice comes from advisors that represent diverse backgrounds. Seek out people who share your values, but not all of your opinions. Good things happen when you surround yourself with smart people who will argue with you and bring an outside-in lens to your business.

Buzz can both accelerate your growth and significantly improve your ability to recruit great people. The next chapter explains why I believe buzz will be the most powerful tool in your marketing toolbox.

• • •

CHAPTER SIXTEEN

How Do You Generate Buzz?

When you hear buzz around the beehive, you know they're making honey in there.

— Terrence Howard, actor, rapper, singer-songwriter

What's the Buzz?

BUZZ IS NOT the marketing that's taught in business schools. It's word-of-mouth marketing. Buzz is generating and accelerating interest in and excitement about your company. It creates an allure. It drives mindshare. It's not free, but it's less expensive than traditional marketing.

Buzz is my band, The Peeple, renting a large bus for cruising the streets until we could fill it with teenage girls who promised to hysterically scream for us—if we could get them into our Battle of the Bands for free.

Think of buzz in the context of a new restaurant. If it's "hot," everyone will talk about it. Customers will make reservations months in advance to be sure they experience it, and they won't mind paying more to dine there. When people stop talking about a "hot" restaurant, it will probably tank.

That works for retailers as well. An Abercrombie and Fitch executive told me a story about the launch of their new store in Paris. "The opening was heavily promoted as a special event, and customers were waiting in what I felt were unbearably long lines to reach our four cashiers. I felt the urge to help, so I hurried to the back room to find a fifth cashier. I ran into Abercrombie's CEO who stopped me in my tracks. He said, 'This is a special event. It's exclusive. People expect long lines.' Then he then pulled one of the four cashiers off of his register and ordered him to sit and do nothing in the backroom to ensure the lines would become even longer."

That story annoyed me. "Didn't your CEO understand that the customer's experience is important?" The executive responded, "That's precisely the point."

Startups can also benefit from buzz. Generating it begins with finding your unique angle. What makes you stand out? What makes you interesting? If you look like everyone else, there's no reason for anyone to talk about you. At ZEFER, we were bringing the power of the internet to the Fortune 1000 (tying our launch to a megatrend) by blending the innovation from new kids on the block with the large enterprise implementation and change management experience brought by seasoned technologists and project managers (our angle). That combination made us stand out from the other internet consultancies. And raising $100 million to launch our company didn't hurt.

How Can Local Networking Build Buzz?

Cambridge Technology Partners was founded and headquartered in Cambridge, Massachusetts. I always was puzzled that we didn't have more Boston-based clients, and I wanted to change that at ZEFER. But I had no idea how a blue-collar guy from Pittsburgh could break into the tightly closed Boston business community. And then I met Karen.

Karen described herself as being connected to "everything Boston." She accepted a position as ZEFER's marketing vice president to create and manage my Boston acculturation plan.

- Step 1 – Become a Northeastern University guest lecturer on the internet economy.

- Step 2 – Join the Boston Chamber of Commerce and polish the Northeastern lecture to present it as the keynote speaker at their monthly CEO breakfast.

- Step 3 – Having established myself as an internet "thought leader," leverage my reputation to join Northeastern University's Board of Visitors.

- Step 4 – Leverage that membership to join the board of the Boston Chamber of Commerce.

- Step 5 – Wrangle an invitation to join the board of either the Boston Public Library, Museum of Fine Arts, Museum of Science, or the Boston Symphony Orchestra (my father-in-law was a librarian, so I chose the Boston Public Library).

- Step 6 – Get connected to the Democratic Party.

Karen created what felt like an Arthur Murray dance lesson. Put your right foot here, count to three, and then put your left foot there... It worked, and ZEFER's Boston business grew to overshadow our other locations.

Karen also helped me both meet and develop new connections. ZEFER made an arrangement with Boston's city government to teach free internet classes two evenings a week to help disadvantaged residents relaunch their careers. Karen leveraged that ongoing commitment to arrange a twenty-minute visit from Senator Ted Kennedy and then-Secretary of Labor Alexis Herman. Our distinguished guests ended up staying more than an hour, discussing our work with my team and engaging with the residents that we taught.

Several months later, my admin rushed into my office looking very excited. "I think I have Senator Ted Kennedy on the phone for you."

I laughed. "Either you're kidding me, or someone is kidding you."

"No," she said. "It's him. It's his voice and his accent."

I wasn't convinced, but I picked up the phone.

"Bill, it's been too long since Secretary Herman and I visited ZEFER's offices. I'm calling to thank you for hosting us. We learned a lot that day and were impressed by what you are doing." It really was the senator!

"How are you doing? And how is ZEFER doing?" he continued. I felt like I was shooting the breeze with an old friend. After ten more minutes of casually chatting, he said, "I'm also calling to ask you for a big favor. As you know, I'm running for re-election this November. I'm one of the longest continuously serving senators in US history, so this campaign is very important to me." He paused, "Would you be willing to nominate me for re-election, on behalf of Boston businesses?"

I was stunned. "I'd like to help, but what would that involve?"

Senator Kennedy explained, "We'll hold the event at your office, with every Boston Democratic Party CEO attending. And you know, Bill, almost all of the CEOs here are Democrats. We'll set up a stage with ZEFER's banner and logo prominently displayed. All of New England's media outlets will attend. You'll begin with a brief introduction of ZEFER, followed by your views on why I would be the best candidate to represent Boston businesses. Senator Kerry will stand at the next podium and second my nomination. I'll close by thanking ZEFER for the impact you are having on our economy and for your contributions to the neighborhoods where you operate. I'll comment on why I believe my policies support both large enterprises and emerging startups like yours. And we'll adjourn so we can informally chat over refreshments with the CEOs attending."

I needed a minute to gather my thoughts. "Thank you so much for offering ZEFER this opportunity," I began. "The exposure, the introductions, the buzz—that would mean so much. I would be delighted to nominate you and host the event. But...I have to be honest." I paused, "I'm not a Democrat."

Now Senator Kennedy needed a moment to gather his thoughts. "Ha, ha, ha," he chuckled softly. Then a louder "Ha, ha, ha," followed by a more emphatic "Ha, ha, ha" that sounded like a belly laugh. Then he whispered, "Bill, let's let that be our little secret."

I happily accepted Senator Kennedy's invitation, and the event was spectacular. ZEFER was on the map in Boston.

How Can You Build Buzz with Staying Power?

You can build buzz by positioning yourself as an expert in something—your industry, the industries that you serve, your technology...anything that your prospects, customers, and influencers might find interesting to follow. Never launch a company newsletter. It takes too long to produce, too long to read, and has a half-life of a single issue. Never hire a public relations firm. They're expensive, and you don't need them to build followers. Instead, you can leverage surveys, interviews, and posts to reach new prospects and build a following.

Surveys generate buzz and are easy to produce. At Mobiquity, we considered ourselves thought leaders. We published bestselling business books, posted thought-provoking whitepapers on our website, and presented at many industry conferences. All of that built staying power for our buzz. But much to my surprise, the most downloaded content from our website was a simple survey reporting on the percent of texters who use a finger, a hand, or both hands to text. That poll required only five minutes to type the question (but only two minutes if you can type with both hands), thirty minutes to process all the results, and another hour to write a short summary.

Interviews are relatively easy to produce. If your startup is generating buzz, interesting people will contact you to network. At Mobiquity, I'd schedule my networking meetings for 11:30 a.m. on Tuesdays. I'd explain that our Boston office held Lunch-and-Learns at 12:30 that day, and the Mobsters would be interested in hearing our guest speak on a topic of their choice after our meeting ended. Every networker was flattered by the offer and readily agreed. Our marketing executive would take notes during the meeting and request a brief interview afterward to post on our website. In a few hours, we built a stronger relationship with a new "friend of the firm," educated and entertained our Boston office, and published fresh content on our website that highlighted the breadth of interesting contacts who liked to hang out with us.

Mobiquity also produced the *Mobile Dose*, a daily brief on the top three mobile happenings. Designed to be read in two minutes, it was texted or emailed promptly at 8:00 a.m., Monday through Friday. Occasionally, the *Dose* would connect readers to relevant content on our website. We hired a student to scour and summarize the daily mobile headlines. Our daily production costs were only $40—and we reached 3,800 daily subscribers in our first year.

Posts on your website are important, but without discipline, they can backfire. Recall your experience when you click on a company's "News" tab on their website and the most recent entry is eighteen months old. Or the posts contain more spelling and grammar errors than your sixth grader's homework assignment. Can we really call it thought leadership if the author cannot spell? Before you laugh too hard, perhaps you should check your own website.

Schedule your posts using an editorial calendar developed by the marketing department. The calendar should:

- state a theme for a period of time;

- define the topics to support that theme;

- identify the author and the submittal date; and

- include controversial subjects—customers will be attracted by your frankness.

Finally, the tone should be professional. Empower the marketing team to manage the process and review and edit all content.

How Can You Find Clients that Amplify Buzz?

Three months after I launched ZEFER, I opened our Chicago office. Did I take this step too soon? How could we quickly generate buzz that would create name recognition and build our brand? Anita, the general manager of our Chicago office, devised a solution: Offer to build the Chicago Bears' first website. We "won" the project by committing to develop it at cost and launch the site in record time—before their first preseason game. In return, the Bears would highlight ZEFER's name on their website. With one of the most loyal fan bases in the US, Da Bears' page views exceeded one million in a short period of time, and the average fan stayed on the site for nine minutes. Better yet, the Bears launched a television campaign to promote the new site, and the commercials ended with a screen that announced, "Web Site Tackled by ZEFER." We were on the map in Chicago!

How Did a Spring Break Experiment Create Buzz?

I met the man who claims he invented the wet t-shirt contest. He was a marketing executive at a music technology company where I sat on the board. He wasn't bragging about his creation. In fact, it embarrassed him. I only discovered his role when I heard a coworker teasing him. I guess if you had created that bit of infamy, you would deserve to be teased. I had to hear his story, and he reluctantly agreed to tell it to me.

I worked my way through college as a professional disk jockey. There weren't many actual pros at the time. I was one of the few who knew how to "scratch," and I intuitively played music that made an audience go wild. After I graduated, I knew it was time to get a real job, and I accepted a position at a pharmaceutical company in the Northeast. But I still had DJing in my blood. A good friend owned a beachfront bar in Ft. Lauderdale. He invited me to use my two-week vacation to fly there and DJ at his club during spring break. We suffered from a brutally cold winter in the Northeast that year, so I happily accepted his invitation.

Monday nights were always slow at his bar. So, my friend tried to generate buzz by converting the dance floor into a temporary basketball court for the evening and recruiting coeds from rival colleges to play against one another. The final match came down to the last shot, and a beautiful, voluptuous blonde drained her shot for a last-second win. I got caught up in the excitement, ran onto the court, and dumped a cooler of Gatorade on her. That's when the wet t-shirt contest was born.

Word got out, and we expanded to three nights every week, then to five, and then to seven with both afternoon and evening matches. We dropped the basketball match but kept the college team format. My friend would dump buckets of water on the contestants while I spun records. The winning team was determined by the response of the primarily male audience—and respond they did. We increased beer sales by 500 percent. I decided to quit my job at the pharmaceutical company. It was the best career decision I ever made.

We wanted to build on our momentum and continued to look for more ways to generate buzz. My friend replaced his bar's tables with bleachers. That reinforced our theme of "rival colleges competing against one another." That also enabled us to double our seating capacity. The coeds could customize their t-shirts as long as they kept their school colors. I believed that making the event more exclusive would add to the buzz, so we required a student ID from a competing college in order to attend. With 350,000 collegians pouring into Ft. Lauderdale every spring, revenues from beer sales, cover charges, and programs continued to soar.

He paused and said, "Mr. Seibel, where did you attend college?"

"Penn State," I replied.

"What school was your biggest rival?"

"At that time, it was Pitt," I said. "It wasn't a friendly rivalry. We hated each other."

"Think back to when you were a junior in college—let's say you were an immature nineteen years old. If Penn State was competing with Pitt in a wet t-shirt contest to determine who had the hottest coeds, accompanied by cold beer and loud music—would you get in line to cheer on your school?"

"I'm not sure," I said out loud. "It seems degrading." But I was thinking, "Hell yes. At nineteen I'd circle that date on my calendar."

The marketing executive's story fascinated me. He hit on many of my own key takeaways for creating buzz:

- find your angle;

- pique your audience's interest;

- build in exclusivity; and

- create momentum.

But I was skeptical. Was any of his yarn true? I asked the company's CEO about the story, and he confirmed it. In fact, during one of the city's crackdowns on unruly spring break behavior, the DJ had been arrested and served a ninety-day jail sentence for inciting lewd and lascivious behavior. And he was still receiving royalty checks from a cameo appearance he made as a DJ in a Hollywood horror movie about spring break. His story was too good to resist, so I'll give him the benefit of the doubt!

Parting Thoughts

Done right, buzz is less expensive and more impactful than traditional marketing. Here's what you need to do.

- Find your angle. Create a following by finding what makes you interesting and then promote it.

- Pique the interest of potential customers. Preserve an element of mystery while hinting at great things soon to come.

- Create allure by building exclusivity into your events.

- Generate timely, digestible content that supports the image you want to create.

- Leverage and expand your connections. Figure out what your Arthur Murray dance steps look like.

- Build staying power. Buzz is all about creating momentum.

The next chapter unveils my secrets to scaling your startup rapidly.

• • •

CHAPTER SEVENTEEN

Hyper-Scaling Your Startup

The person who says it cannot be done should not interrupt the person doing it.

— Chinese Proverb

Why Do It?

MOST STARTUPS WILL never cross the $1 million revenue chasm. But let's say your company is an exception and is powering its way to sales of $10 million. Can you continue to scale at the same pace without changing the way you operate? Or are there new chasms you need to cross? I'm often engaged to help businesses learn how they can scale quickly without fracturing their quality, people, culture, or financials.

By growing revenue rapidly, your enterprise value increases. And your startup reaps intangible benefits as well.

- Recognition as the leader enables you to recruit the best people.

- With a first-mover advantage, it's easier to win customers before new competitors enter the market.

- Fast growth positions you to win challenging and exciting projects from larger clients.

- The faster you scale profitably, the more quickly you achieve the ability to control your own destiny.

Do You Believe You Can Do It?

Your first and most important step toward rapid growth is to *believe that you can do it*. After you convince yourself, convince your team. If anyone disagrees, you'll never achieve it. Next, think through the obstacles to rapid growth and figure out how to overcome them. That focus builds the scalability story that potential acquirers will need to see.

For years, experts believed it was impossible for the human body to run a four-minute mile. The record stood at 4:01 minutes for more than nine years. On May 6, 1954, Roger Bannister broke through the barrier by running the distance in 3:59.4. He attributed his success to visualizing breaking the record and developing a certainty about it. Once the world saw it was possible, it took only forty-six days for someone to break Bannister's record. Since then, almost 1,500 athletes, including more than a dozen high school students, have run a mile in less than four minutes.

Keep Doing Great Work

You're here because you do great work. It's easy to let your quality slip as you rapidly scale. Don't allow that to happen. Continue to over-prepare for everything and sweat the details.

I saved a quote to remind me of the importance of continuing to do great work, and I share it with my team whenever we approach that $10 million chasm.

> In the end, it is attention to detail that makes all the difference. It's the center fielder's extra two steps to the left, the salesman's memory for names, the lover's phone call, the soldier's clean weapon. It is the thing that separates the winners from the losers, the men from the boys and very often, the living from the dead. Professional success depends on it, regardless of the field.

Did a great author write that quote? A famous entrepreneur? A renowned educator? No—it has more humble origins than that!

Beware the Icarus Effect

Icarus was the son of the master craftsman Daedalus. Imprisoned on the island of Crete, Daedalus fashioned wings out of feathers and wax so he and his son could escape. Icarus' father warned him first of complacency and then of hubris, telling him to neither fly too low, where the sea's dampness could clog his wings, nor too high, where the sun could melt them. Overcome by the giddiness of flying, Icarus ignored his father's orders, fell to the sea, and drowned. The lesson for your startup? If you grow too slowly, you'll burn your cash and lose the advantages of an early leader. If you grow too quickly, you'll outgrow your infrastructure and your management bandwidth. Both scenarios will lead to a likely crash.

To avoid the "Icarus effect," CEOs whose startups are scaling rapidly need to manage their egos and rely on early warning indicators that alert them when they are in danger of outpacing their bandwidth and infrastructure. The frugal, slimmed-down startup philosophy appropriate for a young company needs to evolve to allow investment in financial and operations management. It's time to define the key metrics and management processes that will tell you when to hit the gas and when to apply the brakes.

How do you know if you are flying too low? As strange as it might sound, you'll know if you don't experience setbacks. If everything is running smoothly, you're either unusually lucky or not growing fast enough. It's time to ratchet up the pace. As Mario Andretti observed, "If everything seems under control, you're not going fast enough."

And you may be flying too high if you lose a key customer. Or lose a deal you expected to win. Or aren't submitting proposals on time. Or if operating income is sliding. Perhaps implementation projects are taking longer and costing more than planned. That stuff will always occur. But if any of this begins to happen unexpectedly and you don't understand why, recognize the potential early warning indicator. Your business growth might be outpacing your infrastructure and management processes.

Divide Big Problems into Small Problems

After your startup reaches $1 million revenue, it might seem aggressive, but still doable, to set a 50 percent growth goal to reach $1.5 million the following year. You may need to find only one or two new customers to reach it. But the larger your startup gets, the more difficult it is to sustain that growth rate. And continuing to grow revenue by 50 percent every year and maintaining that pace until you reach $100 million is difficult to visualize. There are too many moving parts to manage. Running the business gets in the way of growing the business. Hierarchies begin to create distance between decision makers and customers in the field. The startup mentality to "do whatever you need to do to win new business" becomes dampened. As a result, a company's growth rate typically declines as it grows larger.

That's why you should break your *big* company into a portfolio of smaller companies. Establish individual profit and loss (P&L) statements by geography or product line. Remember to treat each new product or geography as a startup all over again. My guiding principles are:

- customer-facing people should actually face customers, not sit behind a desk at headquarters;

- make as many decisions as you can in the field, close to the action; and

- every new product or geography should operate as a smaller version of the larger company, held accountable for delivering exceptional results to their clients, driving new business, and managing their P&L.

Assign seasoned, ambitious, and forward-thinking general managers who view their piece of the business as their own startup, and empower them to manage it that way. Give them the support that they need from "corporate" and the freedom to decide when they need it. Incent them to drive revenue growth. You'll find it's much easier to rapidly scale a portfolio of ten $1 million *companies* than one $10 million company.

Don't Forget That Your Business Does Need to Make Money

Entrepreneurs can get caught up in the excitement of launching a product and lose sight of the fact that they're supposed to be building a viable business. The former may be more fun, but the latter pays the bills. Small Business Trends reports that only 40 percent of startups are profitable.[38] As your revenues grow, you'll find more opportunities to spend money foolishly. That's when your focus has to change from *growth* to *profitable growth*. Expenses that seemed insignificant in the beginning can become significant when multiplied by more locations and many more employees. That buildup can sneak up on you.

Most of your profitability depends on the decisions your line managers make in the field. Typically, they lack the context or the information to make them wisely. They don't understand that small trade-offs can have a huge financial impact. How could they if no one has ever explained to them how their firm makes money? If you invest the time to explain your business model, they will be equipped to make better financial decisions.

When I returned to Boston to lead Cambridge Technology Partners–Americas, our net income budget was $70 million. My expense budget that year included nearly $50 million for telephone costs, conference and training expenses, external recruiting charges, holiday parties held in twelve offices across the US, express mail, and premiums for travel not booked seven days in advance. Reducing that budget by 20 percent added another $10 million to my bottom line. We expected our consultants to be 72 percent billable every year. Nudging that billable rate up by just 2 percent, our net income increased by another $8 million. As your startup grows, small numbers add up to large numbers very quickly.

If you explain to line managers how your startup makes money and back it up with the right incentives, you will significantly increase your bottom line.

Don't Get Distracted by Shiny Objects

Earlier, I described a startup as an organization in search of a scalable business model and explained that the path to discovering that model is never a straight line. Consequently, I emphasized that it's important for a new venture to be able to pivot quickly to be successful. However, if your company is rapidly growing and approaching $10 million in revenue, odds are that you've found a scalable business model that works for you.

CB Insights reports that losing focus is the eleventh-ranked cause of startups failing.[23] If your model is working, stick with it. You've found a growth curve where every incremental investment of time or money maximizes its impact on revenue. A new curve will, in the best case, have a slower slope and will dilute the funds and bandwidth that you could otherwise allocate to the business model that is rapidly scaling. If your market changes, you may once again have to pivot. But until then, don't get distracted by new, shiny objects.

"Don't You Get It, Dad? It's All About the Data"

Annuities provide a powerful scaling engine. Software companies figured that out early, beginning with timesharing in the 1960s, Application Service Providers (ASPs) in the '90s, and software-as-a-service (SaaS) models soon after that. A subscription model works in many scenarios, including long-term retainers, support and maintenance contracts, and periodic strategy and scenario resets. In my mind, data analytics provides

the most potential. According to BCG, 80 percent of the most innovative companies leverage data to drive advantages in their business.[43]

In 2020, the amount of data produced by humans every day was 2.5 quintillion bytes—that's 2,500,000,000,000,000,000. "By the end of 2020, 44 zettabytes (44,000,000,000,000,000,000,000) will make up the entire digital universe."[44] The opportunity to leverage this overwhelming reality can fuel innovative business models, expert systems, and machine learning—and create opportunities for startups to monetize that data stream.

My son's name is Bill Bailey Seibel (we call him Bales). At twelve years old, he taught me how data analytics can create a better mousetrap and turn a product introduced in 1894 into a killer app.

Soon after I founded Mobiquity, I had a last-minute opportunity to speak to a full room of CIOs about the innovation opportunities driven by the new technology stack: mobile, social, the cloud, big data and analytics, and the internet of things (IoT). I hadn't prepared that kind of presentation and had only one week to create it. I needed help, so I told my teenage daughter, Christina, that I would pay her $20 if she could find an example of a social media app that generated business value. In less than fifteen minutes, she found a terrific example and collected her reward.

Bales was watching and said, "Dad—what about me?"

I replied, "If you can find an example of an IoT killer app, I'll pay you $20."

He walked to his room with his laptop, and I seldom saw him for the next five days. Bales was immersed in the challenge of finding an example.

When I was ready to give up on him, he called out in a very excited voice, "Dad—I've got it." Bales went on, "There's a company named Renkoit that deployed an internet-enabled rat trap across Wembley Stadium in the UK. As soon as a rat is caught, the rat keeper gets a text message on his phone to alert them to get rid of the dead rat and rebait the trap."

At that moment, I was a very proud father. "Bales, great example. Here's your $20," I said.

He interrupted me. "Wait, Dad—that's not the whole story. With that data, the rat keeper knows if the rat population is increasing or decreasing, and whether it's shifting to another side of the stadium. They can use that information to implement a much better extermination strategy. And that creates a great business opportunity for Renkoit as well. They don't just sell the traps—they also sell the data." Bales paused and looked at me quizzically.

"Don't you get it, Dad? It's all about the data."

I smiled and handed him another $20. Still, I had to ask, "Great example, but why did it take you so long to find it?"

"There are a lot of IoT solutions, but it was hard to find one that kills things."

It was my reference to a "killer app" that threw him!

How Do You Build an Ecosystem to Amplify Your Go-to-Market?

Although adding business partners can be an effective way to increase your growth trajectory, the results often fall short of expectations. Partners have their own agendas, and yours is unlikely to stay top of mind. They might remember you if it helps their business, and you might do the same. But neither of you can count on a consistent level of attention.

That's why you should manage a partnership network as a *virtual joint venture*. Joint ventures share a single agenda that both parties are committed to following. Design your partnership based on how it would work if it was a *real* joint venture.

- You'd begin by aligning your customer value propositions (CVP). Why would a customer receive more value if they engage both of you? Where is the synergy? How can 1 + 1 = 3?

- Agree on how you and your partner will communicate your joint CVP to prospects and how to divide partner responsibilities. What does the ideal target prospect look like? How will you find them? Who will find them? What type of content and marketing campaigns should you create? Who will pitch the joint CVP and what training will they need? Establish revenue goals and identify who, from each side of the partnership, is accountable for achieving them.

- In summary, define the roles and responsibilities of each partner. How will the joint pipeline be managed? How will revenue goals be set? Who will "own the customer," and how will that be managed?

By precisely following the same process when forming a *virtual* joint venture, the partnership becomes focused on what's good for the customer, creates commitment and accountability to joint goals, and defines the management processes necessary to achieve them.

How Do You Make "Smart" Acquisitions?

Acquiring the right company for the right price can drive scale while potentially bringing new services and new geographic markets to your business. TechCrunch reports that one in six startups eventually is acquired.[45] Unfortunately, most of the time the acquisition fails. How do you find the right acquisition? And how do you make it work the *day after*?

On my first day in Carnegie Mellon's MBA program, I walked into my first class—Economics. The professor began by sharing his background.

> While completing my PhD, I landed a part-time job working for the president of a regional bank. My assignment, as I understood it, was to build a model that would analyze potential acquisitions and recommend which were the best for our bank to pursue. I developed an analytical model that enabled me to quickly run the numbers, and I found four excellent targets in the first six months. In every case, the bank president passed on the opportunity— without even asking a question.
>
> One day, he walked into my office, tossed a folder on my desk and said, "This is the one I want to buy." I glanced at the folder and recognized that his selection was one I had analyzed and rejected earlier that week. I said, "I've already analyzed that property, and it didn't score very well."
>
> The president stared at me, and then repeated, pausing after every word, "This is the one I want to buy."
>
> "I thought you hired me to provide an analytical framework for deciding on which banks to buy" I argued.
>
> "I'll tell you how I decide which banks to buy," he said, with an emphasis on I. "In this region, most of the banks are family owned. And I know most of the families. When I learn that a bank president dies, I'll call his family and ask if they're open to selling. If they are, it will be easy to fashion a deal that is fair to both sides."
>
> I was perplexed and asked, "Then why did you hire me to develop an analytical model to find the best banks for you to buy?"
>
> "That's not why I hired you," he responded. "I hired you to build an analytical model that I can use to convince my board to approve the banks that I choose to buy."

The professor intended to teach us that we need to clearly understand the question we're addressing before we build a model to answer it.

But his story contained another important lesson. The conventional merger and acquisition (M&A) process that identifies the best-performing companies doesn't always result in a smart acquisition.

I've found that it doesn't work for me, simply because I can never afford to buy a top-performing company. What motivates a top-performing company to be acquired? The most likely answer is that being acquired is a payday—a lucrative cash exit for their management team. Even if the key employees don't leave, they lose their motivation to work "startup hours" to achieve a future payday. If "new" team members can cash out while the earlier employees are still struggling on startup wages, that can create resentment, which may lead to internal factions forming.

Instead, I look for an acquisition to fill gaps in my products, services, or geographies. I target companies that have good bones but are not living up to their potential. Ideally, what motivates my companies to be acquired? They want to be part of—and contribute to—a company that is a top performer. Their motivation isn't a quick payday. It's joining us on our journey to a potential exit that all of us will share in the future.

Acquisitions—The Art of the Deal

Negotiating a deal to acquire a company involves more than agreeing on terms. It's also about building a relationship. But it's challenging to do both at the same time.

ZEFER was attempting to acquire a creative design startup in San Francisco. Although very small, the firm would provide us with a West Coast presence, a few large clients, and an opportunity to build a team around a talented executive. I flew to San Francisco with Fred, my executive vice president of business development, and agreed to meet James and Gary, his partner, at 5:00 p.m. at the restaurant of their choice. Although Fred and I arrived early, James and Gary were already waiting with an open bottle of wine.

James greeted us and said, "I'm very excited about this opportunity, and I want to reach an agreement before we leave this evening. I hope that you can hold your wine, because we are going to drink a lot of it tonight." I winked at Fred. James didn't realize who he was up against.

We quickly agreed on most of the terms, with two exceptions. James insisted that a significant portion of the transaction would be cash, while I wanted an all-stock deal. He also argued for a higher valuation for his company. I could bend on valuation, as long as it would be viewed as fair by the other companies that I acquired. It's important to me that everyone works towards the same exit. We vacillated between arguing our position and backing off to get to know each other better. I'm competitive, so I tried my best to keep up with James' wine consumption. Before I knew it, it was almost midnight, and the restaurant crew was hinting for us to leave so they could finish cleaning. As the four of us stumbled out, James shook my hand and said, "That's more wine than I've ever consumed. But I'm delighted that we reached an agreement. We have a deal!"

Fred and I both immediately fell asleep in the taxi. Upon arriving at our hotel, we agreed to debrief the next morning.

I'm normally an early riser, but I was sound asleep until my alarm rang at 10:00 a.m. I took three Tylenol tablets and a long shower, then sat down with a cup of coffee. I remembered reaching a deal with James and shaking hands on it at the end of the night. But I had no recollection of our final agreement on either of the open items. I drew a complete blank on the most important part of our deal.

A few minutes later, my phone rang. It was Fred. "Bill," he said, "I drank too much last night. I know that we reached an agreement with James, but I can't remember what it was that we agreed to." Now we had a problem. We met in the hotel restaurant for a late breakfast to try to reconstruct last evening's discussions. "I don't think you would have given in on the cash component," Fred offered. "But you might have bent a bit on the relative valuation. I just don't remember."

"If I did bend, it wouldn't have been by much," I replied. "All that I can do is call James, congratulate him on out-drinking us, and explain that neither of us are clear on what we agreed to."

At that moment, my phone rang. It was James. Before I could say anything, he began. "Bill, you drank us under the table. I know we agreed on a deal, but neither Gary nor I can remember what we agreed to. But I do remember that I enjoyed getting to know you, and that I trust and respect you. Just write down what you think is fair, send it to me, and I'll sign it."

Lesson learned: Save the wine until after you negotiate the deal.

Acquisitions—The Day After the Day After...

According to the *Harvard Business Review*, between 70 percent and 90 percent of mergers and acquisitions fail.[46] That's because the acquirer invests more effort in finding the opportunity and negotiating the deal than they do in making it work. Too often, integrating the acquired company is an afterthought. A startup can't survive odds like those.

I've acquired nineteen companies. Best practice is assigning one of my direct reports to be responsible for the acquisition's integration and success. I expect them to make this their top priority for as long as necessary. And I'll restructure their responsibilities and incentives to ensure they succeed. Acquisitions can still fail, but if you focus on the day after, you will tilt the odds in your favor.

Rapidly Scaling Professional Services Firms

Professional services firms have a number of unique challenges that I detail in the Appendix—Lessons Applied to Professional Services. I identify what's different and why that's important.

Parting Thoughts

- Before you take a leap and "press go," your first and most important step is to *believe that you can rapidly scale*. Think through what you want to achieve, identify the obstacles in the way, and figure out how to overcome them. That lesson applies to life as well. Never give up your dreams. The first step in achieving them is to believe that they're possible.

- As you begin to scale rapidly, you will face a trade-off between growth and continuing to do great work. When you do, always choose *great work*.

- Remember the "Icarus effect," and pay attention to the early indicators that signal you are growing too quickly or too slowly.

- When you find a scalable business model that works for you, stick with it. You've found a growth curve where every incremental investment of time or money maximizes the impact on revenue.

- Look for potential annuities in areas like data analytics that can accelerate revenue growth. Partnerships structured as virtual joint ventures and smart acquisitions that are successfully integrated will amplify your go-to-market capabilities.

- Most importantly, don't kick the "making money can" down the road. Build a profitability goal into your culture from the beginning.

Hyper-scaling your team goes hand in hand with hyper-scaling your company. My next chapter explains how to accomplish that.

• • •

CHAPTER EIGHTEEN

How to Hyper-Scale Your Team

The reasonable man adapts himself to the world; the unreasonable one persists in trying to adapt the world to himself. Therefore, all progress depends on the unreasonable man.

– George Bernard Shaw, playwright

YOUR STARTUP HAS become a "real" company. You have:

- created a product or service that delivers on an engaging, impactful customer value proposition;

- recruited your initial team; and

- begun to experience hyper-growth.

Now it's time to step on the gas by:

- finding the talent to enable you to scale more quickly;

- defining and institutionalizing your shared values; and

- preparing your team to lead a business that's growing larger and more complex.

How Do You Scale Your Team Rapidly?

As Cambridge Technology Partners (CTP) began our fourth year in Europe, our financial plan called for our revenue to increase by $25

237

million. That was a huge jump. As a professional services company, that required us to hire 190 new employees across seven countries. To add to the challenge, we had no recruiters, no budget for "headhunters," and very little brand recognition.

Carol was in between projects. I walked to her desk, explained our problem, and asked, "Any ideas on what we can do?"

"You know I've never been a recruiter or worked in human resources," Carol said. "What makes you think I can help?"

I replied, "I'm not looking for best practice. I'm looking for something new and innovative. You've done a lot of interviewing and hiring in your career. And you've always made great choices. You're a great judge of character. For example, you married me!" Carol didn't get my joke.

I continued, "How could we hire exponentially faster without compromising quality?"

"How long do I have?" Carol asked.

"Take two weeks," I replied.

Carol needed only one.

Carol's Hiring Hack

"Let me begin by explaining our current recruiting process," she began. "It's very similar to what you'll find anywhere else. Someone is tasked with sourcing candidates for the highest priority openings. When they identify a strong applicant, they schedule the first round of interviews. That process could take weeks, because it requires matching the applicant's availability to that of four or five interviewers."

Carol continued, "When the first round of interviews finally begins, the process becomes very unorganized. Each interviewer, often selected only because they are available, independently chooses what to discuss in their allotted hour. Very often, all the interviews cover the same ground, while many important topics are neglected. Typically, the interviewers spend most of their time talking, not listening." Carol paused to look me in the eye, making certain that I knew that she was referring to me.

"After the interviews conclude, someone has to gather all of the feedback—that's not as easy as it sounds—and then schedule a meeting with all of the interviewers to share that feedback and get a consensus on bringing the candidate back for another set of interviews. Once again, schedules have to be aligned, the interviews are repetitive and unfocused, and the feedback takes time to assemble. If it's a 'go,' we bring the candidate in once again to meet with you and several of our leadership team members before making the final hiring decision."

Carol summarized, "The process takes much too long, and that makes it difficult to build momentum. The information gathered in the interviews is hit-or-miss. The feedback process is drawn-out, and the basis for the go-forward decision is unclear."

Another pause before Carol said, "I believe we can do better."

She continued, "Let's solve the scheduling problem first. I'll source and prescreen candidates in advance and commit to having twelve of them available for interviews at 5:00 p.m. every Thursday. One week, the sessions will be in London, and the next week in Amsterdam. You need to have a team available at each location, and you need to attend both sessions."

"Next, let's address the hit-or-miss interviews. You'll begin each session by presenting our vision and value proposition to the entire group. Who better than the CEO to do that? And if you do it up front, no one else will have to waste time repeating that information in their interviews. Following you, either our sales or operations executive will talk about the incredible work that we do for our clients. And then someone more junior will speak to our culture and what it's like to work here."

"Since none of that needs to be repeated, each interview can be scheduled to last only twenty minutes instead of an hour. To make that work, each interviewer will focus on only one area—skills, experience, achievements, or cultural fit. If they stay on point, they can get an accurate read in only twenty minutes."

"After three interviews, we'll assemble everyone in a conference room for a coffee break. Remember, some of the attendees are applying for entry-level jobs, others for senior positions. But we'll mix everyone together. I'll start the conversation by casually asking the group for their thoughts on a topical question. We can watch to see how the applicants interact in a group and get a read on their confidence and communication skills."

"After the fourth interview, I'll bring everyone into the lobby for refreshments. That will give the applicants a chance to chat with members of the executive team and interact with some of our employees they haven't met."

"That brings us to our final problem: how to gather feedback and make hiring decisions quickly. As soon as the applicants depart, while everything is fresh in our minds, we'll regroup to discuss each of them. If an applicant gets a 'thumbs up' from all four interviewers, they receive an offer, pending references, the next morning."

Carol summarized, "We'll make better hiring decisions faster and much more efficiently. The applicants will have a more energizing recruiting experience that will build momentum and lead to a higher acceptance level." She paused and asked, "How did I do?"

We hired 198 new, exceptionally talented employees that year versus our target of 190. All but one of them were recruited through Carol's process. She did pretty well.

Our Only Hire That Didn't Follow Carol's Process

That year, Carol and I decided to relocate from Amsterdam to London so we could focus more of our attention on the UK. We needed to hire my replacement. Theo, one of our first business contacts in Amsterdam, heard a rumor about the opportunity and contacted us before we began our search. He was a senior executive from the large IT consultancy that was our initial joint venture partner—and the only one that "got" our value proposition. I was delighted to take the interview.

Theo arrived early at our offices in the attic of 62-64 Keizersgracht, a canal house built in the fifteenth century. He was so easy to talk to, we talked nonstop until lunch. I was confident that he was the right person for the job. As we wrapped up, Theo asked, "Bill, how do you feel about our meeting?"

"I thought it went very well," I replied.

"And so, did I," he responded. "What's the next step?"

"Visit our offices again on Monday," I suggested. "Spend the morning meeting the team that would report to you, just to do a chemistry check. After that, you and I can regroup to chat about how we would work together."

Theo didn't hesitate. "But...but...but...that's how Americans do it. That's *not* how we do it in Europe. "

Not wanting to be "an ugly American," I had no alternative but to say, "Okay. Then what should we do next?"

"You and your lovely wife, Carol, should come to my home for dinner on Saturday and meet Sari, my wife, and our three children. After dinner, you and I can continue our interview in the sauna."

Did he really say, "Continue our interview in the sauna?" I saw no way out. "Of course," I replied. "I should have thought of that. Looking forward to it!"

The moment that Theo departed, I hopped on the phone to call every European business contact that I could reach. "Is he serious?" I asked. "Am I expected to interview a potential direct report naked?" Their answers were consistent. Theo's wife Sari is from Finland. Scandinavians often have business meetings in a sauna. It's likely the answer to the question is "yes."

On our drive to Theo's home, Carol remarked, "It's amazing what a person is willing to do to make their startup successful." She was right. I couldn't see me doing this at CTP's headquarters in Boston.

Theo and Sari's home was charming, their company was delightful, their children were precious, and the meal was delicious. But suspecting that both of us would be stark naked when I interviewed Theo after dinner, I decided I wouldn't eat much. "Just not very hungry this evening," I fibbed.

After dinner, Theo and I walked down a flight of stairs to a large room that resembled a basement "rec" room in the US—except for the sauna. We undressed, and I looked for towels as we entered the sauna. But there were none to be found. We really were stark naked. I sat on a bench, and Theo took the seat perpendicular to mine.

That's when I realized that everything I knew about interviewing did not apply in a sauna. I couldn't look at a resumé or take notes because the steam would dissolve the paper. I remembered that after asking a question, checking for eye contact was a good interviewing technique. But checking for eye contact in the sauna felt creepy. Asking a really tough question and checking body language seemed even creepier. Time passed slowly.

After forty-five minutes, we took a break to cool off. Theo pointed to a black leather couch, handed me a beer, and asked me to sit down. He sat on a matching couch across from me. Still no towels.

After twenty minutes and three beers, we returned to our positions in the sauna and continued our interview. Thirty minutes later it was over—or so I thought. Theo escorted me to a stall with two fixtures, explaining that we would shower to cool off. Oh my God—we were going to shower together. After a few minutes, Theo repeated his question from our previous meeting, "Bill, how did you feel about our meeting?"

I continued to believe that he was the best candidate for the job. I wanted to sound positive, but I definitely did not want to appear overly enthusiastic. My eagerness had already landed me in trouble. "I thought the meeting was okay," I said with hesitation.

"I thought this was an awesome meeting as well," Theo excitedly exclaimed. "And we have one more tradition in Europe. We celebrate successful sauna meetings by scrubbing each other's backs with a tree branch while cooling off in the shower."

"Bullshit!" I no longer cared if I looked like an "ugly American." "You have now crossed the line. If you want this job, you'll come to our offices on Monday and spend the morning meeting the team that will report to you. After that, you and I will chat about how we would work together. And make sure that you're wearing clothes."

Theo just smiled. I believe that he was testing me to see how far he could go.

After dinner, Carol asked, "Bill, how did you feel about your meeting with Theo?" I answered by repeating her earlier remark on our drive to Theo's house. "It's amazing what people are willing to do to make a startup successful."

That Monday, I hired Theo. He was the best hire I've made, in any company, at any time—ever. After I returned to the US, he succeeded me as managing director of CTP–Europe. He also became one of my very best friends. I still wonder how much the sauna had to do with any of that.

Is Culture Fit Important?

I briefly discussed culture in Chapter 5. Is "culture fit" important? Maybe, depending on what you mean by culture. The next time you hear a CEO say, "Our culture is critically important to us," ask them to define it. If it really is critically important, they should have the definition at the tip of their tongue. My bet is that instead they will pause, stare into space for a moment, and then stumble through their answer—almost as if they've never been asked that question before.

When I hear that a prospective employee was rejected because they weren't a *culture fit*, I wonder what that actually means. Often it's a way of saying "He doesn't look like us," or "She's not someone I'd like to hang out with," or perhaps "Just look at the way they're dressed."

Some employers use poor culture fit as a pretext to crush diversity. But diversity is critical to building a high-performing team.

Look up the definition of culture and you'll see something like "the customs, arts, social institutions, and achievements of a particular nation, people, or other social group." Synonyms include "lifestyle," "customs," and "traditions." You're not committed to diversity if you reject someone because they don't share your lifestyle, customs, and traditions.

The summer following my launch of CTP–Europe, I received an email from human resources stressing the importance that every office "shares the same culture." It was sent to remind every location of "the way that CTP is expected to celebrate the upcoming Fourth of July holiday." The bullet points included:

- make sure all locations participate in the celebration the same way (not recognizing that the Fourth of July isn't a holiday in the Netherlands, and certainly is not celebrated in the UK);

- the celebration should begin at 5:00 p.m. EST (which was 10:00 p.m. in London and 11:00 p.m. in Amsterdam);

- the leadership team should grill hamburgers and hot dogs (I never saw a single hamburger, hot dog, or grill in Amsterdam); and

- keep the celebration going until the fireworks begin (a *really* long time in Amsterdam, where the law only allows fireworks on New Year's Eve).

I kid you not.

Culture fit is the wrong criteria for hiring or acquiring. Instead, substitute *values fit*. Values are a person's principles or standards of behavior—one's judgment of what is important in life. Synonyms include principles, ethics, and morals. Culture is defined as the characteristics of a particular group of people, encompassing language, religion, cuisine, social habits, music, and arts. Principles and standards of behavior are more important to a high-performing team than language, religion, cuisine, social habits, and music and art preferences. Go with values over culture.

How to Continue to Strengthen Your Team As You Grow—Metcalfe's "Other Law"

When your company increases in size and complexity, the requirements for your leadership team change as well. A successful sales vice president in a new startup might lack the skills and experience the company needs when it scales to dozens of account managers across multiple geographic locations. What do you do when someone on your team is no longer a good fit?

You probably know Metcalfe's law, which in essence says the value of a network grows as the square of the number of its users. I met Bob Metcalfe several years ago at a technology conference in Nantucket. He was participating on a panel with several CEOs and venture capitalists. Actually, "performing" is more accurate than "participating." Panelists who have shared a stage with Bob say that he made them feel like they need to step up their game. An article in *Wired* once described his style. "Seeing Bob Metcalfe on a panel is like watching Charlie Parker, the famous jazz soloist, sitting in with a high school band."

After the panel adjourned, many of us swarmed the stage to learn more. Someone asked, "Bob, can you tell us what it was like launching 3Com?" I remember his story like it was yesterday. But because I don't always remember yesterday perfectly, I apologize to Bob in advance for any errors as I retell his response.

> I cofounded 3Com in my Palo Alto apartment in 1979 with three colleagues. A potential investor told me we needed to establish roles and titles for each of us. Based solely on the criteria that I was the oldest, our team decided that I should be CEO.
>
> In 1982, our board replaced me as CEO and asked me to accept the role of vice president of sales and marketing. I needed to build my sales team quickly, but I didn't have many qualified

candidates. I asked Dave, a production engineer without any sales experience, to head sales for the entire eastern region. I based this huge decision on two criteria which, in retrospect, seem unwise: Dave was single, and his dad was in sales.

Dave worked hard and learned quickly. Sales began to double. As the company grew, I "promoted" Dave from running the entire eastern region to managing the northeastern region. That might not seem like a promotion, but I explained to him that his new role was much bigger than the job that I gave him two years earlier. Dave understood.

Again, he succeeded, and again, I promoted him, this time to head sales in the D.C. metro area. Sales there doubled, and Dave went down the staircase again to head private label sales in D.C.

As you scale your startup, you'll discover that some people on your initial team can't proportionally scale their performance to keep up with the increased responsibilities that come with growth. In a small, successful startup, the jobs grow faster than the people. In a large company, it's the other way around. You'll be faced with a decision: Should you keep an executive in a role where he no longer has the skills and experience to give you the best chance to succeed? Should you replace him? Or should you hire someone to be his boss and demote him?

But if you believe that he can continue to provide value, you can think about the problem differently. "Promote" him to a job where he will be successful. And explain that this new opportunity has more scope, complexity, challenges, and compensation than his current job offers.

Fast-growing organizations always face the Peter Principle: In a hierarchy, every employee tends to rise to his level of incompetence.

Metcalfe's "Other Law" solves that dilemma: In a fast-growing startup, you can redefine the hierarchy so that every talented employee can continue to rise to higher levels of responsibility—while maintaining their level of competence.

Parting Thoughts

- If your startup grows faster than your ability to recruit new employees, or expands beyond your current leadership team's management capabilities, you either have to adjust your growth or adjust the way that you think about solving those problems. When faced with that choice, it's time to think out of the box. Carol re-engineered recruiting and her Hiring Hack enabled CTP–Europe to recruit more talented employees than anyone believed possible—at a small fraction of the cost. Bob Metcalfe redefined the hierarchy of his fast growing startup so that every talented employee could continue to rise to higher levels of responsibility—while maintaining their level of competence.

- Focus on institutionalizing a set of *shared values*. Values are a person's principles or standards of behavior—one's judgment of what is important in life. Culture is a group's lifestyle, customs, and traditions. I believe that *values* captures a much more important construct than does *culture*.

- Remember, "It's amazing what people are willing to do to make a startup successful." And never forget, if you know that you are meeting in the sauna after dinner, be careful not to eat too much!

It's time to talk about finding your exit. I'll cover that next.

• • •

Part 4

Exiting

*Happiness is not in the mere possession of money;
it lies in the joy of achievement, in the thrill of
creative effort.*

– President Franklin D. Roosevelt

CHAPTER NINETEEN

Finding Your Exit

Do what you love and success will follow. Passion is the fuel behind a successful career.

– Meg Whitman, former CEO, Hewlett Packard and eBay

HAVING AN EXIT plan is both conventional wisdom and bad advice. Never base your operating decisions on achieving a specific exit strategy. There are too many unknowns and too many factors that you cannot control. Instead, focus on building a special company. If you do that, you are setting the best course regardless of any twists and turns that the economy or the market takes.

At ZEFER, I followed that bad advice and developed a beautifully well-thought-out exit plan.

I raised $100 million, with an agreement to return the cash that remained after an exit—without receiving additional equity. That created an incentive to spend, but theoretically to spend wisely. For example, office space was at a premium. ZEFER avoided the exorbitant rental costs from hitting our financial statements by entering into long-term leases and investing capital to renovate the properties. That practice lowered our operating costs and gave us an edge over our competitors that were going public. I applied that principle wherever I could, using "free" capital to make investments that improved ZEFER's bottom line. My board told me our approach was brilliant. It made us much more attractive when we filed our IPO. But as I described earlier, a stock market crash of historic proportions derailed our public offering. That was followed by a major recession that dramatically reduced the cost of office space, leaving us stuck with higher rent than any of our competitors and long-term leases that we couldn't break. After I reduced the size of ZEFER's team, much of our office space sat empty. I had made decisions to maximize ZEFER's enterprise value for a preset point in time but didn't build in enough flexibility. That's when my board asked, "Who the hell made that bone-headed decision?"

Exit plans encourage a CEO to make decisions that maximize a company's value at a targeted point in time. But if the market, economy, industry, or technology changes, brilliant decisions can quickly become bone-headed mistakes.

Don't "Sell" Your Company—Wait for Someone to "Buy" It

My ZEFER experience hasn't stopped me from pondering potential exits. But it's shaped how I think of them. Now, I think about what a good acquirer would look like and which assets would make my company more attractive. But when I'm operating, I try to make decisions that will enable me to build a better company. I focus on profitable growth and customer retention. I try to recruit and develop an exceptionally strong team. I leverage all of that to build a network and to create buzz to ensure my startup ends up on the radar screen of potential acquirers. Instead of launching a process to sell my company, I'll wait for the right acquirer to contact me. I know I'll get a better deal if the acquirer is the one doing the pursuing. I'm in no rush. I can wait for the best opportunity because I don't have an exit plan.

Don't Be Greedy

I've also learned to not be greedy. Often, a smaller exit generates a better result. When I work with a new startup, I'll ask the CEO and their key executives, "What are your personal and professional objectives?" I will never invest my time or money in a startup whose CEO tells me that their ambition is to take their company public or to create the next unicorn. That attitude signals to me that the CEO cares more about ego and fame than about building a successful company. Larger startups:

- take longer to build;

- face lower odds of a successful exit;

- require more venture capital for fuel, resulting in more dilution for the founders; and

- have a smaller pool of potential acquirers that can afford the price.

Traditional wisdom is that "a small percentage of a big number is always better than a bigger percentage of a small number." Often, it's just the opposite.

What Should You Do Before You Get "the Call?"

- Focus on revenue and profit growth, repeatable revenue, and building long-term relationships with blue-chip customers.

- Choose operating metrics that might be important to your potential acquirer and religiously use them to manage your company.

- Build an exceptionally strong leadership team that will convince potential acquirers that your company is more than just you.

- Expand your network to include CEOs of companies in your industry that have been acquired so you can learn more about the market, valuations, and the acquisition and integration processes.

- Connect with several investment bankers to pick their brains about potential acquirers and company valuations and to understand their engagement models. Find the bankers that "get" what your company does and narrow down who you would work with in the future.

- Establish relationships with industry analysts. You don't have to engage them—they are expensive. You will get more attention from the key analysts as a prospect than you will as a client. Analysts are always on the hunt for case studies about customers. Try to get several of your customers to grant permission to share their stories.

- Ramp up your marketing investments. Win awards, find ways to be featured in the press, speak at events, and announce the blue-chip customers that you win. Generate buzz.

In summary, make good business decisions.

What Should You Do When You Do Get "the Call?"

When I receive "the call," I start by saying, "I very much respect your firm and am flattered that you reached out to me. However, I'm not looking to sell my company at this time. I see tremendous growth opportunities in the years ahead that I believe will significantly increase our value. But as CEO, I have a fiduciary responsibility to consider any M&A opportunity. So, I'm open to meeting." The acquirer knows that's bullshit, but it sets the stage. Let the games begin!

After both parties sign a nondisclosure agreement, come to your first meeting prepared to:

- showcase how your operating metrics have continued to improve over time;

- share a list of your key customers, explain why they selected you, and highlight the impact that you have had on them;

- talk about your growth projections and what's driving your optimism; and

- discuss the potential synergies between the companies, for example, customers, products and services, or geographies.

Do not bring an acquisition pitch deck. Remember, you aren't trying to sell your company. You're meeting because you are open, perhaps even intrigued, by the opportunity. If an acquirer asks why you might be open to selling, tell them that you feel it would be easier for you to grow as part of a larger company that has previously experienced the growing pains you are just starting to encounter and that has the financial and sales and marketing resources you need to accelerate your growth. Make the story about building your company more quickly, not about an exit.

Inform your board. Understand their drivers and constraints. Is an all-cash deal more important to them than a higher multiple? Are earnouts (changes to the purchase price driven by your company's performance after closing) acceptable? What level of holdbacks (an escrow of a portion of the purchase price to protect against breaches of covenants and inaccuracies in representations and warranties) would be okay? Also, learn how the board would like to be involved in the process. Typically, one of the directors will be assigned as the point person on the deal.

Decide if you want to launch a sales process in response to the outreach. The potential acquirer that contacted you won't like it if you do. In their mind, that move creates competition for the deal that will drive the price up. And that's exactly why you may decide to do it. If you do launch a sales process, blame it on your board. Hire someone to lead it. Consider engaging one of the investment bankers that "gets" what you do. If you decide not to initiate a sales process, it's still advisable to hire someone to lead your negotiations. You'll get a higher valuation and better terms, without investing 80 percent of your time in the process and without pissing off your potential new boss during negotiations.

Prepare your acquisition pitch deck. It's not the same as your customer pitch deck or your investor deck, even though it will contain material from both. Brag about your leadership team. Make certain that the acquirer knows that the company isn't just you—you have an exceptionally strong team backing you up. Showcase opportunities that confirm your differentiators and your go-to-market strategy. Identify synergies. Highlight the assets that you have built that will act as a "tip of the spear" to an acquirer's business. Help them feel confident that they aren't just buying your revenue stream and that you'll impact their core revenue stream as well.

Make certain that all of your executives will benefit from the sale. Include a few key managers in the sales process. But don't broadcast that you are exploring a sale to the entire leadership team until you have to. Conveying the message too soon could distract them from focusing on running the business. Any operational hiccup at this time could have a devastating impact on the deal.

What Do You Need to Know About Structuring the Deal?

After you and your acquirer agree on the broad terms of a deal, they will prepare a term sheet. It should define:

- the aggregate purchase price and whether the consideration will be cash, stock, or financing;

- "earnouts"—deferring a portion of the price until you achieve your revenue and profit projections;

- purchase price adjustments—adjustments to purchase price based on financial metrics such as working capital at closing;

- the handling and any acceleration of stock options;

- "holdbacks"—withholding payment of a portion of the purchase price until some post-closing condition has been satisfied;

- employees who will be offered employment with the acquiring company and details of "noncompete" agreements;

- how the transaction will be structured for tax purposes; and

- how your investors' liquidation preferences will apply. Make certain that you understand the impact that will have on your proceeds.

How Do You Crack the Code in a Term Sheet?

Invest the time to clearly understand how the deal structure will impact you and your team, both financially and structurally. Who will you report to? How will your responsibilities change? Will anyone lose their job? Engage your personal attorney to advise you.

The term sheet will also specify if the transaction is an asset sale (the purchase of individual assets and liabilities) or a stock sale (the purchase of the owner's shares of the startup). That distinction has tax implications and will determine potential liabilities.

If all of those considerations disproportionly shift the proceeds to the investors, negotiate carve-outs to redistribute a percentage of the proceeds to key employees as an incentive for them to facilitate the acquisition.

All of these factors came into play when a potential acquirer made me an offer to buy the healthcare portion of one of my businesses. It looked like a great deal, carrying a multiple of revenue much higher than I expected. The only problem: I didn't have a healthcare business that I could carve out and sell. I had a consulting company that generated 40 percent of its revenue from healthcare clients. We were organized by geography, not industry. Only six of our four hundred employees were dedicated to healthcare. Everyone else was a generalist. But the valuation was attractive, so my board wanted to pursue it.

Because most of our consultants served both healthcare and non-healthcare clients, we knew that breaking up our teams would disrupt both ongoing projects and key client relationships. We determined which employees would be assigned to each entity just like we did as kids picking teams on the playground in elementary school—a corporate version of rock-paper-scissors. We continued to forge ahead and began to negotiate terms.

The buyer preferred an asset deal, with proceeds that were 40 percent stock and 60 percent cash. Our investors wanted a stock deal because that limited the company's liabilities while reducing taxes on the transaction. They also demanded an all-cash deal. The buyer was willing to concede, but only if our investors agreed to accept a significant reduction in our valuation. They did, and we reached a verbal understanding.

That's when my investors informed me that 100 percent of their liquidation preferences would kick in when we closed the deal. A liquidation preference enables investors to get their money back first, ahead of other stockholders or debtholders, when a company is sold or liquidated. I was shocked to learn their interpretation of "liquidation" would apply to our selling only 40 percent of the business. That certainly was not in the spirit of our agreement and would result in a significant cash distribution to our investors instead of our employees. It also came with tax problems. Under this arrangement, the proceeds would be taxed once when they flowed to our consulting company and taxed again when our investors withdrew their funds. But if we formed a new company and transferred all the non-healthcare assets to the new entity at an artificially reduced valuation, our investors could avoid double taxation. Unfortunately, that created another problem. The surviving company wouldn't have any cash.

I pointed out that the transaction had become much more attractive to our investors at the expense of our employees. The venture capitalists (VC) who owned 60 percent of the company would receive almost all of the proceeds. Losing our healthcare clients, combined with transferring so many of our key consultants to the new venture, would decimate our business. After the transaction closed, we would have to carry an overhead structure that was 40 percent higher than what we could afford. We'd have to terminate a large number of employees and shut down several offices to survive. Most significantly, our company wouldn't have any cash because all of the proceeds would flow directly to our investors. And when we attempted to raise money, we'd be penalized by the artificially reduced valuation that our VCs created to solve their double-taxation problem. It was a terrible deal that was unfair to the employees that built the company. But our investors already knew that.

I requested a carve-out for several of our key employees. The VCs replied, "We won't agree to that now, but we'll take care of you after the deal closes. Don't worry, you can trust us."

I didn't. The acquisition had evolved to a point where I could no longer support it.

Are Binding Term Sheets Always "Binding?"

After you receive a term sheet, do not change how you manage your startup. It's business as usual until the transaction closes. I sat on the board of a consulting company that received and accepted an attractive offer from a software company. They wanted to acquire the firm because they valued the team and wanted to redirect them to work on a new software platform that they were building. The acquirer told them that they were not interested in any of their clients or professional services revenue and suggested that they shouldn't close any new business that would commit their team to new client engagements.

As soon as I heard that caveat, I screamed, "Don't listen to that! The deal might not go through, and you'll be stuck with dwindling revenue and no pipeline. If the deal does go through, the acquirer will rationalize lowering the price because you'll miss your revenue forecast. And your only alternative will be to accept whatever reduced price they offer, because you will have abandoned most of your clients and lost much of your revenue. Don't do that!"

They didn't listen to my advice, stopped selling, and began winding down their current projects. The acquirer reduced the price significantly. The "attractive" deal collapsed, and the sixty-person rapidly growing company became six people trying to survive. Do not let the excitement of any deal distract you and your team from running the business wisely.

Why Should You Be Wary of "Holdbacks?"

One of my software startups was acquired by a very large enterprise software company. As part of our deal, they asked for our assurance that two named key customers would stay on board for at least two years. Those clients were delighted with our solution and our responsiveness, so we agreed that the buyer could hold back several million dollars until we reached that two-year milestone.

Soon after the transaction closed, our buyer informed both key clients that they would no longer honor the software modifications and enhancements that we had committed to before the acquisition. They followed that pronouncement by increasing their support fees while dramatically reducing their responsiveness. They already had hundreds of key customers; one or two incremental clients weren't terribly important to them. Within twelve months, both clients bailed out and engaged a new software vendor who promised them the attention and responsiveness they were accustomed to with us. Our acquirer then informed us that, because the two key clients had left, they would not return our "holdback." It didn't matter that they caused the defections. It just mattered that they had a much larger legal budget than we did.

Avoid holdbacks if you can. And if you can't, precisely define the assurances that you need from the buyer to ensure that you can hit your targets. Formalize the arrangement in the form of post-closing covenants that are documented in the deal.

Why Should You Be Wary of "Earnouts?"

The acquirer will look at your revenue and profit projections and attempt to defer a portion of the price until they are reached. After all, you're the one who projected the numbers. You should be able to achieve them.

However, the assumptions that you used to forecast those revenue and profit levels may change after an acquisition. Your forecast may be easier to achieve because you can now leverage your buyer's brand and larger sales force. But it's more likely that it will be more difficult to hit because you don't have as much control.

I believe that earnouts are also bad for the acquirer, especially for a technology consulting firm. They encourage the acquired company to place their own goals ahead of the parent company's objectives. That can suboptimize the impact of an acquisition.

Parting Thoughts

- Don't create an exit plan that ties you to an outcome at a specific date.

- It's good to have an exit strategy that identifies who the best acquirers are and what you need to do to get onto their radar screens.

- Prepare by meeting with bankers, industry analysts, and startup CEOs that have recently gone through the process. But when you're operating, make decisions that will enable you to build a better company. Focus on revenue and profit growth, repeatable revenue, building long-term relationships with blue-chip customers, and generating buzz.

- Don't "sell" your company—wait for someone to "buy" it.

- If you launch a sales process, engage someone to run it. Trying to lead it on your own is penny wise and pound foolish. You'll divert too much time away from operating your business, leave money on the table by not negotiating as good an outcome, and very likely piss-off your new boss in the process.

- Term sheets can be very complex. Engage your own attorney to understand how the transaction will personally impact you and your team.

- The exit process embraces very high highs and very low lows. It brings with it many opportunities for mistakes that could have a significant impact on your outcome.

Perhaps the best way to understand an exit process is to live through one. Allow me to be your tour guide for ZEFER's IPO roadshow.

• • •

CHAPTER TWENTY

Fireworks on a Foggy Night— ZEFER's IPO Roadshow

The fog of illusion, the fog of confusion is hanging all over all the world.

– Van Morrison, singer-songwriter

Launching ZEFER — 1999

I LAUNCHED ZEFER in March 1999, staked by $100 million from a single investor. We were quick out of the gate and hit $4 million of revenue in our first quarter of business. That first year, we opened offices in Boston, Chicago, New York, and Pittsburgh. Our competitors focused on the "easy pickins" of dot-com startups. I avoided them, instead targeting blue-chip clients including Barclays, Burger King, CitiGroup, GE, Gillette, HJ Heinz, Morgan Stanley, Sara Lee, and Siemens. Seventeen of our clients each generated more than $1 million in annualized revenue in 1999. We ended our first year in business with $33.1 million revenue and 480 employees. Our unprecedented performance, accompanied by the Nasdaq composite soaring 85.6 percent in 1999, compelled my board to unanimously agree to file ZEFER's IPO.

First Quarter 2000

ZEFER's first quarter in 2000 was our strongest yet—a 38 percent revenue increase over our previous quarter. Thirty-eight percent year-over-year is rapid growth but achieving that quarter-over-quarter is a rocket ship, especially for a professional services firm. We grew headcount to 675 employees, and our active client base to seventy-eight including brand names like AT&T, Ford, and Johnson & Johnson. ZEFER had become one of the darlings of the internet. That meant we were celebrities. Every snooty party had to include an author, a musician, a politician, and an internet CEO. Riding that momentum, we began our IPO roadshow on March 28.

Shortly before that, in early March, our sole investor requested that we swap $25 million of their equity commitment for $25 million in their subordinated debt fund—without changing their ownership position. Assuming $25 million in debt without any compensation in return seemed like a bad deal to me, so I pushed back hard. But the conversion of their equity commitment to debt was a device that they strongly wanted to pursue. They argued, "Since we are your sole investor, any interest expense that ZEFER incurs would simply be us paying ourselves back with our own money." Finally, they said, "You shouldn't spend any more time debating this because ZEFER is about to go public, and as soon as that happens, you can pay off the debt." Their request didn't feel right to me, but the board reluctantly agreed. That proved to be a serious mistake.

ZEFER's IPO Roadshow—Second Quarter 2000

In April 2000, ZEFER was completing its IPO roadshow that began with banker and investor expectations of a valuation ranging from $1.8 billion to $2.2 billion. Our three weeks on the road pitching to investors began strong, but the huge, daily market fluctuations impacted our valuation and frazzled our nerves.

It's difficult to describe what an IPO roadshow is like. You'll experience highs, lows, and everything in between. Days are long, nights are short, and you wonder how you can sustain the energy that you need to get through it. I think the best way to paint a picture of the experience is to share, verbatim, the diary of updates that I emailed to ZEFER's employees at the end of each day.

Monday, March 27 (TD Garden, Boston)

Everyone advised me to start our roadshow with a good night's sleep. They cautioned that three weeks on the road, with ninety-eight presentations over fourteen business days, would be grueling. Instead, I started with a late-night Crosby, Stills, Nash & Young concert. I couldn't resist—they were my favorite band since college. Each of Crosby, Stills, and Nash was elected to the Rock & Roll Hall of Fame—four times—as members of CSN&Y, as members of their previous bands (The Byrds, Buffalo Springfield, and the Hollies), as individual performers, and as songwriters. And Neil Young was inducted twice. Fourteen Hall of Fame awards in total. And they did not disappoint.

I don't know if it was driven by the excitement from the concert or opening night jitters but sleep that night did not come easily. I stopped trying at 4:00 a.m. and got out of bed to attend to a long list of last-minute "to-dos."

Tuesday, March 28 (Boston–Baltimore)

We completed our final rehearsal. David Lubin, our vice chair, participated and helped us prepare for the questions that potential investors were likely to ask. Of course, David couldn't resist attempting to convince us to revise our entire presentation one last time.

We compromised and added a section on the *Multiplier Effect*, a phrase we coined that described a phenomenon where the first set of client requirements leads to a strategy engagement, which in turn drives an entirely new portfolio of implementation opportunities. Then we departed to present to the Robbie Stephens equity sales team. Jim (CFO), Cindy (investor relations), Tony (founder of the original ZEFER), and I, along with Travis (our Credit Suisse First Boston analyst) piled into a stretch limo to begin our roadshow.

After sitting virtually motionless in traffic for ten minutes, I asked, "Where is our first meeting?"

"One International Place," Travis replied. So even though the first leg of our twenty-thousand-mile journey was only two blocks from our office, we arrived ten minutes late. The Robbie Stephens team was patiently waiting for us, fourteen people in the conference room connected by video conference to countless others in six locations. Our presentation flowed perfectly, the technology worked, and the Robbie Stephens salesforce seemed to get our message. And David was right. The *Multiplier Effect* message was a hit! After a strong performance responding to their questions, we headed to Baltimore for an early morning meeting with the First Union equity sales force, now feeling very confident.

Wednesday, March 29 (Baltimore–New York–Amsterdam)

We met at 6:15 a.m. and headed to First Union for a 6:45 a.m. presentation. Even though it was much earlier than any of us were accustomed to being awake—much less making a formal presentation— we had no difficulty getting energized. Our pitch to the forty people in the audience, simultaneously broadcast to several other locations, was even stronger than yesterday's delivery. We ended with another robust Q&A session and rushed to catch a train to New York. The five of us were lugging fifteen bags—including eight laptops, six sets of computer speakers, and a week's worth of handouts. Train aisles were not designed to accommodate that kind of traffic. But we were able to push our way through eight cars until we finally found our reserved seats. We were off to New York!

We arrived in New York at lunchtime. Tony stopped several people in the street to ask them if they have heard of ZEFER's IPO yet. No one had. We concluded that we probably needed to give the salesforce a little more time.

We had a few hours before our Credit Suisse First Boston (CSFB) pitch and used it to preview our roadshow pitch with ZEFER's New York team. We arrived at CSFB's offices at 2:00 p.m. and called into a large conference room. The setup felt more like a Senate hearing than an IPO pitch.

Thirty-five salespeople waited for us. Every seat was taken. We were escorted to a raised stage equipped with five individual microphones. Our slides were projected on a screen behind us, and a very small screen at the far end of the room provided us the only clue of what the audience was seeing. Video cameras recorded our presentation and broadcasted it to twelve other locations, making the setting even more intimidating. I couldn't think of a worse time for our technology to crash, and so—of course—it did.

Our five minutes of ad-libbing seemed like hours. But that gave Cindy enough time to find a way to load our backup slides. The animation no longer worked, and most of the graphics were missing—but we got through it successfully. Our audience was engaged and asked many good questions. The entire salesforce followed us out of the room to squeeze in a few more as we rushed to catch our 8:30 p.m. flight to Amsterdam. The long flight gave us time to reflect on our first two days of presenting to our banker's sales teams.

- Our message is compelling, and our differentiators are clear.

- We deliver our story credibly.

- Even with an occasional technical problem, our message resonates with our audience.

We caught a few hours of sleep and felt very confident about the next day's initial meetings with investors.

Thursday, March 30 (Amsterdam)

We landed in Amsterdam at 12:30 p.m., exited customs and immigration, and loaded the cars. Luckily, before we left, we discovered that Cindy had left five of our bags on a luggage cart in customs—including all of our computers!

Jet lag!

Dutch immigration wasn't equipped for Americans to re-enter after leaving. But after about an hour, Jason, another one of our CSFB analysts, returned with the recovered luggage, everything intact.

We checked into our hotel, showered, and departed for two late-afternoon investor meetings. Both went very well. While all of us were running short on sleep, as a former Amsterdam resident, I was obligated to play tour guide and show my team a memorable evening.

Friday, March 31 (Amsterdam–Edinburgh–London)

An early morning meeting with a Dutch investor went exceptionally well. We could feel the momentum starting to build.

The next meeting was in Edinburgh, so we raced to the airport. We arrived to hear "Flight 85 to Edinburgh is having serious technical difficulties and is not going anywhere for a long time." After a tense hour, we learned that a replacement plane and crew were on the way.

We landed in Edinburgh tight for time and arrived at Scottish Equitable with only minutes to spare. Another great meeting! This was beginning to feel like fun! Next stop—Edinburgh Fund Managers for a meeting with two investors. Then a quick sandwich in the car while we traveled to Scottish Widows. The last two meetings went well, but we couldn't read whether or not we had convinced any investors to be buyers.

After four presentations in two countries, we reached the end of our day and headed to the airport for our flight to London.

Monday, April 3 (London–New York–Pontiac)

I tossed and turned for much of the night. Shouldn't "opening night jitters" be cured after a week on the road?

Our morning began at 7:30 a.m. in preparation for our 8:00 a.m. presentation. Andrew promptly arrived, introduced himself as a portfolio manager, and sat at the head of the table. He began by asking, "Why should I buy your stock, other than the fact that CSFB's financial model is absurdly understated—and you should be able to crush it in your sleep?"

All of us gulped down as much coffee as we could drink because we knew that we were in for an intense start to the day. Portfolio managers attend these presentations for a number of reasons. They may have decided in advance to buy—and are there for confirmation. Or, they may be there to resolve some open questions that the red herring prospectus didn't answer. Others are there to be convinced. Occasionally, a portfolio manager is simply curious. Andrew was there for an intellectual debate—and we were ready for him!

After an hour and a quarter of being challenged and standing up to it, the meeting ended. Andrew shook our hands and said, "I really like you guys. I like your story. And I want to come to Boston to see you."

Bloody well done!

Next stop—a luncheon meeting that brought together a number of investors from the UK, Germany, and Switzerland. Our team nailed it— our best presentation yet!

After the luncheon, we hurried off to three scheduled afternoon presentations. By the end of the day, I began to feel disorientated and asked myself, "Did I already say that?" or "Did I just cover the same slide twice?" My most embarrassing moment came as I reviewed the credentials of our management team. I intended to say, "I am very proud that we were able to recruit Doug, the chief creative officer of Viant." Instead, it came out as, "I am very proud that we were able to recruit Doug, the chief corrective officer of Violent." Oops.

Disorientation also resulted in our confusing the statistics that we presented. With every meeting, Tony increased the results from the latest survey on CEOs who "take the internet as their direct responsibility." In five sequential meetings, it went from 22 percent who reported they do, to 25 percent, then 30 percent, 33 percent, and finally to 35 percent. Cindy and I placed a side bet that he would reach 50 percent by the end of our roadshow.

Cindy and Tony made a similar side bet on me. Investors continued to ask about my experience at Cambridge Technology Partners (CTP) and what I learned there. It was important that I convinced them I understood what went wrong at CTP so they would be confident that I wouldn't make the same mistakes at ZEFER. Anticipating that question, I had prepared my answer in advance, and responded by telling them about the *7 Deadly Sins* that impeded CTP's continued success. My problem was that I lost track of where I was in my narrative and never ended up listing exactly seven sins. My low was three and my high was twelve. Fortunately, no one but Cindy was counting.

It was 6:00 p.m., and the day finally ended. But not really. We still had a one-hour drive to Heathrow, a flight to New York on the Concord, a shuttle to a private airport thirty minutes away to meet Walt, our lead CSFB analyst, and then a forty-five-minute flight in a G3 that CSFB chartered for the week. Our flight attendant told me that we were flying on the plane that Denzel Washington had chartered the week before. And the same one that Martha Stewart used for her roadshow last October. Walt commented that she raised $121 million and that her company was now valued at $2 billion. If Martha could do it, so could we!

After we landed in Pontiac, Michigan, we took another thirty-minute limo ride to our hotel. As I got ready for bed, I glanced at my watch that was still set for UK time and realized that we've had a twenty-three-hour day. I had only six hours before my team would meet in the lobby to do it all over again.

Tuesday, April 4 (Pontiac–Minneapolis–Milwaukee–Boston)

Our first presentation was a breakfast meeting without breakfast, where we attempted to conduct a multimedia presentation to two investors in a corner of a hotel restaurant, near the bar.

I wasn't clear about the protocol we should follow. Should we be animated at the breakfast table? I am accustomed to hushed tones at breakfast. Should we whisper? Or should we project? Unfortunately, the hotel kitchen used the blender on the bar next to us, and it seemed like everyone in Pontiac was ordering smoothies that morning. We got through it, but it wasn't one of our best efforts.

Back to the airport, and off to Minneapolis for two more presentations. The first was with Curt, a portfolio manager that Walt warned "can be very antagonistic." Walt was right. After we arrived, Curt began with, "I don't want to see ZEFER's presentation. Just tell me why you want to go public." We were ready for this and provided a solid response.

Curt continued with a series of increasingly difficult questions. Then he paused and reflected, "Let me give you my advice. You appear to be a very solid company with an exciting story and a great team. My advice is 'do not go public.' The market is too crowded. In fact, I see companies like yours every day. And I can tell you that I have not recommended buying their stocks, any of them, for the last nine months. And there is nothing that you can say today to get me to consider changing my position and buy your stock." We glanced at our watches and saw that fifty minutes of our one-hour meeting still remained.

By the end of the meeting, Curt had become excited about ZEFER. He asked to be included on our earnings calls and on any announcements. I didn't know whether or not he would be a buyer at our IPO, but I thought he'd invest in us at some point. When he did, he'd be a long-term holder. And that's more important.

Next, off to a luncheon presentation. On the way, we heard that the Nasdaq was crashing—down another five-hundred points. And the decline was driven by technology stocks. What a week to be pitching our IPO. The market concerns caused our luncheon to be sparsely attended—only two investors. Their attention was elsewhere. No one wanted to leave their desks. Walt told us that he expected to begin to hear direct feedback from portfolio managers the next day.

We were off again to the airport for two meetings in Milwaukee. Both were very positive. And even though we were exhausted, it was almost beginning to feel like fun again.

David's *Multiplier Effect* had not only found its way into the presentation—it had become central. We used the phrase a record of eight times in a single presentation.

We landed in Boston at 9:00 p.m., all of us really looking forward to sleeping in our own beds. But I tossed and turned because I was both worried about the market and investor reactions to ZEFER's story. I'd been told that a jittery market's effect on a company like ours would be substantially less than what it would for a secondary offering. But was the market just jittery? Or would it become much worse than that?

We were dying to hear real investor feedback. Almost everyone that we pitched to understood our story and left visibly excited. But would the market spook them? Would they be buyers? Would they be long-term holders? And did anyone really understand the *Multiplier Effect?*

Wednesday, April 5 (Boston)

I had a great night's sleep at home—six hours in my own bed! Re-energized, I was ready for a day packed with eight presentations.

Our first meeting was with one of the premier portfolio managers in Boston, and their response was very positive. But as we rushed to our next presentation, Walt informed me that the portfolio manager decided not to buy. "You did as well as you possibly could," Walt said. "The portfolio manager really liked ZEFER's story. But in this market, he's not willing to increase his exposure in the technology sector."

I didn't have time to feel crushed. Our next presentation was already beginning. We just had to turn it up another notch. The next portfolio manager began by asking, "Who is the Harvard guy? Is he here?" We took advantage of the opportunity to introduce him to Tony. It felt like this meeting could become difficult. We did not have a chance to cover a single slide. Instead, we were grilled with sixty minutes of tougher and tougher questions.

At the end of the meeting, the portfolio manager summarized: "You know, I didn't even want to take this meeting. I told Walt, before we began, that there was not a chance that I would be a buyer. But you have totally changed my mind. I am in. You guys are great!"

We were now pumped!

Our third meeting went just as well. We now felt ready for Boston's investor lunch—always the toughest stop on every roadshow. Our bankers recounted story after story about Boston lunch bloodbaths. One of our competitors had pitched there yesterday and was "totally destroyed." We were reassured when we saw some friendly faces in the forty-person audience, including David and several other members of ZEFER's leadership team.

Although the questions were tough and occasionally antagonistic, we nailed it! Our most difficult challenge was, "You have only been in business for a year. You are a very young company. And you are going public earlier than any of your peers ever have, and by a large margin. Why?"

Our bold answer: "Because we are ready."

Two of the investors approached us after the presentation and told us, "We see more than twenty roadshows each and every week. This was the best pitch we have ever seen." Wow!

By the end of the day, our energy level became increasingly more difficult to sustain. We had tried our best and felt like we got through the day successfully. After dinner, we left for the airport, then arrived at our next stop, Baltimore, at 12:30 a.m.

Thursday, April 6 (Baltimore–Philadelphia–New York City)

Our first meeting began at 6:45 a.m. Another short night. After that, a two-hour car ride to Philadelphia for three meetings. The mood there was somber. No one was smiling. But the portfolio managers' feedback to Walt was consistently positive. As we were told, you never know whether or not a meeting will lead to a sale. Cindy reassured me that the tougher the audience, the better we do.

We headed to the airport for a flight to New York. We arrived at our hotel by 3:30 p.m., and actually had time for a nap. I used the evening to close the deal to hire our chief operating officer candidate over dinner at Rue 57. Just because we were on the road, we couldn't stop running the business.

Friday, April 7 (New York City–Boston)

At 5:15 a.m., my clock radio stirred me from a deep sleep, playing "For What It's Worth," my favorite song that Crosby, Stills, Nash & Young performed on the eve of our roadshow. Something *was* happening here that wasn't exactly clear. I took that as a sign that today would be a rough day.

Our first meeting at 6:45 a.m. was with a portfolio manager that I wanted to shake. If you believe that there is no such thing as a bad question, keep reading:

- "Was it a coincidence that both your company and Tony's were named 'ZEFER?' Is that why you merged?"

- "Is strategy-led why you transitioned from Siebel (Tom Siebel's software company—no relation to me) to Vantive (a different CRM company that one of our acquisitions partnered with)?"

I never got through to him.

After the three meetings that followed, we received our first dribble of investor feedback. Given the market, we were doing pretty well. But— given the market, we needed to ratchet up our performance another notch.

By the end of our eighth meeting, the team was brain-dead. Getting pumped up for our last meeting was probably the hardest thing that I had ever done. I was ready for the weekend. All of us were.

The team boarded the G3. The last thing that I heard before nodding off is Tony asking, "Dad—are we there yet?"

We arrived in Boston at 8:30 p.m.

Monday, April 10 (Boston–Denver–San Francisco)

Our team flew to Denver on Sunday evening. We began Monday with a morning planning meeting. Everyone appeared relaxed for what we expected would be a relatively easy day. It occurred to me that the phrase "relatively easy day" had evolved to a new meaning. Before the roadshow, I would have described today's schedule as intense: a 6:30 a.m. start, four major investor presentations, a capital markets meeting, a flight to San Francisco, a meeting with Red Herring, another with a potential customer, two hours of media training, then a dinner with the ZEFER–San Francisco leadership team. Seventeen and a half hours—a relatively easy day.

On the way to our second meeting, I called Lindy, my admin in Boston. She told me that she received the photos I had emailed. "Are you guys working?" she asked. "All the pictures are of you dining, drinking, or flying on a private jet. You must really be enjoying yourselves." I didn't have time to respond because our next presentation was beginning.

As we walked into one of the top fund management firms in the world, Walt remarked "Did you notice the lobby? There are no other roadshows here. Three weeks ago, it would have been standing room only. Today you are the only company they are willing to see."

I glanced at the monitor on the trading desk. The Nasdaq was down 250 points. Time to ramp up our energy level once again.

Another good meeting. We discovered afterward that they were in for a full allocation of stock, but only for the trade. In other words, they were not a long-term holder.

The remaining meetings were not remarkable but went well. On the way to the airport, we discussed how we were holding up. Cindy informed us that we had already gone through six sets of PC speakers. I quipped, "We're holding up better than our equipment."

We arrived in San Francisco for media training, followed by dinner with ZEFER's San Francisco leadership team. I fell asleep by 11:00 p.m.

Tuesday, April 11 (San Francisco–San Diego)

A three-hour time difference. I woke to the Nasdaq report—down another one hundred points. We have been on the roadshow for twelve business days, and the market significantly dropped on ten of them. We needed a good break.

We held two morning meetings with potential investors. Almost everyone that we presented to in the last two weeks seemed interested, but not many buy orders had been placed. And those that had were smaller than expected—placeholders in a volatile market.

We were beginning to feel a hint of desperation and hoped that our luncheon meeting would be hugely successful and begin to turn the tide. A large number of potential buyers would be there. Everything must go perfectly.

The meeting began with the projector screen toppling onto a table, upsetting it and breaking the water glasses and setups. We were so used to environmental distractions that we barely looked up. Cindy resecured the screen, but it was damaged, distorting the left half of our slides. We began our luncheon presentation, and it turned out to be the best of the roadshow. We managed to overcome the distractions and, one more time, ratchet it up a notch!

After our Q&A, an investor approached me to tell me that he wanted to be "a big buyer." I asked him, "How big?" He told me he was in for five thousand shares. I smiled and took his business card.

By the end of the day, we felt a little down. We were doing better than I had expected, but recognized that we were in, as Walt described it, "the most difficult two weeks for technology stocks since 1987." We could have used some good news.

We received some! As we boarded the G3, Karen, ZEFER's chief-of-staff, showed me our first analyst coverage, posted on the web. I beamed when I saw the headline, "Why ZEFER Will Blow Away Web Services Rivals." We knew that no one ever generated coverage on their pre-IPO

277

company. And no one ever posted a "buy" rating for a company three days before it went public. Whoever Steve Tekirian was, he made our week. We were pumped again and ready for another day!

Wednesday, April 12 (San Diego–Los Angeles–Kansas City)

We began the day in San Diego. Tony, Jim, and I were totally comfortable with our presentations and had become a little cocky when responding to questions. For example:

Q. When people leave ZEFER, where do they go?

A. Rarely to the competition. We lose more people to starting their own rock bands than to any of our competitors!

Q. It's become a crowded market. How can I differentiate the players?

A. You are absolutely right! Everyone else is pretty much the same, and I can't tell them apart either.

Q. How do you find your clients? For example, how did you find Hillenbrand Funeral Company?

A. The Hillenbrand executives were in a bar and saw a number of our employees, all dressed in black. They bonded with us immediately!

This was becoming fun again, both for both us and the investors.

Three sessions in Los Angeles followed San Diego. We arranged for another aircraft because our crew had exceeded their permitted travel time. Our team had no such constraint. As we drove to the airport for our flight to Kansas City, the car radio alerted us that the Nasdaq had continued to decline. We arrived at our hotel at midnight.

Thursday, April 13 (Kansas City–Houston)

After our sessions in Kansas City, we flew to Houston. When we arrived, we checked with the CSFB syndicate desk and were delighted to learn that our IPO was basically done! The Nasdaq was up for the first time in three weeks, and we were feeling buoyant. I asked Karen to find a music store and buy every CD with the word "home" in the title. I asked the flight crew to order champagne.

As we completed our final meetings in Houston, I kept an eye on the Nasdaq and watched nervously as the index dropped from a 120-point gain to down 80 points in the final hour of trading. We drove to a hangar at a private airport to take our pricing call.

Once again, I remembered Crosby, Stills, Nash & Young's lyrics from "Déjà Vu" at the beginning of our roadshow. And no, I'd never been here before, and I didn't know what to do. But you already know what happened next. I reconvened the group to announce that after ninety-eight presentations in eighteen cities and five countries, I was pulling our IPO. Perhaps we could try again when the market stabilized.

My team supported my decision, and we boarded our G3 for the last time to contemplate our action plan. We needed to craft a message for our board, investors, clients, partners, the press, and most importantly, our employees. Within an hour, we made all of the most important phone calls and crafted a letter to our employees.

But then the logistical issues surfaced. My wife, Carol, was waiting in New York to spend the evening celebrating with us, expecting to watch ZEFER's first trade on the stock exchange floor the next morning. A CSFB analyst found her on a massage table and drove her to the Teterboro airport to wait for us to retrieve her. And what about our employee celebration that we had planned for the day of our launch? My initial reaction was to cancel it. I attempted to call Boston to pull the plug, but I couldn't get an "airfone" connection. While waiting for the call to go through, I opened my briefcase and found the comments that I had written three weeks earlier, in anticipation of our IPO celebration. They began:

> We aren't here to celebrate ZEFER going public. We're here to celebrate the great company that we all built together. We aren't "great" because we went public. We were able to go public because we built a great company—one that leads the industry in the exceptional work that we do for our clients and leads all companies in all industries in growth. We're here to celebrate who we are. And that's not defined by a ticker symbol. It's defined by each of you, each and every day.

If those comments had any meaning upon going public, they were even more meaningful now. I called Boston to confirm that our celebration was still on!

Our plane stopped in New York to pick up Carol, and then we continued home. With an hour of flight time remaining, we still had time to play all of the CDs that Karen found, cranking up the volume on the plane's sound system. She gave us a good laugh by slipping in "If I Had $1,000,000" by the Barenaked Ladies. We opened the champagne and, for the first time in three weeks, relaxed—our emotions mixed.

I knew that we had done our best. And I felt very proud of Jim, Tony, Cindy, and everyone who helped us prepare. I was convinced that we were really building a special company, and that the investors recognized that.

And I was certain that I had made the correct decision.

But I also felt a bit of the same frustration that anyone would feel after investing a tremendous amount of energy in something that didn't turn out the way he hoped.

All of us talked about our mixed feelings and I asked everyone to reflect on the words that I always tell every ZEFER new-hire training class. "The mark of a truly great company is not the number of setbacks you have. You can't build a great company without setbacks. The mark of a truly great company is how fast you rebound from them."

As we landed in Boston, Simon & Garfunkel's, "Homeward Bound," was playing on the plane's stereo, and we were all singing along.

Friday, April 14 (Boston)

I arrived at my office at 7:00 a.m. The final draft of my all-employee communication perfectly captured what I wanted to say, and I distributed it. Waiting in my office for the day to begin, I wondered how everyone would react to my decision.

The first positive sign: All of our recruiters arrived at 7:30 a.m., excited about our ability to continue to offer pre-IPO stock options to new hires. I spent the next few hours catching up and wondering if my guess about the market was correct.

By midday, I talked to at least fifty employees and more than twenty customers and prospects. Their unanimous support continued to grow stronger as it became clear that the Nasdaq was on its way to its largest one-day correction ever. My phone rang, and it was Walt, our senior analyst from CSFB. "Bill, yesterday I told you that this is one of the most courageous decisions that I have ever seen a CEO make. You put your 8 percent share of the company back on the table. If that turned out to be the wrong bet, your investors, board and the press would all be second-guessing you. But I want to revise what I said to you yesterday. It's the most brilliant decision that I have ever seen a CEO make. Congratulations on *not* going public!"

By midmorning, the *Wall Street Journal, New York Times*, and most of the high-profile newspapers were calling us to hear our story. A television station from Tokyo called to ask if we would allow their film crew to fly from Japan to Boston on Monday to interview us. All of the press was positive. I found it ironic that ZEFER received more good press for something that we didn't do, than for everything that we did do.

Walt joined us for our employee communication session and the celebration that followed. And everyone at ZEFER spent the afternoon celebrating that we were truly a great private company!

Zefer celebrates still-private status
Would-be IPO dodged Nasdaq's dive by delaying

By Steve Gelsi, CBS MarketWatch
Last Update: 2:29 PM ET Apr 17, 2000

New! IPOWatch section
Net Stocks

NEW YORK (CBS.MW) -- Usually, companies throw a party when they finally go public.

But Zefer (ZEFR: news, msgs) celebrated Friday because it didn't go ahead with its initial public offering on what turned out to be one of the worst days of all time in the stock market.

Saturday, April 15 (Home)

On Saturday evening, I received an email from Susan, a project manager from our Chicago office. I had met Susan only once, very briefly. Her note was short but captured what I believed most of my team was feeling.

Hi Bill –

I'm a new (sort of—been a contractor since September '99) employee.

I like fast sports cars—had an X19 for a while, and I'm looking at either an MR2 or a BMW—haven't made up my mind. I look for great handling, and a fast, good engine.

But I won't buy anything without good brakes!!

Thank you very much for the brakes!

I have every confidence in the handling and the engine, or I wouldn't have joined.

—Susan

• • •

CHAPTER TWENTY-ONE

The Wreck of the Zephyr

Smooth seas do not make a skillful sailor.

— **African proverb**

I'VE HAD MY share of best-laid plans that were sideswiped by a significant event. Fortunately, Plan B, C, D, or E...would eventually overcome bad luck. But the dot-com bust that began in 2000, combined with the 2001 recession, shattered the dreams of many startups. Nasdaq's peak of 5,048.62, reached on March 10, 2000, was the beginning of a 78 percent free fall—taking fifteen years to fully recover. More than half of the internet companies failed. Of the sixty-eight competitors that I tracked, sixty-five were acquired or shut down. The market value of those that survived fell to a fraction of what it had been at their peak. My expected windfall was in free fall. ZEFER's survival was at risk. In August 2001, sixteen months after I pulled ZEFER's IPO, my board asked me to resign as ZEFER's chair and CEO.

After leaving ZEFER's offices for the last time, I wandered into a bookstore and stumbled onto *The Wreck of the Zephyr*, a children's book written in 1983 by Chris Van Allsburg. I scanned the forward. "At the edge of a cliff lies the wreck of a small sailboat. How did it get there? 'Waves carried it up in a storm,' says an old sailor. But who would believe that waves could ever get that high?"[47] I smiled, bought a copy, and tucked it into my briefcase. That evening, with memories still fresh in my mind, I documented ZEFER's perilous journey. Perhaps I would later discover, in retrospect, what I could have done differently.

Second Quarter 2000

After my "brilliant and courageous decision" to not go public, ZEFER's business continued to boom. We launched new offices in San Francisco and London, and generated revenue of $27 million—a 47 percent quarter-over-quarter increase. That represented a whopping 400 percent year-over-year increase. Had we taken ZEFER public, we would have beaten our street plan of $18 million in revenue by 50 percent.

The stock market's choppiness seemed to settle down, so our board decided to relaunch our IPO process. Our bankers warned that if we filed a second time, there was no turning back. If we pulled our IPO again, ZEFER would never have another opportunity to become a publicly traded company.

Third Quarter 2000

During the summer, our banker's belief that the market would once again support our IPO strengthened. We planned to restart the process by attending Credit Suisse First Boston's (CSFB) two-day investor conference in New York beginning Sunday, August 27. That would provide the perfect venue for updating the key investors whom we had met on our initial roadshow. Following that, if all went well, we would launch an abbreviated pitch process and target our IPO for Friday, September 8.

Once again, all did not go well. One of our largest competitors preannounced an earnings shortfall on Sunday evening, the first day of

CSFB's conference. They projected that their revenue would drop by 15 percent, resulting in a loss for the quarter. That was the first time that any of our competitors had fallen short, and the news triggered a series of downgrades for the broader internet consulting sector that we operated in. Another major competitor followed with a similar announcement on Monday morning. My team's reaction was pure *schadenfreude*—"deriving pleasure from someone else's misfortune." This validated our model! Most of our competitors focused too heavily on winning business from technology startups—business that was disappearing because of the dot-com bubble bursting. ZEFER's model was fundamentally different. We targeted large enterprises that were more likely to stay in business for the long term.

Twenty-seven of our clients were Fortune 500 enterprises, each generating annualized revenue greater than $1 million, and our revenue grew 25 percent quarter-over-quarter. And we continued to beat our street plan. However, I couldn't risk launching our final attempt at an IPO during a period of uncertainty created by the performance of our public competitors. So, I cancelled our second IPO roadshow before it started.

Soon afterward, I received an unsolicited offer to acquire ZEFER. Accompanied by a board member and four members of my leadership team, I flew to Johannesburg, South Africa, to meet the prospective acquirer's executive team. The bonding process did not call for meetings in the sauna. Actually, it was quite enjoyable. Immediately upon landing after a twenty-hour flight, we were escorted to a fleet of four tiny propeller planes—each piloted by a member of their executive team—for a one-hour bumpy flight to a game preserve. Bonding on a two-day safari! Afterward, we returned to Johannesburg for two days of formal meetings that led to an offer, if I remember correctly, of approximately $560 million, which included a generous earnout for ZEFER's key employees. That offer represented a significant return for our investor. However, our board, arguing that just six months earlier we had been valued at much higher levels, and that we had grown rapidly since then, responded with a counter-proposal. Our suitor felt that our counter-proposal was too high. They rejected it and acquired one of our competitors instead.

Fourth Quarter 2000

I saw the first signs of an impending recession. Our largest client informed us that, due to their concerns about the strength of the economy, they were putting their project on hold. That had a $5 million impact on the current quarter's revenue and an additional $18 million reduction that would carry into 2001. If you think that sounds like a major setback—you're correct. Even though the client violated a signed contract, I decided that "the right thing to do" was to be a good partner and support them until they became more comfortable with their future. What else could I do? Sue our largest customer? Even with that hit, we grew quarter-over-quarter revenue by $2 million, generating $1 million profit.

Searching for any new Plan B, we found a small, public technology company that was struggling to successfully compete in the internet wave. They were a perfect candidate for a reverse IPO. That's a process whereby ZEFER would exchange our stock for shares of a public company, enabling us to become publicly traded without going through an IPO. That would create a win-win. They would benefit from our brand, growth engine, leadership team, and internet capabilities. We would gain their back-end integration capabilities and the liquidity that comes from being a public company. We quickly reached a point where both sides showed interest and scheduled two days of exploratory meetings. If everything went well, ZEFER would be a public company by the beginning of March 2001!

Once again, everything did not go well. The day before our meetings were scheduled to begin, I saw this headline flash across the TV screen:

Workplace Massacre; Co-Worker of Victims Arrested

I called to express my sympathy and cancel any further merger discussions.

First Quarter 2001

In late January 2001, the "Wreck of ZEFER" began to unfold. Our prospects admitted that they did not know what their business would look like in the next three to six months. As a result, they told us that they were:

- "stretching their current infrastructure until they had a better grasp on their own internal operations;"

- "taking baby steps, instead of full strides, because of the sluggish economy;" and

- "consumed by the process of budget slashing and hiring freezes."

It was clear that in a major recession ignited by the dot-com bust, our value proposition of "we bring dot-com thinking to the F1000" was no longer relevant to our buyers.

I watched the devastating impact that the recession was having on our remaining competitors.

ON GLOBE   WEDNESDAY, SEPTEMBER 13, 2000

After glitter days of Net start-ups, Zefer faces new dot-com reality

USI and MarchFirst filed for bankruptcy.

Scient, Viant, Organic, and Razorfish each cut more than 50 percent of their remaining workforce and announced plans to cut another 175 jobs the following quarter.

Even the large consultancies were feeling the pain. KPMG cut 550 jobs and announced a $20 million charge, while PWC eliminated one thousand jobs, or 6 percent of their consulting unit.

I learned a painful lesson. If all of your competitors are struggling while you're doing well, it doesn't necessarily mean you have the winning model. It might just mean it's not your turn yet.

Fear overtook *schadenfreude*.

ZEFER's revenue dropped by 49 percent that quarter to $17 million, resulting in a $7 million loss. I revised our professional ambition from "fastest growing" to "outlasting the competition." As a result, we needed to make significant changes to our value proposition, cash management, demand generation, accountabilities, metrics, and key-employee retention efforts. That also required me to lay off 255 talented employees. We renegotiated payments to suppliers. And I convinced my leadership team to follow my lead and convert their 2000 bonuses from cash to equity. I needed to find cash. In February, David Lubin and I flew to Tokyo for a "day trip" and successfully closed $26 million of funding in exchange for approximately 20 percent of ZEFER's stock.

Second Quarter 2001

The wreck continued into the second quarter. Deal sizes dropped, sales cycles increased, and competitive pressure to discount our pricing rose as more dot-coms filed for bankruptcy. The board replaced my chief financial officer with a chief restructuring officer (CRO) who reported directly to my investor. I learned to be wary of CROs. They are not our friends. They are there to spy on us, second guess everything we do, and discretely usurp all of our authority. The CRO assigned to me was exceptional at doing all three. With the compensation package that my board gave him, I suppose he should have been—a six-figure upfront, nonrefundable bonus, monthly compensation three times larger than my salary, and another six-figure completion bonus if our company was sold *or filed for bankruptcy.* I have to admit, I had a problem with that arrangement. It seemed like a lot of money, during a time when cash was key to ZEFER's survival, to pay an outsider, who knew nothing about our business or our industry, to second guess me. I believed that the board could have found someone much more competent to second-guess me for a lot less. And it troubled me that his incentives weren't aligned with those of my leadership team. A huge bonus if ZEFER goes bankrupt? Our investor had stacked the deck.

Second-quarter revenue dropped to $9.4 million, resulting in a loss of $11 million. A significant portion of that was the interest payment to our investor for the subordinate debt that they convinced us to swap for equity. It would have been worse, had I not terminated another 344 employees at the end of May.

Troubled Zefer nearing sale

By TOM KIRCHOFER

A potential buyer was not identified by Herald sources though one

title of "chief restructuring
officer" and was brought on to a

Third Quarter 2001

After only eighteen months in business, ZEFER reached a revenue
annual run rate of $100 million and was profitable—an internet darling
on the verge of becoming a unicorn. But the previous twelve months had
been very difficult for many CEOs. I know they certainly were for me.
There seemed to be one insurmountable challenge after another:

- going public on the very day that the Nasdaq suffered a
  record-setting crash;

- attempting to survive a major recession that devastated
  demand while servicing a significant debt that we shouldn't
  have agreed to carry;

- flying to South Africa and coming back with a strong offer to
  buy the company, only to have it rejected;

- canceling merger discussions just days before they were
  scheduled to begin because of a horrible workplace massacre;
  and

- being hounded by an expensive chief restructuring officer
  who was perversely incentivized to shut down the company.

I'm not one to make excuses—but these were extremely difficult waters
for keeping any ship afloat.

I had run out of Plan Bs. It was a logical step for the board to ask me
to resign. I had no hard feelings. I did have a sense of relief. But that
was overwhelmed by a sense of loss. I have never stopped believing that
ZEFER was a special company.

But I wondered, was that "brilliant and courageous decision" that I made
sixteen months earlier the right one after all?

Parting Thoughts

- Startups come with both good days and bad days. In Chapter 2, I said that on good days, running a startup makes you feel like you are part of a close-knit team that's on a mission from God to change the world. When momentum builds and you start to accomplish something that all the experts, industry analysts, and investors who turned you down insisted was "not possible," you feel unstoppable. That contagious energy triggers the biggest professional high that you can ever have.

- However, I warned you that not all days are good. Most are hard. But like Sisyphus, an entrepreneur refuses to surrender to gravity. It isn't just about enjoying the reward of reaching the mountain top. It's mostly about savoring the experience of pushing that damn rock up the hill. As Chhavi Kumar said, "Embrace the rock. Be persistent. Work hard. Never give up. And be thankful for the journey."[48]

If it's not just about reaching the mountain top, how should an entrepreneur keep score? I share my thoughts on that next.

• • •

CHAPTER TWENTY-TWO

Keeping Score

I've missed over 9,000 shots in my career. I've lost almost 300 games. 26 times I've been trusted to take the game-winning shot...and missed. I've failed over and over and over again in my life. And that is why I succeed.

– Michael Jordan

DURING ONE OF my many chats with Mark Fuller, the founding chair and CEO of the Monitor Group, he noted, "Tell me if I'm wrong, but you look like you are a very happy person." I smiled and nodded "yes." Mark continued, "In my experience, most successful people aren't happy. They're often tormented, and they drive away the people that care about them. That's true for business executives, movie stars, musicians, artists—just about every profession." He paused for a moment to gather his thoughts before he went on. "I think it comes down to what's really important to you. What compels you to continue to 'press go?' How do you keep score?"

"Steve, the Uber driver, taught me about 'keepin' score,'" I joked. "It's the number of startups that I launch as CEO." Chuckling, I leaned back in my chair. But Mark just stared at me, so I knew he was looking for a straight answer. "Seriously," he said, "and I don't want to sound morbid. If you knew that tomorrow would be your last day on this earth, what blessings would you count, and what hopes and wishes would still be unfulfilled?"

I didn't have a quick answer to Mark's question. But I couldn't shake it. That evening, I searched my past for reference points. I thought about

Guglielmo, the tour guide that I met on my honeymoon in Italy and wondered how he kept score. He chose a life where he skied in Zermatt every winter and worked off-season as a tour guide to earn his living. I remembered what he said when we parted ways and thought there might be a clue in how he said goodbye.

"I feel that I know you well enough to confidently say that you and I are very much alike," he said. "But what makes us different is that you are chasing your dreams, while I am living mine every day. I live in the moment and think about how I can make today a better day than yesterday—while you worry about how you can make tomorrow a better day than today." Guglielmo was right, and I wondered what made me that way.

My mind was racing, and I didn't sleep that night. I'm not sure why, but my thoughts went further back to the many times that my dad and I would play baseball in our backyard. He would hit a ball high up on the fence, so that I would have to run backward as hard as I could and leap high in the air to catch it. Then Dad would follow that with a short pop-up that I would have to dive to catch. When I was very young, I'd ask "Can't we just play a real game of baseball?" Dad would reply, "No. It's not about keeping score. It's about trying as hard as you can and enjoying wherever that effort leads you." Eventually I understood and stopped asking.

I had the answer to Mark's first question. I don't care about the final score. It's more about how hard I try and how well I play. I just love the game.

But I still wanted to answer the second part of Mark's question. What is most important to me? It was the middle of the night, and I still had more self-reflection ahead of me.

Building a Special Company

I thought about ZEFER. Before our roadshow began, Carol and I curled up in front of the fireplace to contemplate how our expected proceeds would change our lives. We made a list entitled, "All the Things We Ever Wanted," with a column for estimated costs. Starting was easy. Travel to cool places. A new car. Another new car. Remodeling our Cape home. But when I added "trust fund for our kids," Carol stopped me. "We both want our children to be taken care of. But we also want them to learn the value of working hard for what they want. We don't want them to become spoiled brats." We agreed on a number that provided for their security without messing up their values.

After that, it became more difficult. We didn't care about a private island, a garage filled with antique cars, rare artwork, or a private plane. And we couldn't agree on which sports team to purchase. I guess we liked our lives just the way they were and didn't want them to change very much. When we finished, our estimated cost column totaled less than 3 percent of our expected windfall. So, we agreed to give most of the rest away anonymously.

ZEFER didn't turn out as our bankers expected. Instead of receiving a huge check, I was asked to write one for $1 million. Although a gigantic swing, Carol and I were okay. It wasn't going to change our life either way. Although it was my only "unsuccessful" exit, ZEFER was a marvelous adventure that Carol and I will never forget and a special company that I'll always be proud of. I realized that keeping score isn't about taking a company public or becoming rich. It's about the quest to build a special company and the positive impact that the journey has on my customers, partners, and employees. It's about feeling that I'm accomplishing something that the "experts" believed couldn't be done.

Creating Memories

Several years ago, I served on Profitect's advisory board with Dan Ariely, a world-renowned behavioral economist. Dan is the author of six books, including *Predictably Irrational*,[49] based on the idea that we repeatedly and predictably make irrational economic decisions in many aspects of our lives. Dan explains, "We don't have an internal value meter that tells us how much things are worth. Rather, we focus on the relative advantage of one thing over another and estimate value accordingly." For example, a person baking in the sun on a beach is likely to turn down a $15 ice-cold beer because it's too expensive, even if they are very hot and thirsty. But that same person would spend $22 for that same beer at a New England Patriot's playoff game in the middle of January—when the temperature is in the low teens. *Why we buy* and *what we buy* isn't solely determined by traditional economics.

At every advisory board meeting, Dan would stand after dinner with a glass of wine in hand and share his latest research. His performances were always fascinating, and every one of the board members looked forward to them. At my final meeting, Dan talked about the *half-life* of the value that you perceive when you buy something that you *always wanted*. As I recall, his research showed that the half-life of the car that you just couldn't live without was about twelve months. For a home, it stretched almost two years. For a boat, it was less than six months. And so on...

When he paused, I asked, "Dan, you have been studying and researching behavioral economics for your entire career. You are *the* expert. What is it that you spend your money on? What has the longest half-life?"

Dan didn't answer right away, almost as if he hadn't thought about it before. But then he said, "I spend my money on creating great memories—special times with family and friends. Sometimes they are expensive, but the best ones tend not to be. The half-life of the value of a great memory is infinite. It never decays. In fact, great memories get even better over time. I spend my money on creating great memories."

That was life-changing for me, and, I think, for my family. The great memories that I create are what's important to me, and I've come to believe that they define my life. Great memories are a big part of how I keep score. Perhaps that's why I enjoy sharing my stories with you.

• • •

CHAPTER TWENTY-THREE

Life Lessons

Life is a succession of lessons which must be lived to be understood.

– Helen Keller

Lessons *Earned*

THE IMPORTANT LESSONS in business and in life cannot be taught. Mine were earned from the more than fifty startups that I've touched and the big companies that I've worked for and with. But they also stem from wet t-shirt contests, Doctor Bon Jovi, Little League teams, rock bands, saunas, carpet cleaning ads from the Allentown *Morning Call*, Uber drivers, my children, my wife—and my parents.

I often wonder why a particular memory stays with me. How odd that I still remember the "Tuepenerernr" puzzle that my Mom and I solved when I was twelve years old. Or my Dad's exact words after playing catch when I was only eleven. "It's not about keeping score. It's about trying as hard as you can and enjoying wherever that effort leads you." It must be because it influenced me in some important way, even if I didn't recognize it at the time.

I still remember Mom reading to me when I was very young. But it wasn't the traditional bedtime story. Our time together was more like a book club. Mom would stop and ask questions along the way. And we would chat about the story after we finished. After I learned to read, the book club evolved. When Mom finished a best-seller that she enjoyed, she'd pass it on to me and say, "This book is beyond your reading level. Try to get through it so that we can discuss it." Armed with a dictionary, I wouldn't give up until I was ready for our discussion.

In college, that tradition became bidirectional. I remember arriving home after my freshman year and handing Mom a paperback copy of *Walden Two*. I explained, "It's a utopian novel about a communal experiment designed to create the *good life*—health, no more than four hours of daily labor, time to develop new interests and personal contacts, and plenty of relaxation and rest. The traditional motivators—competition, personal fame, or wealth—are not permitted. Thoreau's *Walden* was one of my favorite books growing up, but it didn't provide a practical path to follow. *Walden Two* does, and I think I might like to follow it."

Keep in mind, that wisdom emanated from an eighteen-year-old hippy wannabe in the summer of 1970. If any of my kids announced anything like that upon returning home after their freshman year, I would have come unglued and pulled them out of college. But Mom never handled my adolescent misadventures that way. "Give me a moment," she said. "I'll be right back."

A few minutes later, she returned and handed me a hardcover book that was the size of two bricks and weighed as much. "*Atlas Shrugged*, written by Ayn Rand, presents another way of thinking about what's important in life," Mom said. "It's about individualism, achievement, and working hard to become the best you can be." She paused before she continued, "You and I haven't held our book club since you left for college. I'll read *Walden Two*, you read *Atlas Shrugged*, and we can discuss both."

Mom seldom told me what to do. Instead, she would introduce me to a different way of thinking about the choices that lay before me. She believed in the power of big ideas and hoped that would help me find my way. Mom was a storyteller like I am. The only difference was that she used other people's stories. I abandoned Frazier's cult and signed on with John Galt!

My Dad was as smart as Mom, but in a very different way. Nicknamed "Skip" after a mischievous troublemaker in the comic strips, he left high school early and didn't earn his diploma until his forties. I don't recall him ever reading a book. He was a tinkerer, a builder, and an inventor.

When Mom read, he passed the time in the garage that he built. As a boy, I spent Saturday mornings there with him. I believed that he could solve any problem and figure out anything—and I still believe that today. I learned how to problem solve from him. He would teach me how to fix things and how to build things. His garage was crammed with past carpentry projects. Dad kept them because they provided the raw materials for future designs. We had a lawn swing that began as shelves, was rebuilt as a dresser, and then converted into kitchen chairs before its final resting place. "How can I rebuild something from this," was a problem that he enjoyed solving.

Dad also taught me how to treat people, and how important it is to enjoy life. Everyone described Skip as the sweetest man in the world. I remember arguing with him when I was a teenager. He was pressuring me to cut my hair. I said, "It does not matter what other people think." My Dad responded, "Nothing matters more than what other people think."

My parents influence continued in very subtle ways. In 1986, my mother mailed me a small package wrapped in brown paper. I still have the note that came with it.

"Life, at times, will be a struggle. It takes courage to change directions— especially when things aren't going too badly. Be confident in your decisions. Don't be afraid to get out of your comfort zone."

Inside was a framed advertisement from the *Wall Street Journal*. She asked me to hang it on a prominent spot on my office wall so that I would see it whenever I looked up. It was titled "Get Out of That Rut."[50] It was the catalyst that finally gave me the courage to leave a cushy Fortune 100 executive position in Allentown and move to Boston to become an entrepreneur.

Oscar Wilde said, 'Consistency is the last refuge of the unimaginative.'

So, stop getting up at 6:05.

Get up at 5:06.

Walk a mile at dawn.

Find a new way to drive to work.

Switch chores with your spouse next Saturday.

Buy a wok.

Study wildflowers.

Stay up alone all night.

Read to the blind.

Start counting brown-eyed blondes or blondes.

Subscribe to an out-of-town newspaper.

Canoe at midnight.

Don't write to your congressman,

take a whole scout troop to see them.

Learn to speak Italian.

Teach some kid the thing you do best.

Listen to two hours of uninterrupted Mozart.

Take up aerobic dancing.

Leap out of that rut.

Savor life.

Remember, we only pass this way once.

– Harry Gray, former CEO, United Technologies

Enjoy the Game

Entrepreneurship isn't a job. It's not just what you do. It's a big part of who you are. For an entrepreneur, business and life become intertwined. But that doesn't have to come at the expense of your relationships with friends and family because many of your lessons earned apply to both business success and a successful life. I'm blessed because Carol has been my partner in both.

Launching a startup and scaling it to become a successful company is difficult. Failure is much more likely than success. Throughout my career, I've shared my stories with my colleagues to arm them with frameworks that may help them overcome the business challenges they encounter. I believe, in some small way, that's contributed to more than one hundred of them becoming CEOs. More than a few of them have become much better at the job than I am.

You might wonder why I continue to "press go." Sometimes I wonder, too. When asked, I tell people that the answer isn't entirely clear.

But if I'm honest, I keep doing it because I get a huge professional high from creating something new and important—sitting across the table from a senior business executive who is asking me to help them solve a critical problem and then successfully delivering a solution that provides value to the company, its consumers, or its patients. Nothing surpasses being able to say, "I helped build that." I decided to become an entrepreneur in order to have a significant impact on the business. Building a special company gives me that satisfaction and also provides me with the potential to impact the many lives and livelihoods that my clients touch. And it does much more. Entrepreneurship spurs the economy. It creates professional opportunities for employees that substantially contribute to personal and career ambitions and will continue to benefit them throughout their careers. And if the company can drive innovation and overturn conventional thinking by redefining an industry—that's the biggest professional high any CEO can get!

When the challenges seem daunting, my thoughts wander to a time in the future. I imagine one of my team members, now much older, telling his grandchildren about the vision that we shared, the ambitious goals that we set, and the impact that we had—not just on our clients, but also on the people that they touched. And then, beaming with pride, saying "I helped build that company."

I'll continue to launch new ventures because I'll never stop enjoying the game!

• • •

About the Author

From the time that Bill Seibel turned twelve, he knew that he wanted to be an entrepreneur—even though he wasn't entirely clear on what entrepreneurship was, how to accomplish it, or how to pronounce it correctly. It took Bill twenty-five more years to join his first startup, after getting a degree in engineering, an MBA, and working twelve years for a Fortune 100 company along the way. Since then, he has been CEO of nine startups and worked with another forty. Although Bill admits that he is still trying to figure it out, he's written his first book to share the lessons that he's *earned* as a serial entrepreneur.

Connect with Bill at contact@BillSeibel.com.

Thank You to My Readers

Thank you for spending this time with me. My sincere hope is that my stories fuel your entrepreneurial passions and my lessons help you achieve your ambitions. If I can help you on your journey, you can reach me at:

bill.seibel@gmail.com

contact@BillSeibel.com

Appendix — Lessons Applied to Professional Services

It must be considered that there is nothing more difficult to carry out, nor more doubtful of success, nor more dangerous to handle than to initiate a new order of things.

– Nicolo Machiavelli

Every now and then, when you are on stage, you can hear the best sound a player can hear... It is the sound of a wonderful, deep silence that means you hit them where they live.

– Shelley Winters

PART ONE

Unique Challenges in IT Consulting

I BELIEVE THAT my lessons in entrepreneurship apply to most businesses. However, technology consulting companies have a number of idiosyncrasies. Before I end, I thought it would be important to explain why they are different and how my entrepreneurship lessons apply to them.

IT consulting companies represent the perfect capitalistic model for aggregating scarce talent and harnessing it to provide positive results for customers. They are easier to launch than other businesses because they can generate cash without requiring a significant investment in software, equipment, facilities, or other hard assets. Because it costs less to launch, it's easier to get started before they find an investor. Although professional services firms don't have the upside that a software company has, they are much less likely to fail. There are a small number of winners in a software category, and the company with the best product doesn't always make the cut. There's room for many more competitors in a consulting category. I also believe that the wide range of engagements that consulting touches provides more opportunities to be creative.

However, having built six professional services firms, I've learned that they face a number of unique challenges. In order to successfully scale a services company, you need to anticipate those stumbling blocks and implement processes that mitigate their impact.

The Production Line Is Different

You can't stamp out high-volume digital copies of consultants. Unlike software companies, consulting firms scale by hiring, training, and selling people's time. Because that business model consumes both time and cash, professional services firms are more difficult to scale rapidly.

It's always difficult to find and hire great people. It's even harder when you need scarce skill sets and experience that are in high demand. The onboarding process for a consulting firm should allow time and resources for training new consultants in your company's tools and methodologies. As a result, you will have to hire your team well in advance of assigning them to billable projects. Timing is critical. If you hire too late you won't have sufficient staff to start a project, delaying revenue and perhaps causing you to lose the deal. But if you hire too early, you'll have to pay expensive consultants "to sit on the bench" without billable work to support them.

Even with perfect timing, the hiring process is still costly. You are doing well if you can hire a consultant, assimilate and train them, and assign them to a billable project within thirty days. Most professional services firms bill their clients at the end of each month. Since most clients pay their invoices in sixty days, typically you will carry the salary of a high-demand, very expensive consultant for 120 days before you recover a dime. With those economics, it's challenging to rapidly grow revenue without raising capital or incurring significant debt.

But it's difficult for professional services firms to raise capital. Most venture capitalists will not even consider investing in a consulting startup. That's because it's tough to scale by selling and delivering projects. Just to stay even, every completed project needs to be replaced by a new project of the same size. Complex projects sometimes go wrong, negatively impacting profitability and the brand. Consultants who are in high demand may leave. Because of those business risks, professional services companies are valued at a fraction of similarly sized software companies. It's no surprise that most investors, in search of a unicorn that will generate most of their fund's returns, are unwilling to consider investing in that risk-reward proposition.

New Technology Waves

Many professional services firms are launched to help their clients exploit a new technology wave. At a high level of abstraction, most technology waves look alike. They start slowly, grow, peak, and eventually decline. Occasionally they crash. If a firm is already riding one wave, it's challenging for them to catch a new one.

It's critical for a consulting company to time its launch correctly. If you enter a market too early, you'll fail. If you are too late, you might miss the opportunity to become the industry leader. But choosing the correct timing requires skill and patience because it takes a while for a new technology to reach its potential. Cambridge Technology Partners (CTP) began by focusing on the client-server technology wave—more than twenty years after that technology was introduced. ZEFER targeted the internet sixteen years after it was invented. Martin Cooper, a Motorola executive, demonstrated DynaTAC, the first mobile phone, in 1973, almost forty years before Mobiquity began. The DynaTAC took ten years to hit the market. When it eventually did, the product still wasn't ready for the mass market because it required ten hours to charge for a thirty-minute maximum talk time, and it sold, in today's currency, for $20,000. But in every case, a tipping point occurs, and the new technology takes off like a rocket ship. It takes a long time for things to happen quickly.

As the technology evolves, businesses envision more use cases and enthusiasm builds. At some point, a spark could ignite and drive hyper-growth. Business executives begin wrestling with ways to exploit the technology's potential and how to separate its hype from the real return on investment. They launch pilots and proof-of-concept exercises to find the answers. The answers vary depending on the technology, but most of the questions are the same.

Some enterprises begin to generate significant benefits by moving from stand-alone applications to leveraging the technology to enable new business processes. Projects become much more impactful, but also larger and more complex. Case studies can call attention to the success stories and detail the failures. Successes fuel the fire.

Eventually the technology becomes mainstream, supported by a large pool of talent with the right skills and experience. New software tools reduce the skills and time required to develop solutions. Packaged applications that leverage the technology to address specific use cases become widely available. The early market leaders find themselves burdened with expensive employees whose skill sets are no longer required—changing them into a high-priced provider in a commodity market.

If a professional services firm catches a new wave either too early or too late, it will fail. If it starts at the right time and can navigate the business changes that are required as the wave evolves and matures, it has a chance of succeeding. But as a technology wave matures, it requires a shift to a new business model, with a different focus, billing rates, organizational structure, and business metrics. In *Managing the Professional Service Firm*, David Maister describes the Brains (thought leaders), Gray-hair (experienced), and Procedure (efficient) models that neatly apply to where a technology consultancy falls within a wave.[51] Here's how I apply those models.

- *Brains* model: Their customer value proposition is, "We have the smartest consultants in the world, and we can work with your executives to create an innovative solution to whatever problem you are trying to solve—even if it has never been solved before."

  As an example, a pharmaceutical company's schizophrenia drug was nearing its patent cliff when they engaged Mobiquity. With sales of more than $6 billion, it was among the top-selling drugs in the US. However, in three years the drug would reach generic status, which could cause its price to plunge by more than 90 percent. In response, the pharmaceutical company was urgently exploring the possibility of launching the first smart-pill—with an implanted chip that could confirm that the medication was taken, as well as providing other services that could contribute to a patient's health. Although the drug would lose its patent protection, the company hoped that their newly developed delivery platform could be patented, and the value it provided would help protect its price. They were seeking a Brains model consultancy and teamed with Mobiquity to introduce one of the first trackable ingested digital medicines approved by the US Food and Drug Administration.

The Brains model is characterized by a top-heavy pyramid, with very high labor rates at the top end, very low rates at the bottom, and utilization rates of about 50 percent. Brains consultancies go to market with a strategic solution sales process that's partner-led and supported by an investment in thought leadership, high-quality focused content, and case studies that demonstrate innovative problem solving.

- *Gray-hair* or *Experience* model: "We have solved your problem many times before and are experts at it. If you are facing that problem, who better than us to help you fix it?" For example, after four years in business, Mobiquity had developed mobile ordering platforms for many of the top quick-service restaurants. Our brand recognition and track record provided us with a significant competitive advantage when pitching to prospects in that industry.

Gray-hair may apply to an industry vertical, a specific problem, or both. Its staffing pyramid is traditionally shaped. Labor rates are average and utilization target rates are 72 percent. Their go-to-market strategy is account-executive driven with "subject matter expert" support, backed by client logos and case studies that highlight expertise in a specific vertical or problem set.

- *Procedure* model: "We have the methodology, tools, and cost structure that enable us to reliably deliver a solution at a much lower price." A procedure consultancy can achieve that by standardizing their approach, by outsourcing their work to lower cost regions, or by employing software tools to increase productivity. It's characterized by a bottom-heavy staffing pyramid, an inside sales go-to-market approach, low labor rates, and very high utilization.

When businesses begin to invest in a new technology, the Brains model is best positioned to drive innovative high impact solutions. After firms begin to accumulate experience in solving particular problems, the professional services market shifts to a Gray-hair model. If a consulting organization recognizes that change, making the shift is not difficult.

When a technology wave reaches the mainstream, experienced consultants are no longer expensive to find, tools are available that deskill the work, and software packages are developed that eliminate the need for a custom solution. That's when the Procedure model rules. Brains and Gray-hair firms are stuck being the high-cost supplier in a commodity market. They can survive, but their growth potential, profitability, and market value are all significantly reduced.

CTP's Failed Attempt to Straddle the Waves

In 1998, the client-server market shifted to the Procedure model. I did not foresee the huge impact of that change. The shift to Procedure caused the average size of my new projects to fall from $2.2 million to $600,000. As a result, I would have to increase the number of projects by fivefold in order to hit my 30 percent growth plan. That was not going to happen. CTP responded by refocusing our business on the new, emerging internet wave and targeting e-commerce solutions. That year, 60 percent of our projects and 39 percent of our revenue were internet related.

CTP's change in focus worked, at least for a while. In 1998, we grew revenue by 40 percent to $612 million, reported an $81 million operating profit, and reached a market cap of more than $5 billion—great results, especially given the shifting market. However, I believed that performance would be difficult to sustain because new consulting competitors were emerging focused solely on the internet. I departed the company in mid-1998 to launch ZEFER. Unencumbered by a business model and a delivery methodology built for an earlier technology wave, ZEFER grew revenue from zero to $134 million within eighteen months.

CTP's 1998 Annual Report showed that they understood that significant change was required. It led with, "The Game has changed. And the companies that play face unprecedented challenges—and opportunities." The second page began, "Cambridge believes that the Internet is not just the next wave. It's not even a tidal wave. It's a tsunami. And there's no safe harbor because it's changing the rules of businesses across all industries." And then the third page, "It's a new kind of problem—

one that requires new kinds of solutions—delivered by a new kind of partner." Unfortunately, they were spot on.

At the beginning of 1999, CTP restructured to a Gray-hair model—moving from a geographic focus to align with industries (for example, healthcare, financial services, and retail) where they had built strong credentials. But that, in itself, fell far short of making them the "new kind of partner" that businesses were looking for. It became increasingly challenging to navigate through the large amount of change required to get there. As a result, CTP's 1999 growth slowed to only 2.6 percent. In the fourth quarter, the wheels came off the bus. The company lost $17.3 million, faced employee turnover of 48 percent, and its stock price fell from a fifty-two-week high of $58 per share to $11.50. The "Icarus effect" was beginning to play out.

The next year, revenue declined by $58 million, operating profit dropped to a loss of $112 million, and the stock price plummeted to $1.38 per share. Between 1999 and 2000, CTP's stock price fell by 98 percent while the new breed of firms were driving the Nasdaq composite to an increase of 400 percent.

Technology consulting companies, with the exception of a few industry giants, are one-trick ponies. The business model, skill sets, delivery methodology, and supporting infrastructure that position them as an industry leader in one technology wave can impede their ability to shift to another. Remember Marshall McLuhan's quote from Chapter 12: "We become what we behold. We shape our tools, and then our tools shape us." When the market shifts, even the strongest firms struggle to survive.

Yaakov Kirschen captured the point in one of his Kozmo cartoons. "The dot.com bubble had burst...but there was no panic... Everyone knew that there'd be a *new bubble* coming along any minute."

• • •

PART TWO

Rapidly Scaling Your Consulting Firm Playbook

EVEN AS CONSULTING startups are navigating through technology waves, they must concurrently chart their course to pass through seven growth stages in order to continue to scale.

Stage 1—$3 million revenue

Your technology consulting startup can reach $3 million in revenue simply by doing great work. But that's not enough if you want to continue to grow. Most firms never reach Stage 2.

Stage 2—$10 million revenue

In order to pass through this gate, you must continue to do great work, articulate a value proposition that is clear and compelling, and have founders who can sell. At this point, you might also need to get your team out of their comfort zone and change their employee value proposition from "We only do cool work, and we only hire world-class brilliant people who want to only do cool work," to "We are building the leading XYZ professional services firm."

Stage 3—$20 million revenue

At this point, your consulting startup must formalize its methodology by defining deliverables and activities and documenting them in a workflow that shows dependencies, and timelines. Include pricing, project management, change control, and risk management. That level of detail persuades prospects that your firm's differentiators are real. To make your differentiators credible, invest in marketing to develop content about your delivery process: whitepapers, blogs, interviews, and surveys. Highlight blue-chip clients. You are what you eat. If you want to be the leading consultancy in a chosen market, you need to win correspondingly high-profile clients. Don't build your sales team until marketing has produced the tools that account executives need. Otherwise, the salesforce won't be productive, and your investment in them will be wasted.

Stage 4—$50 million revenue

It's time to begin to introduce new services or new geographies. In order to continue to scale, your firm needs to define your service delivery methodology to the level of detail required to train large numbers of new staff. Having defined the *what* and *when* in Stage 3, now it's time to define the *how* in order to make the process scalable. Remember that a new service or geography is a startup all over again. Expect familiar growing pains.

Stage 5—$75 million revenue

It's time to expand to multiple services in multiple geographies. If done properly, that commitment can fuel growth to $100 million. It's also time to double down on expanding and developing your management team.

Stage 6—$100 million revenue

Managing the business becomes very complex. There are thousands of moving parts, but it feels like an order of magnitude more. Management processes need to be formalized and documented. More infrastructure is required. In addition, you need to get comfortable saying "no." Everyone will see opportunities everywhere that all look enticing. But any distraction will create more complexity. Focus on doing a very small number of things exceptionally well; that means saying "no" to everything else.

Stage 7—$150 million revenue

A very small percentage of professional services companies make it this far. If they do, revenue from annuities represent a sizable component. Otherwise, the number of new projects that a firm has to win and successfully execute every year to continue to grow becomes too difficult to sustain.

As I discussed before, I believe your consultancy can build powerful opportunities by identifying services to harness the power of data into a sustainable revenue annuity. But most of your clients don't think about their business models that way and aren't organized to take advantage of data as an asset. As my Mobiquity cofounder, Scott Snyder observes, "For most companies, the value of data is an afterthought in developing new products or service offerings, let alone improving their business operations. Instead of starting with how valuable the resulting data may be, they focus on just making something 'connected' as the value."[52] Enterprises have great difficulty shifting their mindset. In most cases, you'll have to find those opportunities for them and sell them on the value.

Occasionally your clients may accidentally stumble upon "data exhaust" opportunities—data streams that are a byproduct of an application which can add significant value to other use cases. Technology consulting firms that identify data exhaust opportunities can create competitive advantages for their clients while creating a data-driven annuity for themselves. For example, a battery company believed they could increase sales by notifying consumers when a battery was about to run out of charge. They embedded a chip into their battery pack and developed a mobile platform to monitor battery capacity. Did that application also create a data exhaust opportunity?

What about smoke detectors? They always seem to run out of batteries in the middle of the night and alert us with shrill beeping. A homeowner is never sure which of the seven detectors installed in their home is the culprit. It's a reasonable bet that a consumer would pay a few cents more for batteries that would eliminate that fire-alarm drill forever.

Would anyone else be interested in that data if consumers could be convinced to share it? The US averages more than 350,000 home fires every year, causing almost $7 billion in direct damage; 2,620 civilian fire deaths; and 11,220 civilian fire injuries.[53] According to the National Fire Protection Association, missing or inoperative smoke alarms are responsible for 60 percent of those tragedies.[54] Clearly, insurance companies would pay a premium for that data exhaust, far exceeding the revenue associated with incremental battery sales—creating an annuity for both the battery company and the consultancy that identified and developed the opportunity. Insurance companies could increase their profits while reducing their insurance premiums for homeowners who opted in and kept their smoke detectors in good operating condition. More importantly, it would save billions of dollars in damages and thousands of lives in the US annually. Win-win-win-win.

• • •

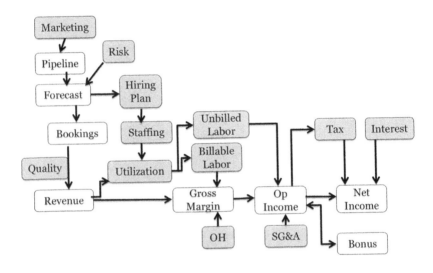

PART THREE

Teaching Your Consultants How to Make Money

IT'S IMPORTANT TO have an incentive structure in place to reinforce the mindsets that you want to build. Encouraging behaviors that contribute to your company making money is one of the most important. A significant percentage of the decisions that drive profitability are made by consultants in the field, not by senior management. At Cambridge Technology Partners, ZEFER, and Mobiquity, every employee was entitled to a yearly bonus based on their salary, role, and individual performance. The bonus pool was funded with a percentage of every incremental dollar of profit the company generated after we reached our profitability target. That made it easy to link "money spent" or "hours billed" to the impact that it had on an individual's bonus. Suddenly, employees felt like they were spending their own money and became more thoughtful before they spent it. And that's exactly how you want them to think.

The model at left illustrates how operating decisions impact a professional services firm's ability to make money.

The metrics in the blocks shaded gray reduce profits, while items in the white blocks increase profitability. Each time I present this chart, I give a "Making Money" quiz to make it fun and competitive for my audience to learn about the business model. I hear at least one wisecrack answer every time. But each question creates an opportunity for me to explain a business principle. For example:

If had we started our four largest projects when we planned to, it would have added _____% to the employee bonus pool:

a) 20%

b) 50%

c) 80%

d) 300%

The correct answer is d) 300%. The lesson is that billable hours for a professional services firm are like airplane seats. If they aren't used, a lot of money is left on the table. When your team understands that they could have tripled their bonuses by getting approved projects started on time, it captures their attention and changes their behavior.

Following are other examples of quiz questions.

- What is the opportunity cost for an eight-person project team to be "on the bench" for one week?

- How much does 1 percent more utilization add to our gross margin? To our operating income percentage? As a percent of the bonus pool?

- How much did delayed project starts reduce our bonus pool?

- How much do our non-billable people cost us each year?

- What is our average sales discount? How much would our bonus pool rise if we charged list price?

- What are the three employee "behaviors" that most negatively impact our bonus pool?

By the time your employees finish a twenty-question "Making Money" quiz, they will have a much better understanding of how they can influence the profitability of the company—and, as a result, increase the size of their bonuses.

• • •

PART FOUR

Valuing Your Professional Services Firm

BOTH INVESTORS AND acquirers value professional services firms at lower multiples than software companies. That's because a consultancy has higher business risks and fewer assets. Assets include:

- employees—but they can leave at any time;

- clients—but unless they are locked in with an annuity stream, they can disappear at the end of a project;

- intellectual property—ideally trademarked or protected in some way;

- brand—the acquisition's name and credentials are recognized and valued by the client base; and

- tip-of-the-spear capabilities—the acquisition will generate incremental revenue for the core business of the acquirer. All the better if you can confirm your impact by pointing to revenue that you have generated for your delivery partners. For instance, for every $1 of revenue that Mobiquity delivered, we generated $8 of downstream revenue for other consultancies. If your acquirer has those downstream delivery capabilities, that's additional revenue for them.

These factors will influence your valuation. You need to know what's important to an acquirer and use that as a basis for negotiation. Valuations can be based on a multiple of earnings that can be as low as two-times EBITDA ("earnings before interest, taxes, depreciation, and amortization"), or as high as ten-times EBITDA, depending on how the acquirer values their assets.

However, if a professional services company can convince an acquirer that they have a high likelihood of continued rapid growth, they may be valued based on a multiple of revenue instead of earnings. For a fast-growing company, that's much better. That approach recognizes that rapidly scaling companies are reinvesting their earnings to drive growth that will lead to higher earnings in the future. The more convincing the growth forecast and the more impact the acquisition will have on the growth of the acquirer's core services, the higher that valuation will be— resulting in a revenue multiplier that can reach two-times revenue.

For example, based on earnings, the valuation of a $10 million professional services company with 10 percent EBITDA could range from $2 million to $10 million. Based on revenue, that same company's valuation could reach $20 million. And if that same company was acquired at the right point in time, when the underlying technology wave was on the verge of entering the Gray-hair phase, the valuation could be much higher.

If you can convince investors and acquirers that you are, or will become, a leader in a new technology wave, you can drive your valuation up significantly.

Sapient is an interesting example because it was a public company that transitioned through several technology waves. As one of the leaders of the client-server wave, their market cap reached six times revenue. After that wave passed, their valuation descended to more traditional levels of 1.5 times revenue. But when Sapient transitioned to become a leader in the emerging internet wave, they were rewarded with a valuation that reached a whopping thirty-four times revenue. After the dot-com bust, their market cap again returned to normal levels. With the acquisition of Nitro in 2009, Sapient quickly pivoted once again, transforming from a website design and infrastructure business into a leader in the mobile wave, doubling their stock price in a year. In February 2015, Publicis acquired SapientNitro for $3.7 billion, much of that value based on the mobile portion of their business.

Clearly, a technology consulting firm that's positioned as a leader in a new technology wave is rewarded with a significantly higher valuation. But leadership status is not just determined by timing. Based on my research, across all of the major and minor technology waves, all the leaders share similar business model differentiators. Key operating metrics include:

- rapid and sustained revenue growth;

- gross margins greater than 45 percent and operating income greater than 15 percent of revenue;

- a value proposition focused on helping their clients grow revenue, not just reduce costs;

- a tip-of-the-spear go-to-market model that drives large, follow-on consulting engagements;

- buzz, brand, and thought leadership; and

- annuities that represent at least 20 percent of revenue.

Don't get me wrong. I'm not saying consulting firms that are recognized as leaders in a new technology wave meet all of those criteria. None of them do. But the ones with the highest valuations always check more of those boxes than any of their competitors do. I've used this research as a framework for designing the business model for every new consulting firm that I've launched. And I've successfully used it to argue for higher valuations from both investors and acquirers.

• • •

PART FIVE

Parting Thoughts

ENTREPRENEURS FACE MANY unique challenges when launching and scaling a professional services firm.

- Recruiting and onboarding scarce skill sets that are in high demand. Timing is critical. If you hire too late you won't have sufficient staff to start a project, delaying revenue and perhaps causing you to lose the deal. But if you hire too early, you'll have to pay expensive consultants "to sit on the bench" without billable work to support them.

- Managing cash flow. Scaling a professional services firm requires more cash than product companies do. Since most clients pay their invoices in sixty days, typically you will carry the salary of a high-demand, very expensive consultant for 120 days before you recover a dime. Negotiating simple changes to payment terms (e.g., invoicing biweekly instead of monthly, or arranging for a down payment) will make a huge difference. Pay sales commissions only *after* receivables are collected. If a payment is late, transfer responsibility for collecting from Accounting to the executive that owns the client relationship.

- Because professional services firms can consume cash at high rate, it's difficult to rapidly grow revenue without raising capital or incurring significant debt. But because consultancies have higher business risks and fewer hard assets than product companies—most venture capitalists will not invest in them. Those that do will value your firm at a much lower multiple than software companies.

- In order to maximize the value of a new consulting startup to potential investors, make certain that you can convince investors that you are positioned to solve a problem that potential clients know that they have, and are willing to pay to have it solved. Confirm this with documented interviews with potential clients. Be clear who your initial targets are, and how that will expand over time. Convince your investors that you have a deep understanding of that market. Explain why your approach is differentiated and is capital efficient. Highlight the team that you have assembled. For most investors, a great team trumps a great idea. And that's especially true for professional services startups.

- If your company has been in business for several years, you will increase your value if you focus on rapid and sustained revenue growth; achieving gross margins greater than 45 percent and operating income greater than 15 percent of revenue; developing annuities that drive revenue; building a tip-of-the-spear go-to-market model that drives large, follow-on consulting engagements; a compelling value proposition; and creating the buzz, brand, and thought leadership that positions you as a market leader.

- Navigating across the seven stages of growth is a significant leadership challenge. Each stage brings new challenges that you will need to anticipate and manage. As you grow, you'll need to develop and rely on early indicators to avoid the "Icarus effect." If your professional services startup grows too slowly, you'll burn your cash and lose the advantages of an early leader. If you grow too quickly, you'll outgrow your infrastructure and your management bandwidth. Both scenarios will lead to a likely crash.

- While managing their way across the seven stages of growth, tech consulting companies must simultaneously navigate across new technology waves. When those waves occur, you must tune your customer value proposition and reconfigure your delivery model.

- Hit profitability early. Even if you are venture backed, get there in two years or less. The longer that you take, the more difficult it will become. The key is to develop a mindset across the company that it's their startup, and they're spending their money. Give them the tools to understand the trade-offs and make the best decisions.

I love building, guiding, and advising professional services companies. If they can anticipate and manage the challenges, they can generate a significant return. Cambridge Technology Partners went public and reached a market cap of over $5 billion in less than seven years. Had the stock market not crashed, ZEFER was expected to be valued at $2 billion in less than 18 months. Mobiquity sold for $182 million in less than eight years. Most importantly, consulting firms generate an exhilarating professional high. If you understand its idiosyncrasies, and anticipate and navigate around its pitfalls, the professional services firm offers a low-risk, high-reward opportunity that may become the "special company" that every entrepreneur aspires to create.

• • •

Praise for *Press Go!*

"Compelling advice to current and future leaders navigating the process of starting, scaling, managing, and exiting high-growth businesses as crafted by a master storyteller. Read and learn."

– Crawford Del Prete, president, International Data Corporation

"Not only does *Press Go* give you an inside look at what it takes to build a special company from the ground up, it also takes you on a heartfelt journey full of entertaining, incredible stories that help you grasp the pitfalls and triumphs of entrepreneurship. I would recommend *Press Go* to anyone trying to hatch a startup or a new venture inside an existing company."

– Scott Snyder, senior fellow, The Wharton School; project fellow, World Economic Forum; coauthor, *Goliath's Revenge: How Established Companies Turn the Tables on Digital Disruptors*

"I've seen Bill in action! He has the gift of anticipating business problems before they occur and always knows what to do to prevent them. He is the expert that you didn't know you needed!"

– Cheryl Smith, retired global business leader; entrepreneur; coauthor, *The Day Before Digital Transformation*

"Bill has helped many entrepreneurs anticipate and overcome the challenges they face launching and scaling their startups. Any would-be entrepreneur who is searching for practical ways to turn dreams into reality must read this book."

– Mark Fuller, founder and CEO, Rosc Global; cofounder, chair, and CEO, Monitor Group; member, World Economic Forum and Massachusetts Governor's Council on Economic Growth and Technology

"Bill masterfully presents his lessons earned from working with more than fifty startups through stories that ensure you will never forget them. New and seasoned entrepreneurs will find his expert advice invaluable. His book is must reading for both."

– Mike Pehl, cofounder, Guidepost Growth Equity; partner, Advent; founder and CEO, multiple technology companies

"A powerful book for every entrepreneur. If you are experienced, it will validate your journey and if you are not, it will help you map the journey."

– Augusto Vidaurreta, serial entrepreneur; coauthor, *Business Is a Contact Sport*

"I love this book! Bill has managed to take lessons 'earned' as an entrepreneur and make them applicable to leadership in larger organizations and, most importantly, in life. An amazing storyteller, his lessons are educational, and his stories punctuate them beautifully!"

– Jody Davids, independent board member; retired global CIO, PepsiCo, Inc.

References

(1) Curt Monash, "Software industry hijinks," *Software Memories*, Monash Research, Mar. 28, 2010, softwarememories.com/2010/03/28/software-industry-hijinks.

(2) Louise Balle, "Information on Small Business Startups," *Chron*, smallbusiness.chron.com/information-small-business-startups-2491.html.

(3) Melissa Wylie, "One-Third of Americans Thought about Starting a Business Last Year (but Don't Know Where to Get the Money)," *LendingTree*, July 24, 2018, lendingtree.com/business/small/small-business-survey-results-june-2018.

(4) Sean Bryant, "How Many Startups Fail and Why," *Investopedia*, Nov. 9, 2020, investopedia.com/articles/personal-finance/040915/how-many-startups-fail-and-why.asp.

(5) Startup Genome and Global Entrepreneurship Network, "State of the Global Startup Economy," *The Global Startup Ecosystem Report 2020*, Startup Genome, June 25, 2020, startupgenome.com/article/state-of-the-global-startup-economy.

(6) Kate Clark, "Unicorns Aren't Special Anymore," *TechCrunch*, Nov. 16, 2018, techcrunch.com/2018/11/16/unicorns-arent-special-anymore.

(7) CB Insights Research, "Venture Capital Funnel Shows Odds of Becoming a Unicorn Are About 1%," *CBInsights*, Sept. 6, 2018, cbinsights.com/research/venture-capital-funnel-2.

(8) Michael Shinagel, "The Paradox of Leadership," *Harvard Professional Development Blog*, July 3, 2013, blog.dce.harvard.edu/professional-development/paradox-leadership.

(9) Joe Iarocci, "Why Are There So Many Leadership Books? Here Are 5 Reasons," *Servant Leadership Learning—Blog*, Cairnway, Oct. 26, 2017, serveleadnow.com/why-are-there-so-many-leadership-books.

(10) Elena Lytkina Botelho, Kim Rosenkoetter Powell, Stephen Kincaid, and Dina Wang, "What Sets Successful CEOs Apart," *Harvard Business Review*, May–June 2017, hbr.org/2017/05/what-sets-successful-ceos-apart.

(11) Cheryl Connor, "Do Older or Younger Entrepreneurs Have the Greater Advantage?" *Forbes*, Sept. 3, 2012, forbes.com/sites/cherylsnappconner/2012/09/03/do-older-or-younger-entrepreneurs-have-the-greater-advantage/?sh=62f2feca3baa (citing Kauffman Ewing Institute report).

(12) Bill Parcells, "The Tough Work of Turning Around a Team," *Harvard Business Review*, Nov.–Dec. 2000, hbr.org/2000/11/the-tough-work-of-turning-around-a-team.

(13) Jaruwan Sakulku, "The Imposter Phenomenon," *International Journal of Behavioral Science* 6, no. 1 (2011): 75–97, accessed Feb. 22, 2021, doi.org/10.14456/ijbs.2011.6.

(14) Johanna Farin, "Dealing With Impostor Syndrome As an Individual And As a Company," QVIK, Jan. 5, 2020, qvik.com/news/dealing-with-impostor-syndrome-as-an-individual-and-as-a-company.

(15) Samantha Garner, "Five Sources of New Business Ideas," *Our Blog*, GoForth Institute, July 18, 2020, canadianentrepreneurtraining.com/5-sources-of-small-business-ideas.

(16) Roger Hood, CEO, E-Z Lyft, email to author, Nov. 17, 2020.

(17) Michael Wolfe, "18 of the Most Ridiculous Startup Ideas that Became Successful," *Quora*, Apr. 28, 2015, quora.com/What-were-the-most-ridiculous-startup-ideas-that-eventually-became-successful/answer/Michael-Wolfe.

(18) Lynda Gratton and Andrew J. Scott, *The 100-Year Life: Living and Working in an Age of Longevity* (London: Bloomsbury Publishing, 2020).

(19) Dominic Endicott, draft article, Apr. 2018, on file with author.

(20) Joseph F. Coughlin, *The Longevity Economy* (New York: PublicAffairs, 2017).

(21) AARP and Oxford Economics, *The Longevity Economy: How People Over 50 Are Driving Economic and Social Value in the US*, Oxford Economics Ltd., Sept. 2016, oxfordeconomics.com/recent-releases/the-longevity-economy.

(22) Dominic Endicott, draft article, May 2019, on file with author.

(23) CB Insights Research, "Top 20 Reasons Startups Fail," *CBInsights*, Nov. 6, 2019, cbinsights.com/research/startup-failure-reasons-top.

(24) The Standish Group, *The CHAOS Report (1994)*, The Standish Group, 1995, standishgroup.com/sample_research_files/chaos_report_1994.pdf.

(25) Dean Davison, "ROI Business Cases Help Differentiate During Economic Uncertainty," *Forrester*, Mar. 23, 2020, go.forrester.com/blogs/roi-business-cases-help-differentiate-during-economic-uncertainty.

(26) Donald Miller, *Building a StoryBrand: Clarify Your Message So Customers Will Listen* (New York: HarperCollins Leadership, 2017).

(27) Walter A. Friedman, "John H. Patterson and the Sales Strategy of the National Cash Register Company, 1884 to 1922," *Harvard Business School Working Knowledge*, Nov. 1, 1999, hbswk.hbs.edu/item/john-h-patterson-and-the-sales-strategy-of-the-national-cash-register-company-1884-to-1922.

(28) Josiane Feigon, "10 Reasons Why Inside Sales Will Displace Field Sales Teams by 2015," *PointClear*, July 17, 2013, pointclear.com/bid/117119/10-reasons-why-inside-sales-will-displace-field-sales-teams-by-2015.

(29) Margarita Yepes, "How Much of a Sales Rep's Time is Spent Selling," *VOIQ* Blog, VOIQ, Feb. 19, 2018, blog.voiq.com/how-much-of-a-sales-reps-time-is-spent-selling.

(30) Scott Brinker, "Marketing Technology Landscape Supergraphic (2020): Martech 5000 — really 8,000, but Who's counting?" *Chief Marketing Technologist Blog*, Apr. 22, 2020, chiefmartec.com/2020/04/marketing-technology-landscape-2020-martech-5000.

(31) Max Altschuler, "Best 150+ Sales Tools: The Complete List (2020 Update)," *Revenue Operations*, Sales Hacker, accessed May 02, 2020, saleshacker.com/sales-tools.

(32) Nishi Saksena, "What Is the Future of Sales?" *TiEcon Blog*, Tiecon 2021, Apr. 26, 2019, blog.tiecon.org/what-is-the-future-of-sales.

(33) Tiziana Casciaro, Francesca Gino, and Maryam Kouchaki, "Learn to Love Networking," *Harvard Business Review*, May 2016, hbr.org/2016/05/learn-to-love-networking.

(34) Tom Richardson and Augusto Vidaurreta, *Business Is a Contact Sport* (Indianapolis: Alpha Books, 2001).

(35) Ilya A. Strebulaev and Will Gornall, "How Much Does Venture Capital Drive the U.S. Economy?" *Insights by Stanford Business*, Oct. 21, 2015, gsb.stanford.edu/insights/how-much-does-venture-capital-drive-us-economy.

(36) Matt Mansfield, "Startup Statistics – The Numbers You Need to Know," *Small Business Trends*, Mar. 28, 2019; updated Jan. 22, 2021, smallbiztrends.com/2019/03/startup-statistics-small-business.html.

(37) Gerald Ross, "Blog #01 – Why Do Only 1:40 Technology Ventures Succeed?" Rubicon Intelligence Unit, 2017.

(38) CB Insights Research, "The 2019 Global CVC Report," *CBInsights*, Feb. 2020, www.cbinsights.com/research/report/corporate-venture-capital-trends-2019.

(39) Dell Technologies and Vanson Bourne, *Embracing a Digital Future: Transforming to Leap Ahead*, 2, Dell Technologies, 2016, delltechnologies.com/en-us/perspectives/digital-transformation-index.htm#pdf-overlay=https://www.delltechnologies.com/content/dam/delltechnologies/assets/promotions/resources/Digital_Future_Executive_Summary.pdf.

(40) Bruce Rogers, "Why 84% of Companies Fail at Digital Transformation," *Forbes*, Jan. 7, 2016, forbes.com/sites/brucerogers/2016/01/07/why-84-of-companies-fail-at-digital-transformation/?sh=4f98b3d8397b.

(41) Alex Graham, "State of the Venture Capital Industry in 2019," *Toptal Finance*, 2019, toptal.com/finance/venture-capital-consultants/state-of-venture-capital-industry-2019.

(42) Jason D. Rowley, "Q4 2018 Closes Out A Record Year For The Global VC Market," *Crunchbase* News, Jan. 7, 2019, news.crunchbase.com/news/q4-2018-closes-out-a-record-year-for-the-global-vc-market/?utm_source=envelope&utm_medium=website&utm_campaign=SocialSnap.

(43) Michael Ringel, Andrew Taylor, and Hadi Zablit, *The Most Innovative Companies* 2016: Getting Past "Not Invented Here," The Boston Consulting Group, Jan. 2017, media-publications.bcg.com/MIC/BCG-The-Most-Innovative-Companies-2016-Jan-2017.pdf.

(44) Jacquelyn Bulao, "How Much Data Is Created Every Day in 2020?" *TechJury*, Sept. 10, 2020; updated Jan. 22, 2021, techjury.net/blog/how-much-data-is-created-every-day/#gref.

(45) Jason Rowley, "Here's How Likely your Startup Is to Get Acquired at any Stage," *TechCrunch*, May 17, 2017, techcrunch.com/2017/05/17/heres-how-likely-your-startup-is-to-get-acquired-at-any-stage.

(46) Roger L. Martin, "M&A: The One Thing You Need to Get Right," *Harvard Business Review*, June 2016, hbr.org/2016/06/ma-the-one-thing-you-need-to-get-right.

(47) Chris Van Allsburg, *The Wreck of the Zephyr* (Boston: Houghton Mifflin Harcourt, 1983).

(48) Chhavi Kumar, "What We Can Learn from Sisyphus and His Rock," *Noteworthy - The Journal Blog*, June 8, 2017, blog.usejournal.com/takeaways-from-the-story-of-sisyphus-and-the-rock-81721c6e499.

(49) Dan Ariely, *Predictably Irrational, Revised and Expanded Edition* (New York: Harper Perennial, 2010).

(50) "Get Out of that Rut," United Technologies advertisement, *Wall Street Journal*, Apr. 10, 1986.

(51) David H. Maister, *Managing the Professional Service Firm* (New York: Free Press Paperbacks, 1997).

(52) Scott Snyder and Alex Castrounis, "How to Turn 'Data Exhaust' Into a Competitive Edge," *Knowledge@Wharton*, Mar. 1, 2018, knowledge.wharton.upenn.edu/article/turn-iot-data-exhaust-next-competitive-advantage.

(53) Marty Ahrens and Radhika Maheshwari, *Home Structure Fires*, National Fire Protection Organization, Nov. 2020, nfpa.org/News-and-Research/Data-research-and-tools/Building-and-Life-Safety/Home-Structure-Fires.

(54) Marty Ahrens, *Smoke Alarms in US Home Fires*, National Fire Protection Organization, Feb. 2021, nfpa.org/News-and-Research/Data-research-and-tools/Detection-and-Signaling/Smoke-Alarms-in-US-Home-Fires.

Made in the USA
Middletown, DE
06 October 2023

40345935R00210